RePlacing Citizenship
AIDS ACTIVISM AND
RADICAL DEMOCRACY

MAPPINGS: Society / Theory / Space
A Guilford Series

Editors

MICHAEL DEAR
*University of
Southern California*

DEREK GREGORY
*University of
British Columbia*

NIGEL THRIFT
University of Bristol

RePlacing Citizenship
AIDS ACTIVISM AND RADICAL DEMOCRACY

———◆———

Michael P. Brown

THE GUILFORD PRESS
New York   London

© 1997 The Guilford Press
A Division of Guilford Publications, Inc.
72 Spring Street, New York, NY 10012

Printed in the United States of America

This book is printed on acid-free paper.

Last digit is print number: 9   8   7   6   5   4   3   2   1

Library of Congress Cataloging-in-Publication Data

Brown, Michael P., 1966–
    RePlacing citizenship : AIDS activism and radical democracy /
Michael P. Brown
        p.   cm.
    Includes bibliographical references and index.
    ISBN 1-57230-210-0 (hbk. : alk. paper). — ISBN 1-57230-222-4
(pbk. : alk. paper)
    1. AIDS (Disease)—Social aspects—British Columbia—Vancouver.
I. Title.
RA644. A25B766   1997
362.1'969792'00971133—DC21   96-52388
                                                             CIP

CONTENTS

LIST OF TABLES
AND FIGURES

FOREWORD

When grassroots groups accept money from the state to provide social services that might otherwise be precluded, do they end up turning their communities into collective *clients*—or, more simply, do they "queer" the state?[1] This version of the assimilation-vs.-autonomy question is not merely grist for idle debate among gay-community-based AIDS groups across North America.[2] Rather, shaping their financial relationship to the state is an ongoing political issue for *all* activists who seek to alleviate immediate suffering but also want to work for long-term change in how people are permitted to order their own social world.

Both the theoretical and the practical answers to this dilemma rely on political analyses linked to the two great modernist narratives: that of emancipation and that of the social contract. The emancipatory narrative celebrates local autonomy and aims for

---

[1]For more on the idea of "queering the state," see Duggan (1996).

[2]I cite gay-community-based AIDS groups only because they have a particular history that has been subjected to considerable scrutiny and debate. Black-community-based AIDS groups in the United States also face a similar dilemma, but with a significantly different history, varying with the degree to which the black middle class had struggled to gain employment in the public health and social welfare systems through which the state served their larger communities, and had militated for the delivery of services in ways that considered the particular problems faced by individuals within black urban communities. At the beginning of the AIDS epidemic, gay communities in the United States, while they had begun to work with public health departments in relation to sexually transmitted diseases, were neither effective players in the welfare delivery system nor an accepted constituency of the welfare system.

consciousness freed from the long arm of the state (even—or *especially*—when the hand wears the velvet glove of social services). Activists and scholars wedded to this framework tend to favor ill-funded grassroots efforts over those of more efficient and predictable state-funded nonprofit agencies, apparently believing that such a loss in efficiency is more than compensated by greater empowerment of individuals (who gain autonomy and clarity about their relationship to the state).

Activists favoring the social contract view, on the other hand, argue that the state is ours—put there by the people—and should be made accountable, even congenial, to those it serves. Receiving state funding and working with the state provide non-ballot-box conduits to the administrators (at heart, people "just like us") of a state created *for* us. By more securely guaranteeing the services due them, more formal arrangements enable affected individuals to devote greater time and energy to other forms of free association and pursuit of well-being. One might imagine the dialogue continuing:

> "But government doesn't work for *everyone* . . ."
>
> "The really needy don't have the time or resources for collective process . . ."
>
> "But if people never learn to self-govern, democracy is meaningless . . ."
>
> "If people don't eat, self-governance is meaningless . . ."

And so the debate has gone . . . at least since the 1950s and 1960s, when the idea of "social movements" took form in response to initially very local acts of civil disobedience—not on the previously *political* front of labor–government relations, but on the new social front of black–white race relations. In the media and in policy circles, "tolerance" became the byword of the day, as civil rights activists sought an end to discrimination and a greater sense of "brotherhood" in society as a whole. As civil rights protests grew progressively more militant and, finally, verged over into violence, commentators began to worry more about what was wrong in society than what was going on inside the hearts and minds of citizens. This new preoccupation led to an overemphasis on macro analyses of social phenomena which, while offering useful insights into the process of social change, forgot about the bodies and spaces in which citizens lived their protests.

Brown is among the "postmodern" social thinkers searching for new, more productive ways to approach the issue of social movements and social change. He sets us down in two largely disconnected (thus far) debates: one among political theorists of radical democracy and those among queer strategists working in relation to the AIDS epidemic. The principal similarity between the two debates is their common interest in tracking the fragmentation of national and subnational identities that were once pronounced "the citizen." For political theorists, radical democracy is still possible, albeit not through the metanarratives of liberation or pluralism that until quite recently has guided politics in the Euro-American world. Hegemony—that shifting, agglutinating form of class domination—should no longer be thought of as the slow but inevitable democratization, through common struggle, of the cast of characters on the political stage, but rather as the amoeba-like action of first engulfing and then subdividing incoherent subjectivities, which in turn form new hybrids—at the level of *individuals* as well as that of *political structures*.

AIDS activism and "queer politics" both stemmed from and continued to perpetuate a crisis in the gay and lesbian civil rights movement, which for a decade or more has been accused of failing to recognize that lability among political actors is the present condition of social politics. Identities are not only hybrid but "performative,"[3] according to several different theoretical positions

---

[3]The publication, in 1990, of Judith Butler's *Gender Trouble* and Eve Kosofsky Sedgwick's *Epistemology of the Closet*, both invoking elements of speech act theory then debated among deconstructionist philosophers and literary critics, launched disjunct usages of the ideas of performance and "performativity." Performance, in its academic sense ("performance studies"), refers to the investigation and theorization of events staged for an audience—in the traditional sense of playing music or doing a play for paying customers who intend to be enlightened or entertained, or in the more avant garde sense of foisting critique and emotional evocations on unwitting bystanders in "public" spaces. "Performativity" is a specialized term associated with J. L. Austin, who, in his 1962 *How to Do Things with Words*, argued that words do not just "mean" they "do," do not only, or even principally, convey "reports" but call situations into being. His reunderstanding of classical rhetorical concerns with speaker-audience-rules emphasizes the iteration and reiteration of claims as the basis for the production of reality.

Emphasizing gender as performance and, later, in *Bodies that Matter*, as subjects hailed (à la Althusser's concept of interpellation) by authorities as gendered bodies, Butler argues that gender is not innate nor even permanently fixed as a social construction, but constantly restated. The gap between each restatement of

framed through the incompatible mix of psychoanalytic, deconstructionist, and poststructuralist social theories. The "queer" offered a refuge for the activists and theorists (and activist-theorists)
fleeing from the constraints of "identity" and the monstrosity of
"identity politics." Whether or not they were familiar with these
academic debates, AIDS activists had little alternative but to accept
performativity and hybridity, the continual reinstalling of a never-
coherent sense of self in relation to the changes in one's body and
in the politics that bear upon it. While ideas of new forms of
democracy and new practices of identity could be—and have
been—exciting for at least some AIDS activists, neither radical
democracy nor queer theory has come up with a truly transformative framework for thinking through that nagging feeling of possibly having "sold out" to the state.

In his participant-observer study of specific AIDS groups and
events in Vancouver, Brown lays the groundwork for a new way of
understanding the relationship between subjectivities and the
state. He retains the notion of citizenship—the prescriptive and resistant practices that relate body to nation through rights, duties,
responsibilities, and membership—but asks us to notice that the
backdrop against which we see citizenship at play—the state, civil
society, and family—is also fragmenting, acting incoherently, and
constantly re-appearing in new hybrid forms. Brown does not pro-

---

gender raises the anxiety-promise that the stated gender may change or disappear.
Hence, dominant culture's insistence on compulsive repetition of acceptible gender
performances.

Sedgwick suggests that sexuality's secretness is produced through a similarly
incomplete and nonterminating process circulating around ideas of the closet. This
she sees not as a deep psychology, but as the modern Occident's distinguishing
epistemological problem: what is the knowing subject's relationship to knowledge
of the self? Sedgwick soon recognized the difficulties in failing to distinguish
among differing genelologies of these ideas, and coedited, with Andrew Parker, a
volume of essays presented at the 1993 English Institute annual meeting. In *Performativity and Performance*, she and Butler (among others) refine the implications and
usages of the two concepts.

Admitting to the complicated usages of the unfamiliar term, I use performativity here to align this part of my description with the idea that identities are not
only not innate, but also require continual repetition to secure their place on a
stage. The latter part of my introduction seeks to contribute to this ongoing debate
in queer theory by reminding readers that the "stage" is also unstable and subject
to constant refiguration in the process of identity re-making. As I indicate in the
main body of this text, Brown's study makes a novel and empirical contribution to
this debate.

pose a new theory of the state or of citizenship—this would require him to move away from the local focus of his study. Instead, he argues that activists must, in their own localities, discover the myriad new trappings of citizenship, the ways a body enacts and acts on the spatial arrangements specified by, and discovered as lacks and surpluses within, the polis.

Grounded in his commitments to radical citizenship and to rejection of "high theory" (overabstraction), Brown, in his search for antibureaucratic and anticlientist citizenship, brings back the "individual" that was treated as inconsequential by a generation of critical theories. But this ambivalent and hybrid actor bears little resemblance to the well-formed, willing ego who speaks well (or at least without "interference"), for whom liberal theorists pine. Brown offers us a body, or rather, a bunch of bodies, that, because they are situated at the nexuses of the fraying relations between state, civil society, and family, possess necessarily fragmentary identities. Sometimes, and in some places, these bodies transform or—are transformed by—the state, family, or civil society in which they enact their ambivalently radical citizenship. At other times, in other places, these citizen-bodies are so deeply embedded in place that they seem barely to know where they are.

But for Brown, "just being there" for a sick buddy or at the moveable memorial AIDS Quilt can express a deep and radical democracy: the bedside of a woman or man rejected by family and the exhibition halls and lawns where the AIDS Quilt temporarily reposes are both postmodern spaces in which affect reemerges as a central modality of citizenship. Following Brown, I want to suggest that body-feeling—that queasy sense of being inside/outside the officially designated places of home, state, and public—does not transcend space but more deeply connects body to place without demanding a fixed—or even *any*—identity as a conduit for being recognizably "citizen" (however plural the faces). This deep *grounding* is nothing like the claim to "humanity" that underwrites both liberalism and Marxism (neither of which considers space as an important construct).

As a geographer, Brown takes very seriously the formative reality of space. Talking about space has become popular in recent political and queer theory, but, Brown argues, most writers think of space as a metaphor rather than a structuring materiality. Using spatial metaphors as a means to provide clever illustrations for concepts that are more properly "abstract" risks failing to notice the restrictions and resistant possibilities that material space—what I would call *territory*, that is, where we are, or are not, allowed to be—present to the social relations produced *in* space and *as* space.

Brown turns a keenly descriptive eye to the interrelationships of people living with AIDS, their "buddies," social welfare providers, and families. His empirical findings question whether the concepts long employed in Marxist and liberal theory enable us to understand the changes in what Foucault would have called the "governmentality" that (what others call) "postmodernity" has apparently wrought. What Brown finds is that the family, state, and civil space are less clearly bounded and (as feminist theorists have also noted), less clearly mappable onto the scheme of public and private space upon which so much liberal and progressive organizing of recent years has rested. For example, "buddies" take up some of the practical and affective labor we have traditionally associated with family. But, while they often practice this affectivity in the home of a person living with HIV, they have been matched up with their buddy through an agency that receives substantial funding from the state.

Even this match-making and support-providing kind of organization does not fit into the usual model of community-based tentacles of the state. Although it is closely related to the state—a "shadow state" for Brown—it is also a decidedly queer space.[4] Brown details a situation in Vancouver that is nearly identical to the structure of state–AIDS community group relations throughout

---

[4]In the early 1990s, activist-theorists working out of landscape planning, urban design, economics, geography, history, and AIDS criticism began to consider more fully how space and bodies produce or erase sexuality. This work, which complexly reintroduces Marxist political economy frameworks into poststructural and postmodern theories which had been deeply critical of Marxism, found one public enunciation in the 1995 "Queer Space" exhibit in New York City and in several panels at that year's Lesbian and Gay Studies Conference and Modern Language Association meetings and, doubtless, other places. David Bell and Gill Valentine's edited volume, *Mapping Desire*, introduces this work, including further work by Michael Brown. The use of "queer" in these debates sometimes refers to urban sexual minorities' territories, but "queer space" is not just where lesbians and gay men might be, but also locales that resist the codifying and regulatory efforts of the hegemonic social order, and that feel uncanny, strange, or disconcerting to those who pass through them.

North America. During the 1980s, the British Columbia provincial government leaders were overtly homophobic, while mid-level administrators recognized the need to fund AIDS projects. Underneath the blustery, officially homophobic policy of "let them take care of themselves!" administrators quietly shifted funds to the Vancouver city government, which, as a more liberal entity, would funnel the money, though inadequate, more or less to where it was needed. While the ultra-conservative Social Credit party then in power officially ruled gay men out of the category "citizen," its administrative arm gave community-empowering money to gay groups. The money helped stabilize a space, a building, in which a community organization could serve its constituents, in their own neighborhood (albeit with but a modicum of the continuity and efficiency that a modern bureaucracy, at its best, could afford).

Without question, AIDS Vancouver was connected to the state. But it was also a "gay-positive" space, a place in which the trauma and mourning specific to the epidemic were not only permissible affectivities, but even part of the "corporate culture." This strange hybrid of shadow state and queer corporatism is not an aberration, but a new kind of community place. However much liberals dislike the campiness of day-to-day management style, and however much progressives may be suspicious of the fluidity between such an organization and the state bureaucrats, this kind of agency (an AIDS service organization, or "ASO" in bureaucratic jargon) is now the norm in North America. Employees often move between jobs in ASOs and their related government agencies. Sometimes state workers leave their bureaucracies for what they experience as the greater freedom and political connectiveness of the community-based, corporately queer space. In order to find greater professional fulfilment, or to make inroads within the government, others move from their on-the-job training in "AIDS administration" to official government positions. Yet others abandon this hybrid space to work in smaller, "homier" groups that emerge on the fringe of—and are sometimes funded through[5]—the shad-

---

[5]The From All Walks of Life ("AIDS Walk") initiative and the later copycat bike rides and races pooled fund-raising efforts into a single major event that could receive significant media attention and provide an opportunity for educating and publicizing the current state of the epidemic. The funds raised from these efforts were then divided into medium-sized and small grants for smaller groups or to seed

ow-state ASO. However, problematic the new spaces are, their very stability has put *an address on AIDS,*[6] making it possible to publicize the epidemic *here and now,* not mysteriously always someplace else. As Brown demonstrates, the corporately queer shadow state broke down the perimeter of civil society–family–state because it could circulate ideas through the mainstream media and attract increasingly diverse volunteers and support from outside the gay ghetto.

Brown's careful attention to the hybridity of new spatial formations has direct implications for enacting radical politics, especially for contemporary thinking that has not adequately assessed the state and the civil society as constantly evolving stages for politics. In both radical democracy theory and queer theory, ACT UP, with its democratic procedures and keen eye to agonistics, should count as a success. But Brown suggests that the striking failure eventually of ACT UP Vancouver reflected not so much a failure to collectively act out participants' fragmentary subjectivities, but rather related to the group's basic misunderstanding of new political spaces, particularly how the state and civil society had hybridized in creating new instrumentalities for implementing Vancouver's AIDS policy and care delivery system. Brown argues that ACT UP Vancouver understood itself to be performing political critique; *a civil space that was distinct from the state.* Misunderstanding the queer shadow state as AIDS Vancouver "selling out" and *becoming-state,* ACT UP may have momentarily jeopardized the on-

---

new projects. For all the criticism of the handling of funds in some of the cities that sponsored such events, they did manage to produce handsome grants for groups that otherwise lacked the resources or skills to do such fund-raising on their own. An exploration of this kind of corporate giving might yield similar results to those in Brown's analysis of state–activist relations; that is, in the age of global capitalism, grassroots groups may find themselves merging spaces with mainstream corporate concerns.

[6] I offer this little pun on the many "put a face on AIDS" campaigns conducted by the mass media and by AIDS groups. The plurality of images that these means of visualizing the epidemic made possible was, I think, partly contingent on the media's ability to locate a variety of people living with HIV or AIDS through groups like AIDS Vancouver. From the standpoint of forging the collective sensibility across racial, gender, and class differences to which the any pluralizing gesture must point (unity in difference, difference in unity), Brown's field work shows that the volunteering activity, however problematic as a solution to social welfare problems, provided a venue for the form of bravery that pluralism ought to demand: becoming different within difference, rather than becoming indifferent to difference.

going clandestine shift of state funds into the more mainstreamed but corporately queer organization. ACT UP saw itself as a radical vanguard encompassing fragmentary postmodern subjectivities, but this "performativity" was understood in relation to a hypostatized idea of the spaces of intervention. In presuming a sharp distinction between civil society and state, ACT UP could not recognize the breakdown between civil and state, between both and family, that AIDS Vancouver, and its buddy program in particular, produced. Brown suggests that the hybrid and fractured new political spaces offered many more possibilities for radical alteration and immediate response to crisis than ACT UP was able to identify or affect efficaciously.

This is not to suggest that Brown sees the mega-organizations, hybrid as they are, as unequivocal spaces of radical democracy. Indeed, he suggests, they do "clientize" those who use them, if only by privileging the "needy" part of persons living with HIV over their other, contradictory (and nonneedy) selves. Brown adds empirical weight to the difficult-to-document reports that the majority of care*giving* buddies are HIV seronegative. But he also offers us the comments of some who are HIV seropositive caregiving buddies, who are contemplating their own potential need for a buddy in the near future. Rippling clientization has its mirror in the several buddies who, because they "do" the same things for friends as for designated buddies, have trouble recalling how many buddies they have worked with; their lack of clarity over their own roles suggests that these gay communities have been "buddy-ized" as much as "clientized."

Further investigation might reveal the extent to which identities among people in the hardest-hit urban gay communities (as with a variety of other fractured communities with long-term enmeshment with social welfare agencies) now tolerate the aseptic style of the state agencies that have merged toward them. Paradoxically, the buddy programs may have helped reinvent a kind of asexual glue for the most traumatized gay male communities. Clearly, buddy programs transform domestic space, but this may entail a creeping (and creepy!) form of sexual behavior change. Brown suggests that two distinguishing features characterize buddy programs—a prohibition on sex between buddies, and the tragically situated meeting of once virtual strangers. I wonder whether these qualities may have weirdly transformed one kind of democracy among strangers ("anonymous sex") into another that pro-scribes rather than writes itself through queer sex. The "no sex" rule, though probably violated more often than anyone cares to admit, tries to gloss over the intense affectivity, even eroticism, that emerges in so close a relationship among strangers.[7] A pro-found geographical shift has taken place in that intensity, main-tained even with people with whom one often had sex, that was once promoted and sustained in erotic economies that viewed anonymity not as a lack of commitment, truth, or "communica-tion skills" but as an insistence on the absolute democracy of sex among men. Historical attention to the geography of queer com-munities will give us the framework to understand more complete-ly the effects of our sexual survival strategies (both those "before" the epidemic and those intended to stem it).

I want to see more work that moves in the direction of recog-nizing that the problems of fracture and hybridity affect both identity and space. Just as there are different kinds of rules for forming and re-forming irreconcilable subjectivities, so the status and malleability of spaces differ. Space must absolutely be thought as "real," but the rules through which spatiality produces effect and affect are complex, and bear investigation in their own right. Brown's intensive study of how space worked at one point in time, and in one place, can be supplemented by further work, not on a Theory of Space, but on describing the practical logics through which space is realized.

We might want to distinguish between something like "virtual space" and "actual space," recognizing that most of the time the hybrid space we inhabit is simultaneously becoming-virtual ("dis-placing," "dis-affecting") and becoming-actual (stopping us in our tracks, body-affecting). Laws that govern housing rights (as such, or through extension of antidiscrimination codes) intend to pro-vide the means to actualize a habitational space. The denial of housing to a person living with AIDS reveals the hybridity of the space of home, the malleability of the practical logic of home. The homeless person living with HIV or AIDS is experiencing the actu-alization of a virtual-space exclusion. But there is a crack in an-

---

[7]The late Arthur Bresson's film *Buddies* (1983) deals precisely with such issues as buddies, lovers, sex, and death. Unaccountably, the film has disappeared from the canon of "AIDS films."

tidiscrimination law: it cannot be actualized, but it does not become unreal. Housing laws are far from abstract or unmaterial; they materially govern a particular kind of space—the space where bodies rest, which they call their own, at least for the duration of a rental contract. The virtual space of protected housing remains, even if this person cannot link an actual apartment to the virtual space. From the standpoint of placing their belongings and body, they experience virtual disappearance and actual exclusion: we cannot ensure housing for you, we cannot protect your body, these laws are not *your* laws, you cannot put your body *here*.

Then *where is* such a body?

In the most literal sense, it might be *on the street*, a kind of no-status space of temporary siting. But, in a more general sense, this body is not in the state because it cannot make the law work, but it is also not in the home or in a civil setting because it is a nomad, transecting other people's private spaces, lacking any resting place of its own. The law retreats from its general regulation of housing to declare that the person living with HIV's body is not covered. The dis-closed body on the street is realer than real, as the state and home evaporate in his (or her) face. In this logic of space, the person living with HIV becomes fragmentary, not unreal, but displaced, disaffected, virtually and actually outside the spaces of home and state, in public but without civil rights.

These leftover spaces, these gnomon, these unsituated spaces of occupation, need fuller exploration of the kind Brown undertakes in Vancouver. The AIDS Quilt, he suggests, creates a transient situation, a placement of bodies—it stops us in our tracks and produces a sometimes violent affect. ACT UP, too, sometimes *grounds* that violent affect as rage, "unleashed" as "power." Vancouver's Stanley Park, a space of paradoxical placement, suggests that cruising park grounds may be another virtual space of community, of radical citizenship. The absolute materiality of cruising grounds and their occupation—by queers—is neither official nor representable, either in the sense of media representation (all we can see is people being arrested for doing something that should have been done elsewhere) or in the sense of participatory democracy. The cruising body ceases to be a cruising body once it leaves Stanley Park. It might be a gay man—even a gay MP!—who describes his cruising experiences. But in the moment of speaking for a class dislocated from its sole space of meaning, in the moment of democratically representing it as a class, this body ceases to be a *cruising* body.

"Finding a place for ourselves," or finding ourselves as place, as queer(ed) bodies, has always been paradoxical, open-ended, and insecure, despite a certain recent nostalgia for "home." Brown has opened the door to a very different way of imagining and acting on the hybrid spaces that we fragmentarily inhabit and only transiently control. Like the frame-shattering work of early gender performance theorists, Brown is among those whose work demands that we think and do politics differently. He takes up the critique of identity politics not to turn against identity, but to turn toward *place*, to press on with the vital project of discovering not just that bodies matter—but where, and through what complex of spatial logic, bodies matter.[8]

CINDY PATTON, PH.D.
Emory University
Atlanta, Georgia

REFERENCES

Austin, J. L., 1962, *How to Do Things with Words* (Harvard University Press)

Bressan, Arthur J. Jr., Dir., 1985, *Buddies*, USA

Butler, Judith P., 1990, *Gender Trouble: Feminism and the Subversion of Identity* (Routledge, New York)

Butler, Judith P., 1993, *Bodies That Matter: On the Discursive Limits of Sex* (Routledge, New York)

Duggan, Lisa and Nan Hunter, 1996, *Sex Wars: Sexual Dissent and Political Culture* (Routledge, New York)

Parker, Andrew and Eve Kosofsky Sedgwick, eds. 1995, *Performativity and Performance* (Routledge, New York)

Sedgwick, Eve Kosofsky, 1990, *Epistemology of the Closet* (University of California Press, Berkeley)

---

[8]I allude here to Judith Butler's *Bodies That Matter* (1993), which takes up hybrid identifications in relation to the concepts of interpellation and performativity. Although this is an extremely important book in advanced arguments about the performative dimension of identity, Butler stops short of fully exploring the malleability of the "stages" on which such performative iterations occur.

PREFACE

The inspiration for this research took form on a very wet December night in Seattle, Washington. Ducking into the mall on Capitol Hill (the city's gay neighborhood) to escape the driving rain, I came upon a woman seated beneath a large ACT UP banner. She was wrapping Christmas gifts for small donations to the cause. ACT UP is a direct-action group that fights for the rights of people living with AIDS. We began chatting and I told her about my Ph.D. research. I was interested in new forms and locations of city politics and had come to Seattle from Vancouver to investigate whether certain local issues—including recent beatings of gay men in the city—might be worth pursuing. She nodded politely without looking up from her wrapping. A moment passed before she looked up and said, "Well, gay bashing is certainly interesting and relevant, but if you're going to study anything, why not study AIDS? I mean, that's the most important city politics I know of."

Before this conversation, as a student of urban political geography, I simply had not seen AIDS as a topic relevant to city politics. In part this oversight arose from the current scholarly emphasis on urban political economy, with restructuring and development issues looming large in the past decade. But in part it also had to do with my own orientation to AIDS. As a gay man, I was certainly aware of the changes wrought by the epidemic on gay subculture. More personally, my older brother, Terry Brown (1959–1991), had died of AIDS-related causes a month earlier. He had been active in an AIDS organization in Worcester, Massachusetts, but rarely spoke about his efforts. Facing my loss, I realized just how closeted—and politically relevant—his often concealed city politics were. I returned to Vancouver the following month and began an ethnography into the local responses to AIDS. So, I should begin my acknowledgments by thanking that ACT UP member for pointing out the obvious to me.

More narrowly, this study formed my doctoral research at the University of British Columbia. I am also grateful to a large number of people who helped me during my time there. The graduate communitiy at UBC in the early 1990s provided a stimulating intellectual setting in which to consider the relations between politics and place. I would especially like to thank Alison Blunt, Anne-Marie Bouthillette, Kate Boyer, Noel Castree, Dan Clayton, David Demeritt, Robyn Dowling, Andrew Hamilton, Suzy Reimer, Matt Sparke, Anna Skeels, Michael Smith, and Bruce Willems-Braun for nurturing that invigorating, dynamic environment. Gerry Pratt, Derek Gregory, David Ley, and Nick Blomley were each helpful readers and together made up a challenging supervisory committee that let me find my own way through it all. Susan Clarke, Michael Dear, Gordon Clark, Cole Harris, Andy Jonas, Larry Knopp, Robert Lake, Sallie Marston, Don Mitchell, Bob Ratner, Lynn Staeheli, Clarence Stone, Robert Wilton, and Jennifer Wolch also provided useful comments and criticisms at important junctures. I should also thank my editor at Guilford, Peter Wissoker. Without his support and enthusiasm for this project, this book would never have been published.

Given the intensive nature of my research, it is not surprising that I have a great many people from the field to thank. AIDS Vancouver and the AIDS Committee of Toronto were kind enough to let me reproduce their graphics. I would especially like to thank Judy Weiser for granting me permission to use her photos of the Quilt display. I also have to thank the many people across the city of Vancouver who were kind enough to grant me interviews and generally get in their way, especially the staff and volunteers at AIDS Vancouver, the Vancouver Persons With AIDS Society, and the NAMES Project. These were places where it was normal to meet extraordinary individuals. I hope their members do not find their trust was misplaced. Ted, Patrick, Mark, Garnet, Meaghan, Judy, and Quita—I am indebted to each of them for their help, insights, guidance, and their hugs. I hope that the people who participated in this research, even if they are no longer participating in AIDS politics, can take something useful from this finished product. I realize, however, that theoretical meditations are not always helpful in the middle of a health crisis. For this reason, I want this research to give something back to the community in more tangible ways as well. I explicitly undertook a program of oral histories with participants. Those transcripts will be archived locally so that there will be a recorded history of AIDS politics in the city. Like so many other writers on AIDS, I will also reinvest any proceeds I accrue from this book into local AIDS organizations. As I have profited from their insights and perspectives, so should they.

As this book has been a long time in the making, various bits and pieces of it have appeared elsewhere. Portions of Chapters 1 and 2 have appeared in *Environment and Planning A* (1994, Vol. 26, pp. 873–894) and *Environment and Planning D: Society and Space* (1995, Vol. 13, pp. 159–183), and I thank Pion Ltd. for permission to reprint them. The bulk of Chapter 3 has been published in Steve Pile and Michael Keith's *Geographies of Resistance*, and I thank Routledge for letting me reprint it here. An earlier version of Chapter 5 appeared in *Ecumene* (1997, Vol. 4, pp. 27–45), and I thank the editors for permission to reproduce the bulk of it here. Since my arrival at the University of Canterbury, I have also been lucky enough to receive two generous faculty research grants that assisted in the completion of the book. Technical assistance from Janet Bray, Sue Christophers, Andrew Oliphant, Pete Mayell, Michelle Rogan, and John Thyne is gratefully acknowledged as well.

Finally, I must thank my friends and family. Dawn, Tony, Marie, Todd, Michael, and the "Out on the Shelves" crew have been mainstays of support. Cindy, Lee, Amy, Chris, Elizabeth, Viv, Pete, and Jen have also provided encouragement despite the miles and the brevity of Christmas Eve parties. Special thanks have to go to Jonathan for his love and support, but for all his patience, too. Most of all, though, this book is for TB, who lived the argument it advances.

MICHAEL BROWN
Christchurch, New Zealand
August, 1996

Of course, for TB

Chapter 1

"NEW SPACES" OF RADICAL CITIZENSHIP

FLASHBACKS

A friend and I walk slowly along Piedmont Street, an inner city neighborhood in Worcester, Massachusetts. It is a hot and humid New England summer day in 1986. As we approach the infamous corner of Main Street and Piedmont, an intersection well known for sex and drug trades, the decayed urban landscape seems washed out from the haze. Yet, clearly I can see a large white billboard above a boarded up three-decker. It reads something like "Warning! AIDS and Hepatitis B Have Not Been Controlled In The Piedmont Area!" We scoff at the usefulness of the city's outreach strategy. I am sure the stark billboard did little to promote the lives of the citizens under its Spartan face, many of whom speak Spanish, not English. Still, I always think of that sign whenever I pass through that intersection. And after all these years, it is still burned into my mind, my "heart's geography."

My sister has come to visit me in Vancouver, and while sightseeing we stop for lunch on Granville Island, a popular public space in the city. Across a bustling restaurant I catch the eye of a man I have interviewed for this research who happens to

be HIV positive. I can see he is in an intense and hushed conversation with a woman. I recognize her as a buddy volunteer at AIDS Vancouver. Buddies are volunteers who provide emotional and practical support to people living with AIDS and HIV. The man discreetly nods to me, but the woman does not see me, and he quickly returns to their discussion. I cannot help but wonder if the woman is his buddy, volunteering to provide support through the simple gesture of a lunch date.

During an interview with a very spiritual woman in her seventies who volunteers extensively for local AIDS causes in Vancouver, I asked her if she put her work in any sort of global context beyond Vancouver. She smiled warmly and summed up the philosophy that led her into AIDS volunteering several years ago, before she ever knew anyone who had AIDS:

> *"I went to hear Mother Theresa one day when she came to Vancouver. And she said she had so many young people who come up to her and say, 'I want to come out to India to help you. I want to come and work with you.' And she said, 'I tell them, "No. There is work to be done* in your own town, where you live!, *and be content to work to the best of your ability in the place that God put you."' That's what she said. And that's how I feel. I'm a bit too old to think about global things, and things like that. I mean, I'm very aware of the global situation and how the rest of the world is affected by [AIDS]. But I don't feel that I'm an 'activist' as such in that way. I feel that if I do what I can right here, for people who are here—that's my job."* (emphasis in original)

Should we detect "citizenship" in any of these vignettes? If so, *how* and *where?* Do we tend to recognize politics only in state actions like the Main Street billboard, or should the buddy providing emotional support in a crowded restaurant count too? Should the elderly woman's volunteer work at a local agency be considered charity—or *citizenship?* These questions, arising during moments of my daily life, raise a broader conceptual question for political geographers. Where is *the citizen*—the political individual claiming rights, duties, responsibilities, and membership in a political community? Where are citizens' struggles being waged on contemporary issues like AIDS? Only a decade ago, scholars confidently asserted that the state was the predominant focus for political geography (Dear, 1986). But at the close of the twentieth century a loud refrain insists that there are "new spaces" of politics beyond state-defined locations (e.g., Magnusson, 1992; Shapiro, 1992; Pattie, 1994; Hoffman, 1995). But, then, *where* are these newer spaces vis-à-vis the AIDS crisis (itself scarcely more than a decade old)?[1] What is the significance of these new (or at least shifting) political geographies in the city?

To answer these questions this book reports on an ethnography of the local responses to AIDS in Vancouver, Canada, from 1992 to 1993. As a modern holocaust that conjoins issues of identity with political rights and obligations, AIDS is perhaps one of the most appropriate crises through which we might gain an understanding of the relations between radical democratic citizenship and geographic space. In the pages that follow I consider the actual locations where the politics of AIDS occurs in order to bring a geographic perspective to bear on new forms of citizenship. I wish to show how (changing) sites of citizenship help both to enable and to constrain new forms of political identity, which in turn modulate how citizenship is defined.

This book "spatializes" the three spheres of social life outlined in classical political theory: the state, civil society, and the home and family. My specific aim is to consider in geographic terms the most recent theoretical attempts to widen the parameters of politics. To that end I take up Chantal Mouffe's (1991, 1992, 1993) work on radical democracy and citizenship as the basis for a revitalized leftist politics. Mouffe is one of a growing number of political theorists interested in recuperating ideas of citizenship for progressive politics (see also Trend, 1995; Heater, 1990; Roche, 1992; Vogel & Moran, 1991; Bock & James, 1992; Evans, 1993). Her work on citizenship is examined here not only because of its widespread influence but also because a crucial step in her argument rests on political theory's need for a more geographic imagination. She per-

---

[1]To give a *very rough* indication of the extent of "crisis" during the research period, 1994 epidemiological data indicate that, of 1,746 total cases of AIDS reported in British Columbia, 1,246 (71%) had already terminated in death (Rekart & Wong, 1994). In Canada over 10,000 people had been diagnosed, while 6,930 of them had died (Health and Welfare Canada, 1994). See also Wigwood (1993).

sistently argues that we must look for "new spaces" of citizenship in order to reject modern, foundational, and fixed axes of politics. In spite of her advocacy for space in political theory, the actual geographies of those political spaces remain uncharted. Instead, this geographic rhetoric is only used to conceptually de-center the citizen away from fixed identities common to liberal and communitarian theories.

Since Mouffe herself does not provide a geography of these new political spaces, we lack a clear understanding of the relationship between "new" material spaces and new identities associated with citizenship. It is not clear, for instance, where these new spaces of citizenship might be, nor what their relations to "older" spaces are. These gaps in understanding are widened further by the various social changes these spaces and social relations are presently experiencing. The decline of the welfare state, the rise of the voluntary sector in civil society, and the changing form of the family and its locations of support—these trends complicate any naive quest for "new" locations of citizenship around an issue like AIDS service delivery and care. Each of these restructurings suggests a myriad of citizenships and locations. Thus, by conducting an ethnographic search for citizenships' spaces in a single city at a particular point in this pandemic, this book makes no claim to be the definitive work on radical democracy—or even on AIDS politics—since they themselves are quite heterogeneous![2] Instead, its aim is more modest, namely, to offer a single intensive empirical investigation into the almost always highly abstract debates of (critical) political theory in order to emphasize the significance of geography in radical democratic theory.

Concurrently, this book also argues for extending further the "geographic imagination" (Gregoy, 1995) in the study of urban politics. Urban political inquiry (usually pursued under the rubric of "political science" and rather distinct from political theory) remains tightly focused on state-centered spaces in its search for politics (Magnusson, 1992; Kirby, 1993; e.g., Judd & Swanstrom, 1995).[3] The rise of new social movements has refocused attention

---

[2]For a more comparative work, see Perrow and Guillen (1990) and Altman (1988, 1994).

[3]On the sharp division of labor between political scientists and political theorists, see Gunnell (1993). For odd examples of attempts to bridge the gap in the study of urban politics, see Arkes (1981) and Schabert (1989).

in the past decade away from state forums like elections or legislatures and toward spaces of civil society like neighborhoods or sites of public protest (Castells, 1983; Offe, 1985; Lowe, 1986; Berkowitz, 1987; Berry, Portney, & Thompson, 1993). Nonetheless, the study of urban politics has only just begun to grapple with expanded parameters of where "the political" might be found in the city (not only across public-private divides but also into public arenas not defined by the state), and has rarely engaged poststructuralism, which insists precisely on a *more complex* understanding of politics and identity. Before attempting to chart these emerging new spaces of citizenship, let us review how the citizen has been understood in contemporary political theory.

CITIZENSHIP

We understand the relations between political obligation, rights, and inclusion in political community through the concept of *citizenship*,[4] which is a political identity of entitlements and responsibilities that is (potentially) equally shared in a liberal democratic society. Urban politics has long been characterized as a likely (if not favorable) venue for citizen participation and identity formation.[5] The state, especially the local state, provides an array of spaces and situations where citizens claim rights or entitlements, or evince obligations to the wider political community. City hall, the voting booth, the welfare office, the community meeting: each of these venues illustrates a familiar state-centered location for political identity to take perform. At a wider scale, the city itself comes to be recognized as a political community, where membership through residency defines the citizen. As noted above, these portrayals of the citizen are typically conceptualized through relations of state service delivery and formal public participation.

---

[4]For useful reviews of these relations, see MacIntyre (1984), Mann (1987), Ignatieff (1989), Pateman (1989), Fraser (1989), Marston (1990), Jones (1990), Watney (1990, 1991), Heater (1990), Kymlicka (1990), Rose (1991), Shklar (1991), Vogel and Moran (1991), Mouffe (1991, 1992, 1993, 1994), Bock and James (1992), Roche (1992), Resnick (1992), Marston and Staeheli (1994), and Painter and Philo (1995).

[5]For examples see Wood (1958), Syed (1966), Wicwar (1970), Dahl (1968), Mill (1958), and Hill (1974). For a Vancouver example, see Hasson and Ley (1994). For a critique that focuses on the structural limitations on urban politics' democratic potential, see Magnusson (1985).

Conventional Debates

Two approaches to citizenship currently dominate Western political theory: liberalism and communitarianism (Mouffe, 1992). *Liberalism* is the hallmark of modern democracy (Gray, 1986), focusing on the proper relationship between the individual and the state. In liberalism, politics are defined as actions the citizen takes to get the things s/he wants from the state or other citizens, while mitigating the state's interference in this pursuit of happiness. It is efficiently summed up in Harold Lasswell's (1950) definition of politics that well characterizes urban political inquiry: "politics is about who gets what, when, and how." In liberalism, citizens are conceptualized as corporeal holders of rights. Society reflects and secures citizens, holdings formally in a written constitution, which confers a largely legal status on the citizen. Characteristically, liberal citizenship is socially thin; there is no substantive sketching of community (Sandel, 1982, 1984). Instead community is defined as a set of legally defined citizens, who each rationally pursues his/her own concept of "the good." Hence, liberals insist on what Mouffe (1992) calls "the priority of the right over the good." In other words, the individualized citizen defines for her/himself what is good, and his/her rights positively secure the quest for it. Community cannot usually impinge on those rights, nor can it define what is good for the citizen. Liberty is thus challenged when rights are denied or squelched (Berlin, 1984). In those instances, it is infringed by the state or other citizens when they block a citizen's pursuit of the good. The relationship between morality and politics, then, is largely a private-public one—distinct and separate, though in constant tension. Morality is where we—privately—decide what is good and bad; politics is how we go about getting what is good publicly.

Communitarianism offers a widely accepted and ongoing critique of liberalism in modern democratic theory. It is often noted for its tendency to lament the loss of classical Greek notions of citizenship and participation (MacIntyre, 1984; Ricci, 1984). Its view of politics is more ethereal: politics is where we, as a community, decide who we are as a people and what kind of society we deserve (Elkin, 1987). Communitarians insist that liberalism's fundamental flaw is its lack of community, and more specifically the moral consensus that defines such a political association. Thus, communitarian critics are quick to point out that theoretically there is no truly, noninstrumental way that liberals can join with one another in pursuit of communal goals. Thus, they disagree with liberals, who say that community is only possible when it provides mutual good ends to each citizen. Citizenship, for communitarians, is about the communal, participatory relationship individuals have with the state or polity. Often the state and community are likened or equated, as with romantic notions of (local) government (Hegel, 1991; cf. M. P. Brown, 1992). The benefits and obligations of membership in a political community are emphasized by communitarians. Thus, contrary to liberalism, communitarianism suggests a priority of the good over the right. In other words, communitarians point out to liberals that we have communal standards of what is good and bad, that we do not simply each decide our own moral codes in a social vacuum. Under this approach, individual rights can justifiably be subordinated to the good of the community. Morality and politics, for communitarians, often become the same enterprise (see also Wolfe, 1989).

Poststructural Interventions

Perhaps the most challenging influences on the very discourse of political theory have been the various strands of recent poststructural thought (White, 1988). While these works are by no means entirely consensual, together they criticize several tenets of modern Western philosophy. Their most radical impact for theories of citizenship comes from a reconceptualization of the human subject.[6] Poststructural philosophy rejects a coherent, unified, and centered subject in its understanding of social life (see Smith, 1988). To quote Sarup (1993):

> Poststructrualists . . . want to deconstruct the conceptions by means of which we have so far understood the human. The term "subject" helps us to conceive of human reality as a construc-

---

[6]Besides the critique of a unified subject, poststructuralism also challenges the belief in historicism (i.e., the belief in an overall trajectory to history), meaning (the belief in a straightforward relationship between signifier and signified), and philosophy (the confidence modern thinkers have placed in its capacity to reveal *the* truth). For accessible discussions see Weedon (1993), Sarup (1993), and Pratt (1994).

tion, as a product of signifying activities which are both culturally specific and generally unconscious. The category of the subject calls into question the notion of the self synonymous with
consciousness; it "decenters" consciousness. (p. 2)

The implications for citizenship are immensely profound, especially for hegemonic liberal definitions. Various lines of thinking
within poststructuralism, for instance certain strands of feminism,
queer theory, and radical democracy, have each posed challenges
to the long-standing categorical certainties of liberal democracy
(Jones, 1990; Mouffe, 1992; Young, 1990; Russo, 1991; Watney,
1991; Carter, 1992; Tatchell, 1991; Evans, 1993; Berlant & Freeman, 1993). These movements have highlighted the reductions
and exclusions left in the wake of liberalism's citizen (Pateman,
1989; Fraser 1989, 1990). Most notably (given liberalism's hegemony), they reject its typically fixed, a priori identity as an unencum-
bered, instrumental, heterosexual "Liberal Man." That static identity has circumscribed the public sphere to the exclusion of certain
struggles. For instance, many feminists have shown how liberalism
denies that politics can take place in the private sphere (Elshtain,
1983; Siltanen & Stanworth, 1984; Sasson, 1987; Pateman, 1989;
Fraser, 1989; Benn & Gauss, 1983; Brownhill & Halford, 1990;
Rose, 1993). Consequently, conventional attitudes towards the political do not look for (thus do not find!) the citizen being political
in the home or in the family (though see Rose, 1990; Staeheli,
1994a, 1994b; Bell, 1995; Marston, 1995). Relations of intimacy,
love, caring, and friendship are only exhibited by citizens—according to classical liberal theory—to the extent that they nurture and
civilize the individual in order to maximize his/her participation
in the public sphere (Elshtain, 1983).[7]

Poststructuralism would agree with communitarianism that
liberalism overstates the importance and efficacy of the singular

---

[7]As Kymlicka (1990, p. 250) points out, these are actually two different conceptualizations of the private sphere. The first is the Lockean distinction between
the social and the political; the second is the Romantics' distinction between the
social and the personal. This distinction is taken up more fully in Chapter 5. While
Kymlicka insists that neither strand of liberalism completely locates the family in
the private sphere, he concedes that liberals have not drawn the family through
these distinctions, nor have they examined the family's structuring of both private
and public spheres.

citizen. That said, it would also contend that communitarians ignore the realities of modern democracy that emphasize liberal individualism. Personal liberty—from either the state or aspects of civil society like fellow citizens—can be threatened and must be protected (Held, 1990; Keane, 1988). Thus, Mouffe is suspicious of sacrificing individual liberty for the sake of recovering a strong participatory ideal premised on a singular (often romantically premodern) axis of community. Sometimes there should be a priority of the right over the good. Interestingly, however, poststructuralists have yet to specify exactly when those trumps should be played (White, 1988).

Yet, a poststructural theory of radical democracy should not be equated with a return to a premodern, communitarian notion of the citizen. It rejects the romantic or classical notion that there can be a single moral code in modern society. For radical democracy takes on the liberal point that the lack of a common good is precisely what characterizes modern democracy, what Lefort (1986) has problematically labeled the "empty space" of modern politics. Thus, it denies communitarians' substantive idea of a common good for a political community. A political community is plural, composed of several different social groups and personal identities. Here again we can see the rejection of a unified theory of the subject. Thus, premodern, simplified axes of community or virtue endemic to communitarian notions of citizenship are rejected. Mouffe (1992, 1993), for instance, rails against collapsing social differences into a singular notion of "the citizen," which both liberalism and communitarianism (for very different reasons) do. Consequently, praxis begins not from a predetermined subject-identity of the citizen founded squarely on a simplistic, single axis of community, but rather from how the *elements* of citizenship (namely, rights, duties, or obligations, and the forging of political community) arise or are suppressed in actual contemporary political struggles (Walzer, 1989; Young, 1990; Shklar, 1991; Mouffe, 1993). Identities of the citizen remain open, socially produced, often contradictory, and in flux (Laclau & Mouffe, 1985; P. Smith, 1988, 1991).

That said, radical democratic thinkers would not want to take the modern distinction between morality and politics too far. They would point out that this separation is exactly what cheapens modern politics and makes it so meaningless and instrumental.

The good, poststructuralists argue, should not be defined substantively, nor instrumentally. Rather, they note, there are some fundamental principles that members of society do agree on (White, 1988). Mouffe uses the concept of the *res publica,* drawn from Oakeshott's (1975) work, to discuss the connections attending citizenship, based on these agreed-upon principles, what she calls "a grammar of politics." The *res publica,* as Oakeshott suggests, is a common political language or civil discourse that produces political community. As Mouffe (1991) describes it:

> Those rules prescribe norms of conduct to be subscribed to in seeking self-chosen satisfactions and in performing self-chosen actions. The identification with those rules of civil intercourse creates a common political identity among persons otherwise engaged in many different enterprises. This modern form of political community is held together not by a substantive idea of a common good but by a common bond, a public concern. It is therefore a community without definite shape, a definite identity, and in continuous reenactment.
>
> Such a conception is clearly different from the premodern idea of the political community, but it is also different from the liberal idea of political association. For liberalism also sees political association as a form of purposive association, of enterprise, except that in its case the aim is an instrumental one: the promotion of self interest. (p. 77)

Oakeshott's conservatism leads him to deny conflict at the site of these agreed-upon principles or language. Mouffe alternatively argues that the *res publica* is indeed a particular hegemonic project, yet insists that there is the potential for conflict and counterhegemony because there are multiple interpretations of those meanings.[8] Here, again, it is helpful to quote her at length:

> Politics is to a great extent about the rules of the *res publica* and their many possible interpretations; it is about the constitution of the political community, not something that takes place in-

---

[8]While Habermas (1984) and Benhabib (1992) adopt a similar logic in suggesting a performative framework through which a less coercive, more democratic public sphere might be constructed, their commitment to a universal theory of morality underwriting that sphere distinguishes them from Mouffe. As a poststructuralist, she would insist that the very adequacy of those rules, that is, the structuring of the *res publica* itself, must be perpetually questioned by radical democrats.

side the political community, as some communitarians would have it. Political life concerns collective, public action; it aims at the construction of a 'we' in a context of diversity and conflict. But to construct a 'we,' it must be distinguished from the 'they' and that means establishing a frontier, defining an 'enemy.' Therefore, while politics aims at constructing a political community and creating unity, a fully inclusive political community and a final unity can never be realized since there will permanently be a 'constitutive outside,' an exterior to the community that makes its existence possible. Antagonistic forces will never disappear, and politics is characterized by conflict and division. Forms of agreement can be reached, but they are always partial and provisional since consensus is by necessity based upon acts of exclusion. We are indeed very far from the language of civility dear to Oakeshott! (Mouffe, 1991, p. 78)

In this passage Mouffe addresses the fears of radical critics of citizenship who have seen the term's appropriation by neoconservativism (for examples, see Kearns, 1992). Here citizenship is criticized for its incorporative, hegemonic role, squelching differences and alternative struggles, and legitimating state retrenchment (Mann, 1987; King, 1987; Giddens, 1987; Rose, 1990).

Radical Democratic Citizenship Conceptualized

Given Mouffe's steering between the rocks of liberalism and the hard place of communitarianism, it remains unclear just how radical democracy scholars are supposed to search for—and practice—citizenship. Where are these radical citizens? Where should they be? Mouffe (1995) uses a philosophical compass to guide her search by drawing a distinction between "politics" and "the political." She argues that, while *politics* can refer to situations where people collectively struggle toward a common end, what makes those situations *political* has to do with the way those struggles occur. Two characteristics of social relations of citizenship seem to be most relevant. The first is that radical citizenship must be *agonistic*; in other words, it must strive for effect and material change in people's lives. We can see this point reflected in her definition of politics, where a group of people come together agonistically, to achieve some sort of collective ends that matter. On the second definition, Mouffe finds the work of political philosopher Carl Schmitt (1976) especially helpful in clarifying her search for radical citizenship by specifying the utterly *antagonistic* nature of the political. Writing in the 1930s, Schmitt attempted to unhitch the political from its basis in the nation-state. He wanted to move away from a substantive definition to one that would provide flexibility and utility over a wide variety of social situations. Thus, he sought to move the issue away from definitions of politics and toward what makes those politics especially political. His drive was toward a purely abstract conceptualization of the political. The key for Schmitt was an "antagonistic moment" when friends or allies squared off against enemies while pursuing their collective ends. Now, certainly Mouffe does not completely import Schmitt's model of the political into her own theorizing.[9] But she finds his line of thought helpful in capturing the spirit of modern politics, where diverse ends are sought after and there is a lack of common morality, though not necessarily the absence of *any* moral consensus (e.g., Mouffe, 1993, pp. 117–134; 1995, p. 24). What is especially attractive to Mouffe is that Schmitt's criteria for the political allow it to be recognized in a wider array of social relations than simply those centered on the (nation-)state. *The political,* in other words, *can happen anywhere.* Drawing together all of these insights, she explicitly defines citizenship as follows:

> . . . a common political identity of persons who might be engaged in many different purposive enterprises and with differing conceptions of the good, but who accept submission to rules prescribed by the *res publica* in seeking their satisfactions and in performing their actions. What binds them together is a common recognition of a set of ethico-political values. In this case citizenship is not just one identity among others—as in liberalism—or the dominant identity that overrides all others—as in civic republicanism [or communitarianism]. It is an articulating principle that affects the different subject positions of the social agent . . . while allowing for a plurality of specific allegiances and for the respect of individual liberty. (Mouffe, 1991, p. 79)

Given the flexible yet substantive component of poststructural formulations of citizenship, radical democracy seems the appropriate theoretical entrée into the new forms and locations of city politics.

---

[9]For instance, she is suspicious of his essentializing tendencies (this discussion is taken up in greater detail in Chapter 6).

THE GEOGRAPHICAL IMAGINATION
OF POLITICAL THEORY

If any number of social relations may be expressions of citizenship, it follows that we must broaden our spatial search for political engagement. And at first glance radical democratic theory seems to recognize this necessity. Repeatedly in her texts, Mouffe reiterates the need to investigate *new spaces* of radical democratic citizenship. For instance:

> . . . it is clearly impossible to identify either the state or civil society a priori as *the* surface of emergence of democratic antagonisms. (Laclau & Mouffe, 1985, p.180, emphasis added)

> . . . what has been exploded is the idea and the reality itself of a unique space of the constitution of the political. What we are witnessing is a politicization far more radical than any we have known in the past, because it tends to dissolve the distinction between the public and the private, not in terms of the encroachment on the private by a unified political space, but in terms of a proliferation of radically new and different political spaces. (Laclau & Mouffe, 1985, p. 181)

> Our societies are confronted with a proliferation of political spaces which are radically new and different and which demand that we abandon the idea of a unique constitutive space of the constitution of the political, which is particular to both liberalism and civic republicanism. (Mouffe, 1993, p. 20)

> As we approach the end of the century, we are witnessing a vast process of redefinition of collective identities and the creation of new political frontiers. (Mouffe, 1994, p. 105)

But for a geographer what is bothersome about these passages is that they are only meant to convince the political theorist to rethink the *subjects* of radical democracy—not the locations for them. While these arguments may seem to show a more geographic sensitivity to citizenship (beyond, say, its familiar association with the nation-state), they actually appear to be rhetorical metaphors aimed at de-centering the subject of radical democracy. I worry that Mouffe is only using the word "space" metaphorically, as a gesture to widen the array of de-centered social identities that come to mind when we conceptualize "the citizen." Her goal is to ponder who these citizens are, not *where* they are found engaging in politics.

Similar spatial discourses have appeared across the humanities and social sciences recently, and geographers have been quick to criticize them. They have objected to the panoply of spatial metaphors currently popular in cultural studies on a number of grounds that are relevant to the discussion here (see Pratt, 1992; Barnes & Duncan, 1992; Ley & Duncan, 1993; Price-Chalita, 1994). N. Smith and Katz (1993, p. 68) argue that "there has been little, if any, attempt to examine the different implications of material and metaphorical space." Massey (1993) notes the irony that spatial metaphors are often used outside the discipline of geography to convey a static, fixed attitude about space, while geographers themselves have struggled with ways of representing the constantly changing, fluid nature of space, place, and scale.

In fact, more recently Massey (1995) has argued that radical democracy needs to be thought about in more explicitly spatial ways. These criticisms suggest that, however rhetorically enticing (or similar) Mouffe's agenda might be to geographers, her failure to discuss the implications of *material* space on political engagement suggests that "the geographical imagination" of political theory is narrow and underdeveloped. That argument can be lodged against Mouffe's spatial arguments on a number of levels. Most broadly, her discussion fails to acknowledge the point that all social relations are always spatialized, a point geographers have been arguing in social theory for over a decade (Gregory & Urry, 1985; Massey, 1984). Radical democratic thinking never seems to consider that citizens are always engaging in politics in actual locations.

And yet this is the very point that geographers have been making lately. There has been a resurgence of interest in the question of citizenship by geographers recently (see Smith, 1989; Marston & Staeheli, 1994; Painter & Philo, 1995; Rose, 1990, 1991). Demonstrating what Painter and Philo (1995, p. 109) have called a sociocultural sensitivity, which political theory has tended to lack, these interventions have challenged political theory's rather abstract conceptualizations of the citizen in a number of spatial settings: the home (Bell, 1995; Fyfe, 1995a), the local (Rose, 1988; Marston & St. Germain, 1991; Staeheli, 1994), the national (Marston, 1990; Pincel, 1994; Kearns, 1995), and even the global (Kofman, 1995). Like Mouffe, geographers have been pressing for visions of citizenship in a multiplicity of spaces (MacKian, 1995) in order to advance and connect political struggles on the left. I wish to extend this spatial flexibility of citizenship by demonstrating how radical democracy's geographical imagination must change if its chief goal is to be pursued fruitfully.

If we open up citizenship to numerous social identities it has not been previously associated with, we must also open it up to a wider variety of material spaces across (in this case) the city.[10] Spatialized social processes do not necessarily connote static or fixed placements for political engagement, however. In other words, changes in locations themselves can contribute to or inhibit the emergence of citizenship in social relations not previously considered "political." Thus, I want to enhance the radical democratic project by demonstrating that the spatial emphasis of its framework is indeed more than mere metaphor. To pursue the project successfully we must consider how citizenship affects, and is affected by, its various spatial contexts. If we do not, we are left with new identities associated with political engagement in the same old static and unchanging locations. An extreme example is instructive and perhaps also explains why I approached the research ethnographically. According to Mouffe's argument, examining the city politics of AIDS would impel us to see a wide array of participants' social identities across lines of (among others) class, race, gender, and sexuality and focus on how these multiple discourses sometimes overlap and sometimes affect one another through the citizen's political practice. But those politics would likely take place in the same old places they always have: the voting booth, city hall, the neighborhood meeting. Such a paltry geographical imagination leaves us with a fairly sophisticated rendering of the citizen-subject but a simplistic account of the spaces citizens are affected by, and, in turn, affect. Citizenship, then, must take place *somewhere* but not just *anywhere*. This is precisely why Lefort's metaphor of "empty spaces" in modern democracy is so dangerous conceptually. At present, radical democracy lacks any sort of geographical imagination. Where are these agonistic, antagonistic cit-

---

[10]We must also reconceptualize political spaces as a number of different geographic and temporal scales, as well. I take up these matters more explicitly elsewhere (Brown, 1995b, 1995c).

izens? The question is important not just empirically but also because it has significant *theoretical* consequences. Because struggles
shape and are shaped by their spatial context, where they take
place matters.

I began this research with Mouffe's premise that citizenship
can be articulated in a wide variety of social relations, in many locations. Consequently, as the ethnography unfolded, I delved into
as many different forms of the responses to AIDS as possible, in order to get a sense of the plurality of political subjects working on
AIDS issues in Vancouver, speaking with anyone involved in local
responses to AIDS who was willing to speak with me. My aim was
deliberately not to anticipate where I thought new political identities (i.e., citizenship) ought to take place. I spoke to elected city officials, provincial and city bureaucrats, a host of volunteers, family
members, and people themselves who are living with AIDS, tracking the locations of their political engagement with the AIDS crisis. As their collective stories amassed, I certainly documented the
variety of spaces where citizenship took place beyond the narrow
confines of the state. But what also struck me was how inadequate
concepts typically used in political theory to describe social life
(the state, civil society, and the family) were to convey the structuration of space and political (in)action during the AIDS crisis.
These concepts, while heuristically useful, became awkward, cum-
bersome, and static when spatialized. If we are to introduce a multiplicity of citizen(ship)s, we must rethink the spaces through
which they act or are structured.

WHERE ARE CITIZENS AND CITY POLITICS?

In a certain sense, political theory retains such a high degree of abstraction that any discussion of material spaces through its discourse might be misleading.[11] Nonetheless, before we begin a

---

[11]For arguments relating to the highly abstract nature of political theory from
within that discourse community, see Dunn (1996), and Gunnell (1993). See also
Postone (1992). It is interesting to note that Dunn, for instance, argues passionately
for an understanding of political theory that is fundamentally historical and temporal. He sees no complementary need, however, for a geographical or spatial perspective.

search for new spaces of politics, it seems prudent to understand just what sorts of spaces political theory has tended to plot. The discourse of political philosophy has tended to hive off social life into three more or less distinct spheres in liberal democracies: the state, civil society, and the family. This triptych can be found in a wide variety of historical and contemporary political philosophy, even in Mouffe's own work.[12] Given that all social relations are always spatial, these spheres of social life have come to be connotatively (and often denotatively) associated with particular locations in the city.[13] Consequently, I began with this loose organizing heuristic to classify the spaces of citizenship I witnessed in Vancouver. What became clear as the study progressed, however, was not simply that politics had shifted away from state-centered spaces toward those of civil society and the family (as many critical theorists would predict). Rather, I became frustrated by the disagreement between the conceptual clarity and mutual exclusiveness of those categories and actual changes to (the social relations in) those spaces that made them flow into one another. That messiness signaled not just de-centered subjectivities but also the de-centered quality of citizens' spaces (both new and old) in city politics. The multiple meanings and interpretations of citizenship have hinged on these blurring edges that conceptually separate state/family/civil society. In paying so much theoretical attention to plural, de-centered political actors, radical democratic thought has perhaps neglected to consider the implications de-centered spaces themselves have on citizenship. What follows, then, is a sketch of political theory's geographic triptych, infused with an argument that recent changes (demonstrated with data specifically from the Canadian context in light of this ethnography) in these locations theoretically may permit us more geographical imagination in shaping radical democracy.

---

[12]See also, for instance: Hegel (1991), Pateman (1989), Kymlicka (1990), Okin (1991), Cohen and Arato (1993), Held (1990), Keane (1988), and Elshtain (1983).

[13]Notice from the quotes on page 13 that Mouffe herself refers to the state and civil society as "spaces," albeit metaphorically. That these three sets of social relations have come to be associated with particular places in the city may seem obvious to geographers, but bear in mind that political theory has tended not to engage in empirical inquiry, beyond the anecdotal example. The materiality of these three spaces and, more precisely, the effects of their restructurings are difficult to incorporate in such an abstract tradition of scholarship.

The State

The state, of course, typically has a bounded territory and at key sites through that terrain exercises its sovereign authority. Studies of urban politics typically have drawn our attention toward these state-centered spaces: the legislature, the city hall, the voting booth, even the point of contact with public service delivery like the welfare office (for instance, Helig & Mundt, 1984; see Figure 1-1). The state embodies the classic, orthodox location of citizenship. It is the institution that defines citizens communally and liberally identifies its citizens as bearers of specific rights and responsibilities. The restructuring of the state and economy in recent decades, however, has made it more difficult to locate citizens' spatial relation to the state so readily. Clark and Dear's (1984) state apparatus argument, where they demonstrate the multifacetedness

FIGURE 1-1. The state: Vancouver City Hall. Photo by author.

and sheer number of institutional locations of the modern bureaucratic state, immediately diffuses any tight spatial focus to more diverse locations. This arrangement leads to a focus on relations between facets of the state and state-influenced institutions (Kirby,
1993). Magnusson (1992), for instance, has noted the rise of new
social movements based on identity politics, and the globalization
of capitalism and social movements means that the state can no
longer be the sole—or even primary—locus of attention in political inquiry. He argues that we must "de-center" the state in political studies. The retrenchment of the welfare state in several Western democracies since the 1970s is arguably one of the broadest
complications to any simple location of the citizen at or near the
state (M. K. Brown, 1986[14]; Guttman, 1988; Mishra, 1990).
Michael K. Brown has specifically tied retrenchment to the changing morphology of the state, which has been missed in arguments
about the downsizing of welfare. As he states:

> There is ample reason to believe that recent policy changes
> amount to more than a mere slowdown in the rate of growth
> but arguably less than a life-threatening crisis. The welfare state
> may be intact, but subtle alterations in its shape and structure
> have occurred, which in my view have begun to undermine the
> postwar vision of the welfare state as a force for social justice and
> political inclusion within capitalist societies. (1986, pp. 6–7)

His argument implores us to rethink the state as the sole location where citizens (as recipients of state welfare) could be found.
A crucial element in state restructuring has been the rise of service
provision by the voluntary sector rather than by the state itself.
Wolch (1990) has insightfully termed this body "the shadow state"
because of its indirect but important relationship to the state
through funding and contracting. In British Columbia, shadow
state service delivery has long been a favored arrangement (Ismael
& Vaillancourt, 1988). However, recent work has documented its
significance in the past decade specifically (Donaldson, 1985;
Butcher, 1986; Rekart, 1993). The shadow state complicates any
simple geography of the state because its organizations mediate
between the community of service recipients and state bureaucra-

---

[14]This is actually a different Michael Brown.

cies. Figure 1-2, for instance, depicts the intricate yet massive financial links between the state and shadow state in British Columbia. Rekart (1993) sampled 133 voluntary organizations and found that the *majority* of their funds came from the B.C. government rather than from other state or nonstate sources. What are the implications of these close relations for spaces of citizenship? At the most general level, they describe a not so clear-cut categorical distinction between state and civil society. The geography of these new relations suggests that we need to look beyond traditional geographies of the state because the morphology of the state is shifting. AIDS politics occurs at a time when complicated relations between the state and nongovernmental organizations are becoming more complex and interconnected. Consequently, I pay particular attention in this study to how those shifts place politics in new locations—both beyond and inside state-centered spaces—that conduce to new forms of citizenship.

Civil Society

Civil society is perhaps the most obtuse and difficult sphere in political theory to locate. It can refer to a wide variety of public

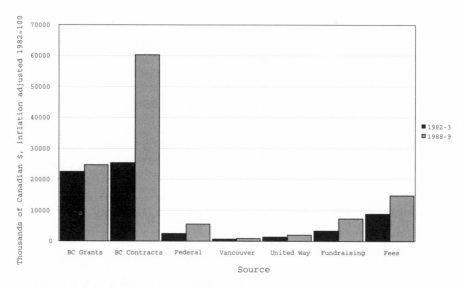

FIGURE 1-2. Shadow-state funding of 133 British Columbia nonprofit organizations, 1982, 1988. (Based on J. Rekart, 1995.)

FIGURE 1-3. Civil society: Public space, Robson Square, Vancouver. Photo by author.

spaces in the city (Mitchell, 1996). Civil society encompasses locations outside of, or beyond, the state (Urry, 1981; Hegel, 1991: Cohen & Arato, 1993; Johnston, 1994).[15] The term has been used typically by liberal political theorists to describe the limits of state power in social life. Nonetheless, it is characterized by public interaction, especially among strangers, or private (i.e., nonstate) contractual relationships (Tester, 1992). The defining feature of civil society's social relations is voluntary associations, especially those aimed more at common ends than at individual desires (Cohen & Arato, 1993). "Civil society," then, often popularly conjures up images of public spaces in the city: spaces used by popular protest groups to attract the attention of fellow citizens (Figure 1-3).

This sphere of life has, of course, come under increasing attention and interest by theorists of new social movements (e.g., Gamson, 1991). New social movements and grassroots organizations have become important qualifiers to political theorists' description

---

[15]While Cohen and Arato (1993) insist on locating the family within the boundaries of civil society, typically theorists see the family as constituting a separate sphere of life, and I retain that distinction here. Cohen and Arato's argument is more normative than descriptive; they argue that placing the family in the context of voluntary associations would give it a more democratic structure than it has had historically.

FIGURE 1-4. Civil society: Grassroots organizations—in this case the Vancouver Gay and Lesbian Centre. Photo by author.

of civil society as increasingly vapid, instrumentalized, and without the ability to nurture forces of social change in advanced capitalist contexts. Authors as diverse as Boyte, Bellah, Offe, Castells, and Cohen and Arato have acknowledged civil society's potential site for citizenship. Here, political activity does not take place *necessarily* at or through the state, but in voluntary associations that identify with new social movements. Thus, we can situate relations of civil society not merely in public spaces of the city but also in the grassroots community organizations that bring strangers together in common, voluntary pursuits (Figure 1-4). In such locations volunteers delivering public services have become an important aspect of urban politics.

Data on volunteering bear these arguments out. Table 1-1 summarizes a 1989 survey that shows that nearly one-third of Canadians polled volunteered in some ongoing capacity, while over half considered themselves more informal volunteers (Duchense, 1989, pp. 18–19, 85).[16] Multiculturalism and Citizenship Canada estimates that over 13 million citizens do volunteer

---

[16]Formal volunteers are defined as people who "willingly perform a service without pay, through a group or organization" (p. 97). Informal volunteers are defined as those who help on their own, *not* through an organization or group (p. 93).

TABLE 1-1. The Voluntary Sector in Canada, 1989:
Percentage of Formal and Informal Volunteers, by
Metropolitan Area

	% Formal volunteers	% Informal volunteers
Canada	27	66
St. John's	28	60
Charlottetown	23	66
Halifax	34	71
Saint John	29	78
Chicoutimi-Jonquiere	nd[a]	76
Quebec City	18	67
Montreal	17	59
Trois-Riveres	nd	72
Sherbrooke	nd	63
Ottawa-Hull	29	76
Sudbury	nd	61
Toronto	21	54
Hamilton	20	68
St. Catherine's–Niagara	27	79
London	25	65
Windsor	nd	78
Kitchener-Waterloo	30	74
Thunder Bay	nd	85
Winnipeg	35	66
Regina	27	61
Saskatoon	44	77
Calgary	38	70
Edmonton	38	75
Vancouver	23	53
Victoria	33	67

[a]nd = No data.
Source: Duchese (1989).

work, the average volunteer giving 191 hours per year. This labor is equivalent to 617,000 full-time positions and worth approximately $13.2 billion (Can.) per year.[17] These data widen the spaces where we ought to look for the citizen in society, as well as complicating the distinction between civil society and the state. Public locations beyond the state that bring different political actors together offer tremendous promise to extend what gets defined as

---

[17]Data available from Volunteer Vancouver, #301-3102 Main Street, Vancouver, B.C. V5T 3G7. See also Duchense (1989).

politics, or who gets defined as a citizen. An issue like AIDS, whose immediacy and stigma have meant that traditional (state-oriented) locations of politics are often ineffective, seems particularly well suited to take place in locations we would describe as "civil society." These potentials for social change, however, are not always successful everywhere, in part because "civil society" is not the only way to define "new" locations in city politics.

The Home and Family

We tend not to think of the family as a spatial concept, and yet its ongoing association with the home betrays that social institution's alleged aspatiality (Dowling, 1997). In political theory historically, the home was the location where private interests were formed. These interests were, in turn, brought into the public sphere and put to bear on the state by citizens. In this arrangement, the family was prepolitical. It was a nurturing environment for the citizen (Elshtain, 1983; Pateman, 1989). Feminism, of course, has challenged liberalism's facile public-private dichotomization of social life (Benn & Gauss, 1983; Pateman, 1989; Okin, 1991; Fraser, 1989). It has demonstrated how women have been effectively excluded from the category of citizen in liberalism, which sequestered women in the private domestic—and apolitical—sphere. Feminist theory has long insisted that the family, and by implication the home, was indeed a political site. With the rise of the postwar welfare state—and through issues like foster parenting and children's rights—the relationship between the state and the family has been increasingly politicized (e.g., Ursel, 1992).

Politics in and around the home also appear through the changing morphology of the family. A decline in the traditional nuclear family form has led to the questioning and exploration of different forms of kinship (Koontz, 1992; Stacey, 1991; Weston, 1991; Browning, 1993; Benkov, 1994). This restructuring widens the spatial possibilities for where to look for "family" and the politics of home. A recent study on the family declares, "There is no universal definition, but many definitions [of the family], each emphasizing different aspects of the family. . . . Family definitions depend, to a large extent, on who is doing the defining, and the purpose for which the definitions are provided" (quoted in Priegert, 1994, p. A-5). The ratio of Canadians in families to those not in families has been decreasing over the past 25 years, as Figure 1-5 shows. While

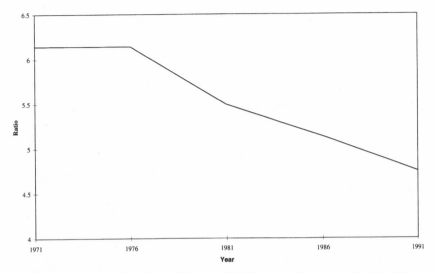

FIGURE 1-5. Ratio of Canadians in families to those not in families. *Source:* Based on La Novara (1993).

the vast majority of Canadians live in families (83% in 1991), the percentage of individuals not living in families has increased from 13% in 1971 to 17% in 1991. Married couples comprise a majority of Canadian families (77% of all families in 1991); nonetheless, alternative forms of family arrangements are on the rise. Common-law families made up 10% of all Canadian families in 1991, up from 6% in 1981. The number of lone-parent families has doubled between 1971 and 1991 (La Novara, 1993).[18]

While these national statistics demonstrate the shifting form of the family, they nonetheless fix it heterosexually. None of these data, for instance, considers same-sex couplings. Familial relations, then, cannot be isolated in the home (or in particular forms of the home). Paralleling these restructurings has been an increasing theoretical recognition that any singular, fixed definition of home is problematic (Massey, 1994; Veness, 1993, Mack, 1993; Sarup,

---

[18]"Families described in this report are generally defined in one or two ways. Census families include married couples and common-law couples with or without never-married children living at home, as well as lone-parent families. Economic families, on the other hand, refer to all groups of two or more persons who live in the same dwelling and who are related to each other by blood, marriage, common law, or adoption" (La Novara, 1993, p. 7).

1994). Rather, the home needs to be considered more as a type of space that should provide a degree of comfort, privacy, and intimacy (Douglas, 1993).

Furthering these processes, AIDS has traumatized the already often complicated, tenuous relationships between gay men and their biological families (Preston, 1992). AIDS has forced the family to come to grips with gays and lesbians, as persons with AIDS confront their families with the facts of their sexuality and their terminal illness, as well as their needs for familial care and support. In addition to providing or requiring familial-type support because of AIDS, gays and lesbians are now confronting society with same-sex partnerships, or their own self-consciously constructed kinships that have come to be called "families we choose" (Weston, 1991; Browning, 1993; Benkov, 1994). Struggles over domestic-partnership benefits are the classic example of these restructurings, but the rise of kinship networks to support people living with AIDS can also complicate the distinction between state and family. State and volunteer-affiliated careworkers have joined, or replaced, familial caregivers as new forms of kinship are forged by people living with AIDS.

Combined with ongoing restructurings of the family, AIDS caregiving opens up the possibility that the citizen can be found in the home and family. Struggles for rights, duties, and membership in political community are often forged there through the need for alternate or augmented forms of kinship support. Radical democracy's willingness to locate citizenship within *any* social relation means that, in the context of the local response to AIDS, we must be open to a geography of citizenship that includes the home and even public spheres of private interaction amongst kin. Spatially, then, we can certainly consider the home as a potential site for citizenship. But we should also consider the many public spaces where an intimate, familial environment can be created as well since, as both Pateman (1989) and Kymlicka (1990) note, private space can often be forged within the public sphere of civil society.

AN INTRODUCTION TO THE STUDY

With the aim of expanding radical democracy's geographical imagination, I began a political geography of the AIDS crisis in

Vancouver from January 1992 through June 1993. I became a participant observer at AIDS Vancouver, and later at the Pacific AIDS Resource Centre (PARC). I was also a volunteer at the NAMES Project Quilt display. This research strategy enabled me to gain an in-depth understanding of the ways AIDS politics had come about and were unfolding. I should note that I did not become a formal volunteer at AIDS Vancouver. At the time, there was a waiting list of volunteers, and, were I a volunteer, I would be channeled into only one branch of the organization. My understanding of the organization as a whole (not to mention other shadow state groups) would be greatly hindered by that scenario. I could not become a member of the Vancouver Persons With AIDS Society (PWA), as it is only for people who are HIV positive. Needless to say, when these organizations moved in together at PARC, my capacity to understand their operations was greatly improved.

I was very conscious about my research being viewed as possibly parasitic. All social research is obtrusive to some degree or another, but doing an ethnography on AIDS can be especially so (see also Stacey, 1988). I wanted to be able to give something back, but the volunteer option was not possible. In a roundtable discussion I had read, AIDS activists Jan Zita Grover and Michael Callen worried over the loss of historical documentation as an ongoing problem for AIDS activists (Callen, Grover, & Maggenti, 1991). The crisis has been so immediate and there has been so much death in such a short span of time that there might be little left to future generations by way of historical record:

> GROVER: There is a great need for oral histories, for example, and for archives of material taken from nonofficial, nonscientific discourses, so that twenty-five years from now we can write histories from within, rather than having to deal with AIDS according to the official histories, which will almost exclusively use scientific materials. In San Francisco, the Lesbian-Gay Historical Society is starting an AIDS history project.

> CALLEN: I know that both the Lesbian Herstory Archives and the Gay Archives have been very public about wanting to obtain AIDS stuff. I have in my own possession a tremendously valuable oral history. I take my tape recorder wherever I can, and I have some incredible stuff. I'm acutely aware of the historical value of this material, and I'm trying desperately to save it and find a place for it. (pp. 242–243)

For this reason, I complemented my ethnography with a series of 120 oral histories with people who had been or were currently involved in Vancouver's AIDS politics. Because of the wide variety of respondents (from family members to workers in the Ministry of Health), I used an informal, open-ended approach to the oral history component. For purposes of reliability, however, three broad questions were always asked:

1. Please describe what it is you do/have done in the local response to AIDS.
2. How did you come to do these things?
3. How have you seen things change? How have they stayed the same?

The data that were supplied permitted me to gain a more systematic understanding of the underlying ethnography. It also gave "the local response to AIDS" a chance to speak for itself.[19] In the chapters that follow, these activists are quoted extensively in order to bring a fully historical geography to bear on radical democracy. Their voices help to provide a fuller context to understanding what the local response to AIDS was like in Vancouver in the early 1990s.

The four chapters that constitute the case study of this research are inspired by Mouffe's guiding principle that we should investigate new spaces of radical citizenship, and by the reality of interaction among these conceptually discrete spheres. The restructurings of state, family, and civil society are treated in Chapters 3–6. Each substantive chapter focuses on the confluence or overlap of these three spheres in actively promoting radical democratic citizenship: state and civil society (Chapters 3 and 4), state and family (Chapter 5), and civil society and family (Chapter 6).

Following radical democracy's guidelines, I expected the best empirical example of poststructural citizenship in civil society would be ACT UP (AIDS Coalition to Unleash Power) Vancouver, a direct-action civil disobedience coalition known for its theatrical

---

[19]Though, clearly, respondents quoted in my own text are not necessarily speaking on their own terms, as critical ethnographers have so often pointed out (e.g., Clifford, 1988). I have relied heavily on Frish (1990) to guide my collection and recording of these oral histories.

and highly effective hijackings of public space. ACT UP, however, made only modest inroads in Vancouver, and Chapter 3 interprets that failure as a reluctance of its members to acknowledge the already changed relationship between Vancouver's voluntary organizations (which began in civil society) and the state apparatus.

The overlap and simultaneity between civil society and the state in local AIDS organizations is the subject of Chapter 4. Here I examine the way citizenship in the voluntary sector or "shadow state" is articulated amidst ever shifting social relations in hard-to-define political spaces. Local AIDS organizations that began as grassroots, gay-oriented community spaces are becoming highly integrated into the state apparatus, as well as bureaucratizing in their own right as demand for services rises. I examine the reshaping of these spaces by looking at the negotiations of identities between citizen and bureaucrat in employees of AIDS Vancouver, as well as the polarities evident among members of the Vancouver Persons With AIDS Society.

In Chapter 5 the boundary between state and family is made more problematic through an account of the relations between AIDS Vancouver "buddies" and their clients. The tremendous variability in the way these relationships of support are sustained challenges us to see citizenship in locations like the home, the bedside, and even the coffee shop. We must therefore see it in relationships that are full of love and tenderness and especially support as much as those that take the form of social work and personal advocacy. Repeatedly, I was told by respondents that this fuzziness, this lack of definition and boundaries between "state" and "family," was precisely what made buddy relationships work as support systems for people living with AIDS.

The need to understand the cultural aspects of defining present-day citizenship's location was nowhere more resonant than at the Vancouver display of the Canadian NAMES Project Memorial AIDS Quilt, which I describe in Chapter 6. Here was a space where family members, friends, and acquaintances interacted with complete strangers. It was a space that combined elements of a space of grieving in the family and one of public education in civil society. This new space of politics challenges Mouffe's insistence that the citizen can be found only where Schmitt's "friend-versus-enemy" distinction obtains. The Quilt was a deeply political site—but one that did not hinge on any "antagonistic moment."

In sum, while Mouffe has begun to provide a complex understanding of how citizenship can be expressed through a wide array of social relations, the categories she uses to bracket those spheres, when spatialized, become awkward when describing the geography of AIDS citizenship because the spaces themselves are still rapidly undergoing change. That is to say, they *themselves* are decentered, in flux, and have been undergoing extensive restructuring during the AIDS crisis. It is on that flux that I focus while considering the structuration of any new definition of citizenship to our traditional understanding of state, civil society, and the family. In order to place that discussion in better context, Chapter 2 offers an historical geography of AIDS in the city and the politics it impelled.

Chapter 2

——⋅——

AIDS AND THE
GAY COMMUNITY
IN VANCOUVER

VANCOUVER AS A NEW SPACE
OF CITIZENSHIP

In early July 1996, Vancouver hosted the 11th annual International AIDS Conference. Well over 5,000 papers were presented, and nearly 12,000 people attended the conference. Attention centered on drug-combination therapies called protease inhibitors, which have shown some promise in slowing the virus's reproduction, but the drugs remain extremely expensive. Still, the focus of the conference was not entirely medical or scientific. International and local activists repeatedly called for a national AIDS policy. There was also a sense that in the fight against AIDS this host city had come a long way in an incredibly short period of time. By mid-1996 it seemed that Vancouver had become the center of AIDS discourse. Yet, only 15 years earlier each of the local participants at the conference was each doing something quite different, and no one had ever heard of the human immunodeficiency virus (HIV). The choice of venue for the International AIDS Conference cannot simply be explained by Vancouver's emerging status as a world-class city or a gateway to the Pacific Rim. The city has been at the forefront in responding to the AIDS crisis ever since this mysterious illness began to affect North American gay men in the early

1980s. This chapter in part recounts how Vancouver grew to be a new space of citizenship in AIDS politics.

To date, most in-depth accounts of North American AIDS politics have been focused on only three cities: New York (Chambre, 1991; Kramer, 1989; Kayal, 1993; Kuklin, 1989; Perrow & Guillen, 1990), San Francisco (Arno, 1986; Ruskin, 1988; Perrow & Guilen, 1990; Fernandez, 1991), and Los Angeles (Geltmaker, 1992; Walton, 1996).[1] This concentration makes partial sense in that geographers have established that there was a high incidence of HIV and AIDS in these places during the 1980s.[2] Furthermore, since these urban areas exhibited the first and most intense signs of epidemic in North America, these cities may have the most developed histories of AIDS. They are not the only places, however, responding to the AIDS pandemic. Such a narrow and precise lens on urban AIDS politics can trick our geographical imaginations into assuming that we need to look only at these three cities to understand local AIDS politics in North America. We may forget that there has been a local politics of AIDS *everywhere.* In other words, the many geographies of AIDS are lost to the metanarratives of only three American cities.

Bearing that point in mind, this chapter demonstrates how Vancouver itself became a new space of radical democratic citizenship. More specifically, it charts historically how citizenship grew

---

[1]Shilts (1987) takes a comprehensive perspective in presenting the historical geography of AIDS in North America. Nonetheless, his account is also largely centered on these three cities. For a more global view of community responses to AIDS, see Altman (1994).

[2]Geographers have almost exclusively taken up the AIDS pandemic from a spatial science perspective. For examples, see Cliff and Haggett (1989), Dutt, Monroe, Dutta, and Price (1987), Dutt, Miller, and Dutta (1990), Gardner et al. (1989), Gould (1991a, 1991b, 1993), Loyotonnen (1991), Shannon (1991), Shannon, Pyle, and Bashshur (1991), Shannon and Pyle (1989), Smallman-Raynor and Cliff (1990), Ulack and Skinner (1991), Wallace and Fullilove (1991), and Wood (1988). They can be compared to more scientific epistemologies of AIDS (e.g., Fauci, 1991). For broader critiques of science and AIDS, see Banzhat (1990), Beauchamp (1991), Callen (1992), Callen, Grover, and Maggenti (1991), Crimp (1988a, 1988b, 1989, 1992a, 1992b, 1993), Crimp and Rolston (1990), Newman (1990), Geltmaker (1992), Dorn and Laws (1994), Kearns (1994), Brown (1995a), S. J. Gould (1991), Grover (1988, 1992), Haraway (1991, 1992), Horton (1989), Latour (1987), Olander (1991), Patton (1985, 1989, 1990), Rappoport (1988), Wacher (1990), Watney (1987, 1988, 1989), Watts and Okello (1990), and Williamson (1989). For an overview on the subdiscipline of medical geography, see Smith (1986).

to be articulated with an emerging gay subjectivity in the city. That process was met with decided opposition from the state and elements of the wider political community, which acted to exclude gays and people living with AIDS from the very category of citizen. Signifying the importance of state, civil society, and home to the formation of radical democracy, this chapter narrates that local history through each of these three locations.

HOME IN THE WEST END

The rise of gay neighborhoods across North American cities has been well documented. In many ways, the historical geography of Vancouver's gay community parallels experiences in other cities (Shilts, 1982; D'Emilio, 1983; Castells, 1983; FitzGerald, 1986; Kinsman, 1987). The West End, just adjacent to the central business district (CBD) on Vancouver's downtown peninsula, has come to be the central space for the gay community in the Lower Mainland, if not western Canada more broadly (see Figure 2-1). The West End, with some of the highest-density census tracts in Canada, is a scenic high-rise apartment neighborhood that is touted as the best in urban inner-city living. Gay men made the neighborhood their own for a variety of reasons over the past 30 years or so. An elderly man who has spent his entire life in the West End insisted that the area had been gay long before the sexual revolution and zoning changes in the 1960s:[3]

"The West End's been a gay community for as long as I can remember. I was a teenager there. Lived right across from the old motor vehicle branch testing station, between the White Spot and Denman Street. But whatever gay community there was in Vancouver, for as long as I can remember, was focused around the West End. Even in the fifties. A lot of the old mansions were rooming houses. And some of them divided into

---

[3]It is interesting to note that his recollections pace some of the recent historical geographies of gay communities in North America, which argue that there were (more or less) visible gay spaces long before the rise of the urban gay neighborhoods of the 1970s (e.g., Chauncey, 1994; Newton, 1993; Lapovsky-Kennedy & Davis, 1993).

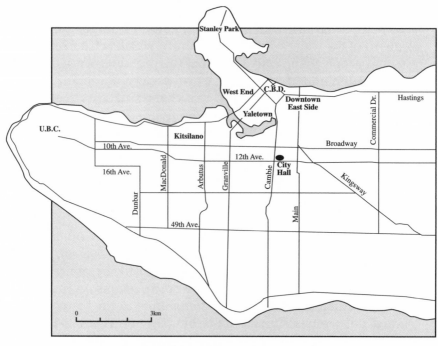

FIGURE 2-1. Map of Vancouver.

suites, so it was still a densely populated area. The bars weren't
around there then, maybe because of the zoning laws. Maybe
they couldn't get commercial licenses for that area."

Zoning changes in the late 1960s established pull factors in
the neighborhood for gay men. Formerly a single-family residential area, the West End was rezoned for high-density apartment
blocks, designed to contain urban residential sprawl and encourage inner-city lifestyle living. These apartments (and later condo-
miniums) attracted single, young gay men who did not need the
residential space the suburbs had promised and who collectively
could afford inner-city rents (Figure 2-2). Attracting a diverse
group of gay men from across Canada, the West End gentrified
through the sixties and seventies. Vancouver became "the San
Francisco of Canada": it was imagined nationally as an escape
from the closets of not only small-town Canada but even from
those cities where gay men's preexisting local ties prevented them

FIGURE 2-2. Home in the West End. Photo by author.

from coming out and exploring their sexuality. As the city's only openly gay alderman explained:

> "And the West End is Boystown. It had been well identified as a gay community ever since the sixties. It's a textbook case. The West End was rezoned in 1956, and it took about five years for the boom to really start. But between 1962 and 1972 almost every building over five stories that you see between Burrard and Stanley Park was built. It was an unparalleled period of construction and development. And most of what that provided was one-bedroom apartments for lower-middle-income younger people. Well, if you had gone out to design a gay neighborhood, you couldn't have done a better job than that. So every [gay] kid that was growing up from Moose Jaw to Prince Rupert soon, one way or another, gravitated towards that neighborhood. And the bars were there and the restaurants and the whole emergent sense of identity. And it was very much, of course, influenced by the culture of San Francisco."

My oral histories are replete with tales of gay men moving from other parts of Canada for the freedom that Vancouver promised: it was a place *where* they could *be* gay. While no precise statistics on gay migration into the city are available, my interviewees recalled a definite and ever increasing migration of gay men throughout the seventies and eighties. A gay baby-boomer summed up the experience when he said, "I came to the West End because I liked the sense of freedom and liberation associated with that place in the period of the late seventies. Unbelievable period!"

The number of gay bars in the city grew through the 1960s, and by the late 1970s they clustered in the West End and Yaletown (Fairclough, 1985; McLeod, 1996). Gradually they became more visible as public spaces by the early eighties. The atmosphere of sexual liberation and the emerging gay consciousness through the 1970s, as well as an increasing number of social organizations, augmented feelings of liberty and freedom, and community (Fairclough, 1985). Respondents who had lived in Vancouver for several decades readily identified these trends. One man in his forties recalled:

"Through the Seventies it was wild! Just wild! I guess you could say the discotheques and the 'glitter era,' everybody was quite high all the time. I mean you go out to a bar and everyone'd be doing acid and just dance their brains out. The gay bars were mixed straight and gay. About 10 years ago the bars moved into the West End, Numbers being the first in the West End, and then Celebrities and the Denman Station, and then the Odyssey. Oh, there was another old one way over on Robson about 10–12 years ago called Neighbours. And that was a real hopping bar. Oh, I forgot about Buddies! It opened up about the same time as Numbers They were the two in the West End. They were all basically downtown: Richards Street, Seymour Street. They're all gone now. One of the oldest bars in town is the Shaggy Horse. And I went to that—it was the first bar I went to. It was called The August Club then. It was really bizarre, and really seedy. It had drag shows. I didn't know what was going on. I was like, 'Why do they have women here entertaining?' I didn't know they were drag queens [laughs]. So by the 70s it started changing, you know, average guys and girls coming out of the closet. And it seemed safer during the sexual revolution. We had more freedom."

Thus, according to popular local history, securing a gay enclave in the city occurred without the intense political conflict common in other emerging gay areas. To paraphrase numerous individuals, "There never was a Stonewall in Vancouver."[4] This lack of confrontation was usually explained culturally, with an emphasis on Vancouver's being "West Coast," or a "lotus land" with a relaxed attitude about differences. One gay man in his early sixties recalled:

> "In my opinion this city's had a very tolerant attitude, for as long as I can remember—much more so than other cities I've lived in throughout North America, as a matter of fact. Toronto, Calgary, Edmonton, a couple of places in the States. I lived in New York for a while, but that doesn't really count there because it's a melting pot of everything. But Vancouver has always had, in my opinion, a far more tolerant attitude about being different from the norm. I can remember, and this is going back to the very early fifties, right across the country The Castle [a bar] was known as a fruit hangout. . . . During the war American servicemen were barred from going there because of that fact. And yet the local citizens didn't seem to mind There was no problems with the police or anyone. It was sort of, 'You do your own thing. We do ours.'"

Another early founder of AIDS Vancouver agreed:

> "I think Vancouver has a reputation, and justly so, for a certain degree of tolerance. There's the aspect of a large urban center. And there's also the aspect of the West Coast. There is this geography of the West Coast of North America being much more open to new ideas and spirituality and all of this

---

[4]For example, respondents often cited the Toronto's bathhouse raids in 1981 (see Kinsman, 1987, pp. 206–211) or its "Brunswick Four" episode of 1974 (see McLeod, 1996, pp. 147–150) as illustrating Vancouver's comparative lack of radical gay politics. The 1969 Stonewall Inn riot in New York City pitted gay men against police and is typically cited as the flash point of the gay-rights movement (see Duberman, 1993).

sort of stuff. So I think Vancouver was influenced by that. I think there's more tolerance."

He went on:

> "The difference between Vancouver and almost every other major city—certainly Toronto which had the raids on the baths in the seventies—was that we've never had a cathartic, bonding event. The city has always been 'laid back,' you know, liberal, do-your-own-thing, go-to-Wreck-Beach, have a good time. Tolerant of all kinds of behavior, welcoming to newcomers. And with a political leadership that has either never seen any particular interest in doing any political gay bashing. Just the opposite. It's been very supportive. I mean you could argue there's oppression, homophobia, that sort of thing, but nothing concrete."

Nevertheless, this alleged culture of tolerance did not always translate into ready acceptance of gays and lesbians into the political community. Through the 1960s and 1970s police surveillance of gay nightclubs was routine, and there are reported cases of raids on bars (Turner, 1964; "Police hassling clubs . . .," 1974) . Requests for the city to fund a social service center for gays and lesbians were soundly rejected in 1974. The city feared it would be promoting homosexuality through such funding ("Gays seeking . . .," 1974). Popular columnists repeatedly condemned gays and lesbians throughout the seventies, and city papers refused to run classified advertisements for gay and lesbian organizations ("*Sun*'s ad policy. . . .," 1975). In 1979 one such case was taken to the Supreme Court of Canada against the *Vancouver Sun*. The paper won, on grounds of freedom of the press (Richstone & Russell, 1981).

Despite this litany of homophobic actions, a single, unified gay and lesbian rights organization never materialized in the city.[5] The early 1970s saw the rise of a number of fairly single-issue gay

---

[5]Though perhaps the oldest gay organization in the city is the Dogwood Monarchist Society, founded in 1971. It is a coalition of drag queens and their fans. In Vancouver, the society has typically been seen as apolitical, though it has acted as a fund-raising vehicle.

and lesbian organizations, which often arose in response to specific controversies (McLeod, 1996, pp. 253–254). These were short-lived organizations, however, and broader based organizations like GATE (Gay Alliance Toward Equality) did not survive.[6] Even during its heyday the group did not garner widespread participation from the gay community, according to longtime Vancouver residents. If gay Vancouverites recalled tolerance from straight Vancouver, it seemed to be based more on ignorance than acceptance won by a well-organized urban social movement. Nonetheless, by the end of the decade gays had built a home for their community in the central part of the city.[7]

It was in this air of quiet community building that AIDS politics emerged in the 1980s. As early as 1981 there were rumors throughout the West End of a disease targeting gay men. Stories were filtering up from San Francisco, though information was sketchy. For example, a woman who traveled between San Francisco and Vancouver in those days recalled:

"So I moved here [in 1980], and had this whole core group of people which are still my friends. There was no talk about AIDS then. Nobody knew what it was. It's funny though. Back then in San Francisco in about 1981–82 I remember I had a friend who died of hepatitis, and I thought that was the weirdest thing. How can anyone die of hepatitis?"

Doctors in the West End, whose patients largely consisted of gay men, also began to notice strange epidemiological trends. They were also alerted to similar bizarre maladies concentrating in urban gay men elsewhere by the Center for Disease Control (CDC). One well-known doctor in the neighborhood recalled:

"As we slid into '82 it was getting to be more people. Skin things started to come up. And I remember quite well a phone call with [another West End doctor], who said, 'It's re-

---

[6]GATE actually had a number of chapters across Canada (see McLeod, 1996).

[7]The lesbian community in Vancouver is situated along Commercial Drive in a working class district several kilometers to the east of downtown. It formed slightly later than the gay ghetto, through the 1980s. For a discussion of the significant differences between gay and lesbian neighborhoods see Adler and Brenner (1992).

ally strange how many gay men are presenting with this kind of. . . .' It wasn't KS, . . . —but it was strange. And we're up to the late summer of 82, because I remember saying to him, 'How strange you should phone about that because we're having a meeting tomorrow or next week about how we might try to quantify some of this strange stuff that we're seeing.' "[8]

At St. Paul's Hospital, located in the southeast corner of the West End on Burrard Street, staff conceded that early cases of AIDS during this time were no doubt seen there but were passed off as other illnesses until infection trends were identified in 1981 and 1982. By 1983, it became clear to most gay West Enders that there were sick and dying gay men locally, and the problem was growing rapidly. Another doctor noted how geography played a key role in St. Paul's future as a leading center for HIV/AIDS care and research:

"I think initially people came here because they were being looked after by family practitioners who had their offices here, and most of them lived here in the West End. So they first came here because they were close. I think they continued to come here, though, because they recognized that even though there was some discrimination, it wasn't nearly as strong as the discrimination they experienced at other hospitals. Now, one of the interesting aspects that I can remember in about 1984, when I assigned the first AIDS case to a medical student, a third year medical student. They work up patients for the first time, take histories, do physicals, etc. And I can distinctly remember asking myself whether I should phone the head of the department or the dean and ask them if it was appropriate to assign a case. And that's a reflection of the sort of level of fear and apprehension. Well, I didn't phone the dean."

---

[8]This local epidemiological astuteness led to the Vancouver Lymphadenopathy study, which began at St. Paul's Hospital in November 1982, an ongoing study of people living with AIDS, which was continuing through my fieldwork. It is one of the best longitudinal studies of AIDS in the world. For more information contact the B.C. Centre for Excellence in HIV/AIDS Research, #608- 1081 Burrard St., Vancouver, B.C. V6Z 1Y6.

An infection control nurse had similar recollections:

"I can remember going up on a nursing unit one day and a nurse was in a private room. Patient had gone down for X-rays, and she was in making the patient's bed. She had a gown on and a mask on and gloves. There was no need for it! That patient was not incontinent. So I said, 'Can I talk to you?' And I helped her finish making the bed, dressed like I am right now in a skirt and a blouse, not wearing a uniform. And I said, 'I know the person who is in this room. In fact I came up to see him. And I know that he's not incontinent. Why have you got a gown and gloves and a mask on? I know you've been to the in-services we've done [on how HIV is transmitted]. And you and I have talked about it between us. Do you not understand how it is and isn't transmitted?' 'Oh yes. But there's no information out there yet to say that it's not transmitted in some other way.' This is back in '83. And you know we became the Centre [for Excellence in HIV/AIDS Research and Treatment] because of our geographic location. So if they hadn't looked after someone [with AIDS] yet, it would only be a matter of time before they did. There was a lot—oh, the education I did! We used to say if there was one disease they hadn't covered in talking about HIV it was laryngitis."

Apprehension was so high in the West End that a group of gay men began quiet meetings to figure out what could be done. Their recollections capture the growing uneasiness and sinking realization that the neighborhood was in the early stages of a catastrophic health crisis:

"It was simply unimaginable that something like this could be happening. It was far too nightmarish a scenario to actually be grasped. And also it was politically unacceptable to acknowledge that a lifestyle that had really been developed around sex—whether you like it or not, so much of what distinguished the gay community was sex—could have been so fundamentally disastrous, tragic. Anyhow, because I had been active in the community and knew a lot of people, and had some community organizing background . . . I got a visit from a friend named Ron Alexander. That was his 'stage name.' He was a figure skater, had been very active. And I can remember very well his anger at the refusal of people in Vancouver to recognize what the hell was going on. And somebody—at least—had to call a meeting. And he said, 'Well, look, you've been involved doing this kind of thing, how do you go about doing it?' This was '83—pretty late when you look back. And that's not too hard to do. So we got together some other key people we were going to need to do this."

"The first meeting I remember going to was on a Sunday morning in the gym for men on Granville Street. We sat around on the weight equipment. And I think there was three or four of us there. Most of them are still around, strangely enough. Bob Reimer was there. John Carswell was there. Mike Maynard was there. And then subsequently there were meetings in the basement of St. Paul's church. And we met for ages before anything actually ever happened. Then the group got bigger. David Salter was there. Daryl Nelson was there (he was on the Parks Board for a while). Then Gordon Price came on. And in my opinion he was the first effective chairperson. He finally started focusing people on, you know, 'let's not just sit here night after night talking about what's wrong. Let's talk about what we can do.'"

Seeking expertise, they called Paul Popham of the newly formed Gay Men's Health Crisis (GMHC) in New York. He came to Vancouver and spoke at an information night at the West End Community Centre on March 12, 1983. Shilts (1987, pp. 246–247) describes the meeting in some detail, focusing on "Patient Zero," a Canadian airline attendant alleged to be a leading figure in the transmission of HIV across North America. Vancouver activists, however, recall the fear and apprehension that pervaded the packed hall. It was not clear exactly how the virus—if in fact it was a virus—was transmitted. The virus itself was not publicly identified until early 1984. The term "AIDS," had just recently been coined by the CDC in mid-1982. Before then it went by various names, including GRID (Gay Related Immune Deficiency) and "gay gut." People feared attacks on their sexuality because of this link. More to the point, gay Vancouverites feared that the sickness and death that was plaguing U.S. cities would inevitably cross the border. Later, at a restaurant, Popham stressed the need for a local support and service organization to the forum organizers. AIDS Vancouver was officially formed later that year, and was the first AIDS service organization (ASO) in Canada. Operated at first completely on a volunteer basis, the organization held its meetings and conducted operations out of people's homes throughout the West End until it finally opened an office in that neighborhood in July 1985.

The fears and recognition of the need for a quick response were well warranted in Vancouver. During the 1980s, new AIDS cases in British Columbia increased rapidly, gradually leveling off during the early 1990s (see Figure 2-3). More to the point, British Columbia was the province exhibiting the greatest demand for AIDS initiatives in the country. By the late 1980s British Columbia had the highest rate of AIDS per capita in Canada (see Figure 2-4). Bear in mind that this was at a time when there were few treatments available for AIDS-related infections. And while it is quite problematic to disaggregate numbers of HIV positive people into "acquisition categories," both official statistics and commu-

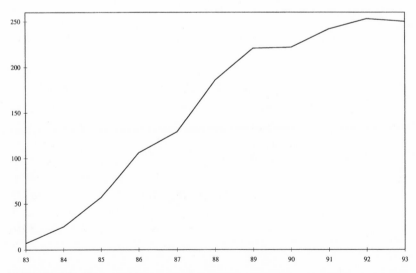

FIGURE 2-3. New AIDS cases in British Columbia, 1983–1993. *Source:* Rekart and Roy (1993) and Rekart and Chan (1993).

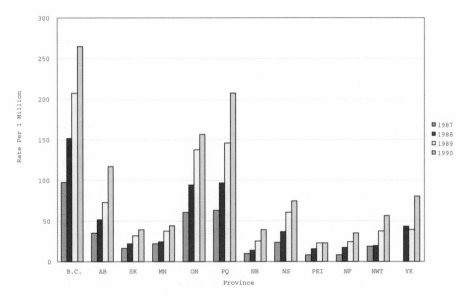

FIGURE 2-4. AIDS rates in Canada by province, 1987–1990. *Source:* Health and Welfare Canada, 1990.

nity perceptions suggest that the disease overwhelmingly afflicted the gay community, and foremost in Vancouver (see Figure 2-5).[9] More specifically, the city of Vancouver was by far the location where HIV was at its most intense rate of infection (see Figure 2-6).

The interesting political point to be made, however, is that through the 1980s AIDS issues exerted strong *internal* pressures inside the gay community that were hardly felt before. For the first time gay Vancouverites had to form a broad-based coalition to meet hard material needs quickly (such as drug treatments, financial aid, housing, food, medical supplies, etc.). Before AIDS, there had not been much to link gay men (and lesbians) across their social differences (see Cohen, 1991; Adam, 1992). Nor did gay men ever before have to deal with the state *as* gay men so publicly or collectively. One long term activist and counselor underscored the internal differences in the gay community that AIDS cut across as she recalled conversations she had with the men who formed the

---

[9]For a critique of this mode of representation, see Brown (1995a).

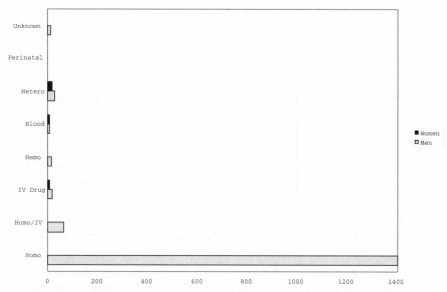

FIGURE 2-5. AIDS cases in British Columbia, by risk group, to 1993. *Source:* Rekart and Roy (1993).

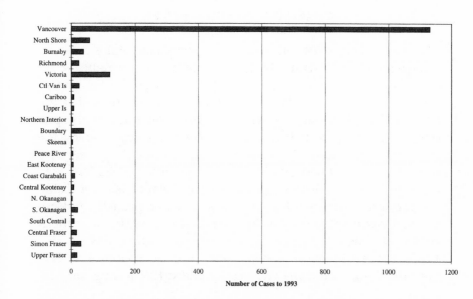

FIGURE 2-6. AIDS cases in British Columbia, by health unit, to 1993. *Source:* Rekart and Chan (1993).

Vancouver Persons With AIDS Society (a self-empowerment and advocacy group):

> "I don't know how they all got together exactly.[10] Certainly a lot of them when I saw them individually said that, in regards to the group, they regarded most of the others as people they would not normally have any sort of relationship with. And so it was very difficult for them to be in a group with these people on the basis of a terminal diagnosis. Different classes. Different social circles. Just different interests. The fact that they were all gay was not enough that they should all be friends, right?"

Thus, AIDS became the first material issue related to identity politics for gay men in the city. AIDS service organizations, in turn, quickly became ongoing outlets for volunteering and financial charity by and for the gay community locally. There were not just internal forces, however, impelling a local response to the crisis; it is important to communicate the tremendous external pressure on the gay community to form its own shadow state.

A HOMOPHOBIC STATE

Vancouver's culture of tolerance was directly (and quite publicly) challenged on AIDS issues by the provincial Social Credit (or Socred) government throughout the 1980s. The Socreds were a right-wing coalition of Liberals and Progressive Conservatives that (up to 1991) had dominated provincial politics for much of the preceding 50 years. In 1986 the party leadership was won by the charismatic Bill Vander Zalm, who governed until 1990. The party had long espoused neoconservative calls for entrepreneurism, government downsizing, and privatization. Premier Vander Zalm, however, was a staunch Roman Catholic who repeatedly and unabashedly attempted to press his moral views directly into official government policy (Persky, 1989; Mason & Baldrey, 1989; Leslie, 1991). Issues like abortion and AIDS received special attention from the Cabinet and the Premier. Typically, HIV testing, medical

---

[10]For a comparison of the differences in AIDS activism across Canadian cities, see the excellent article by Rayside and Linquist (1992).

services, and research were funded, albeit quietly and minimally. AIDS education, prevention, and support services were deemed problematic, however, and were publicly denied funding. Despite an aggressive policy of "restraint" and welfare state retrenchment (see Magnusson, Carroll, Doyle, Langer, & Walker, 1984), Socred arguments against funding AIDS initiatives were not based on fiscal conservatism but decidedly on moral opposition to premarital sex and gays. A senior bureaucrat in the provincial Ministry of Health offered this characterization:

"Hindsight is 20-20 vision, but retrospectively it seems to me that there were some serious mistakes made on both sides (government and community groups). And that probably reflects a relative immaturity as much as anything else in dealing with that kind of issue. The community groups were very vociferous. They didn't mind standing up and disrupting meetings and having die-ins in the streets. And for a conservative government like the Social Credit government was, that's tough to handle. The other thing that we had, because it was focused on the gay community, there's no question that there was a massive dose of homophobia in the cabinet and our institutions, and a fair bit of it in the ministry itself. 'Well, hell, that's their lifestyle! They created the problem, let them live with the problem.' It was sort of a blame the victim kind of approach, as opposed to looking at it more holistically. And we had a hell of a time for a few years of getting the message across in the ministry, but more particularly within the rest of government that we had to invest in trying to prevent the spread of disease. It was tough sledding for a while."

Through the 1980s and into the early part of this decade a number of specific, explosive issues collectively demonstrated the government's homophobia and moral reading of AIDS to the gay community (McInnes, 1989). In 1988–1989 the Premier stopped a video produced by the Ministry of Health from being shown in movie theaters. He banned it because it promoted condom usage; an "acceptable" video was eventually released. AIDS Vancouver was repeatedly frustrated by the province's refusal to fund explicit safe-sex brochures designed for gay men. In the early 1990s, Bill 34 was passed, which gave the provincial government sweeping powers to quarantine people suspected of knowingly transmitting HIV. Around the same time, when AZT (azidothymidine) came on to the market, British Columbia became the only province in Canada not to subsidize the drug completely, instead requiring that patients pay 20% of its cost themselves, which many could not afford. All the while, Vander Zalm and his Cabinet ministers repeatedly stressed their personal objections to gay and lesbian "lifestyles." For example, the Socred Forest Minister referred publicly to AIDS as a "self-inflicted wound" in 1989—without reproach from the Premier or Health Minister (Leslie, 1991, p. 146). Most controversial, perhaps, was the Health Minister's 1987 remark that AIDS Vancouver could "take care of their own kind," though he insisted it was not a slur (Barrett, 1987, p. B-3; Simpson, 1989; see also Weeks, 1989; Ouster, . . ., 1990). These controversies galvanized the gay community in the West End. A comment from one AIDS Vancouver employee in early 1992 captures the perception of neglect and homophobia—along with the gay community's immense frustration:

> "A lot of what's around has only been around for a few months or a year. And that's related to the provincial government—that fascist, fundamentalist, right-wing regime. Hearing the stories that are starting to get out now from some of the ministry people about what was really going on, it's scandalous. I feel these people should be made accountable and sued for negligence. I'm very angry. I'm very angry! It's set things back in this province many, many years. They completely ignored it. Did not want to address it. Felt that AIDS had to do with some crummy fags that really weren't important anyway. And that's the absolute fact of it."

GAYS RESPOND IN CIVIL SOCIETY

While British Columbia has had a long history of relying on semiprivate organizations to provide welfare services (Ismael & Vaillancourt, 1988), its increased use of the shadow state over the past 15 years has been amply documented (Donaldson, 1985; Magnusson, 1986; Butcher, 1986; Reimer, 1992; Rekart, 1993). In the case of AIDS, a rapid emergence of shadow-state activity has proceeded since 1983. The range and quantity of service providers are demonstrated in Table 2-1 and mapped in Figure 2-7. These agen-

TABLE 2-1. The AIDS Shadow State in Vancouver, 1992

Advocacy

AIDS and Disability Project
ACT UP Vancouver
British Columbia AIDS Information
   Exchange
British Columbia AIDS Network
Vancouver Persons With AIDS
   Society

Counseling

AIDS Vancouver
The Street Project
Vancouver Native Health
Vancouver Persons With AIDS
   Society

Education

Aboriginal AIDS Awareness
   Project
AIDS and Disability Project
AIDS Vancouver
British Columbia Centre for
   Disease Control
Vancouver Health Department
Healing Our Spirit
Latin American AIDS Awareness
   Project
Needle Exchange Program
Safeco/British Columbia Ministry
   of Health
The Street Project
Vancouver World AIDS Group
Woman and AIDS Project
YWCA

Financial Aid

AIDS Vancouver
Street Youth Services
Vancouver Persons With AIDS
   Society

Food

AIDS Vancouver
Downtown Community Health
Vancouver Meals Society
Vancouver Persons With AIDS
   Society
Help lines
AIDS Vancouver
British Columbia Centre for
   Disease Control
Canadian HIV Trials Network

Home Support

AIDS Vancouver
Vancouver Health Department

Housing

McLaren House
Helmcken House
Vancouver Persons With AIDS
   Society

Legal Aid

British Columbia Civil Liberties
   Association
Vancouver Persons With AIDS
   Society

Support

AIDS Vancouver
Healing Our Spirit
Vancouver Health Department
St. Paul's Anglican Church
Vancouver Persons With AIDS
   Society
Women and AIDS Project
Positive Women's Network

Testing

British Columbia Centre for
   Disease Control
Vancouver Health Department
Safeco
Vancouver Lesbian Centre

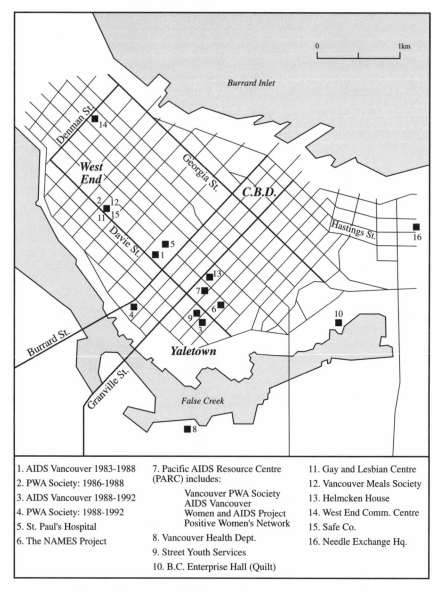

FIGURE 2-7. Map of the AIDS shadow state in Vancouver.

cies historically have clustered around the West End and have more recently congregated in the adjacent Yaletown district (just south of the West End across Granville Street) because of cheaper rents and space availability (Brown, 1995b). Two agencies dominate. AIDS Vancouver (AV) is the principal education, prevention, and support service organization in the city. It was founded in the wake of the meeting held in March of 1983. During my fieldwork it had a paid staff of 20–25 and a volunteer base of over 300. The Vancouver Persons With AIDS Society (PWA) is a self-help group that encourages empowerment and "advocates" for people who are HIV positive or who have AIDS. It had a membership of over 1,200 during my research. Following its self-help mandate PWA broke away from AIDS Vancouver in order to better articulate the voice of people living with AIDS. The coalition formed originally around three men—Kevin Brown, Warren Jensen, and Taavi Nurmella—in 1986 and quickly grew through informal networking.[11] Members of AIDS Vancouver who were HIV positive or who had AIDS, frustrated with the Socred's reactionary attitudes, pushed the organization to take a more explicitly antagonistic stance toward the government. The leaders of AIDS Vancouver declined to do so, concerned that it might jeopardize the organization's nonprofit tax status and funding. A PWA member recalls:

"This was spring of '86. And they were just splitting from AIDS Vancouver and starting PWA. One of the reasons was that they wanted funding for alternate therapies, and AV was fairly hesitant about funding that. This is now the complementary health fund. And of course at that time AV was fighting very hard to get any funding anywhere. And I think they were petrified that if the medical establishment didn't approve of what they were doing then the various levels of government would simply say forget it. I could see both sides. I could understand the frustration that PWA felt, but I could also understand the politics behind AV's decision."

---

[11]The first PWA self-help group began in October 1984 under the auspices of AIDS Vancouver. Meeting originally in people's homes and later at St. Paul's Hospital, the group officially separated from AIDS Vancouver in April 1986 (Goldberg & Collins, 1991).

An associate PWA Society member recalls the tensions similarly:

> ". . . the strange thing was AIDS Vancouver was trying to get its tax number, which of course means nontaxable donations could come in. This probably would have been around '85. And it was initially refused by Revenue Canada because there was a political mandate included in the mission statement. That was to advocate for the rights of people with AIDS and HIV infection. And as a result of that AIDS Vancouver had to amend its constitution to remove its advocacy mandate in order to raise the money to carry out the support services that it wanted to do. That sort of vacuum in the advocacy business eventually led to all sorts of hassles and the emergence of the Vancouver Persons With AIDS Society. . . . And having dropped the advocacy funding the PWA group within AIDS Vancouver got very angry that there wasn't enough noise being made. And nobody really understood the niceties as to why that had to be done. And so the PWA group eventually emerged out of AIDS Vancouver in 1986. And it became its own separate society."[12]

After a brief period of tension where the two organizations remained apart, they set up house together in a Yaletown office block dubbed "PARC" (Pacific AIDS Resource Centre) in the summer of 1992 (see Figure 2-8).

Ironically, in spite of government opposition and gay community support, these organizations have consistently received funding from the province, as the preceding comments above hint. Local autonomy in British Columbia is tightly circumscribed by the province (Magnusson, 1986). City health departments are principally an arm of the Ministry of Health. Even so, by 1985 the city health officer, along with the new director of the provincial Centre for Disease Control (a branch of the health ministry), had realized

---

[12]Interestingly, this interviewee goes on to note: "In the meantime the PWA Society set up with an advocacy mandate and got a tax number like that. God only knows why! The Positive Women's Network can't get their tax number right now. They've got to go through some hoops before they can get it. As I understand it, there has been a change in [federal] policy in the interim. The policy is now that political activity incidental to your primary mission is acceptable, whereas in the old days if you mentioned political, no way could you have a tax number."

FIGURE 2-8. The Pacific AIDS Resource Centre (PARC). Photo by author.

that AIDS Vancouver's services were invaluable, because the health crisis would only get worse. Therefore, it needed to be subsidized despite government homophobia. They devised an approach whereby the province would transfer money to the Vancouver Health Department, which, in turn, would quietly earmark it for AIDS Vancouver (and later the PWA Society and McLaren Housing Society) alongside more public city grants to the agencies. This funneling (well known by people in ASOs but not the public more generally) enabled the organizations to cover overhead expenses, thereby helping to stabilize their position in the city, and more importantly eased some of the intense financial pressure on the gay community. As a City Health official recalls this arrangement, he puts an ironic twist on Clark and Dear's (1986) *State Apparatus* argument, which asserts that the multifacetedness of different apparatuses serves to channel and displace conflict from one part of the state to another:

> "So I had a lot more flexibility [than the province]. In fact one of the things I should have mentioned is that during that time I laundered a lot of money for the province. [A ministry bureaucrat] would give me money that—you know—was legal. I would receive it, report to council that I had received this

money, and then I would allocate it. And it would look like I was allocating where I wanted to spend it. The truth was, [we] had worked out where it would be allocated. Some of that money was for the specific gay and lesbian education money, which would have blown the minds of some of those politicians if they knew the kind of thing they were funding. [Money was going to] AIDS Vancouver at that time. And we're still doing that funding through AIDS Vancouver. So we became a way of getting money to them. Interestingly, the Minister of Health knew we were doing that, but he didn't want to involve the Cabinet or the Premier and that sort of thing. So the ruse was 'We give money to the city, and the city does with it what it wants.' I would go to the Mayor and say, 'Look, I really don't have a lot of flexibility; this is what we want to do.' But also we were able to get money for our own campaigns. And so the condom ads and that sort of stuff were being supported by the province, even though officially they weren't."

According to provincial health bureaucrats of the day, the Premier and Cabinet allowed the secretive and minimal funding to proceed because, by 1985, the crisis had become too great to ignore. Nonetheless, the scheme gave the impression that the city was funding AIDS organizations while the Socreds were ignoring dying gay men and only representing their Christian fundamentalist supporters. This budgetary arrangement did have the favorable consequence of further augmenting gay solidarity and support for local AIDS organizations. A Ministry of Health bureaucrat summed up the situation as follows:

"The perspective of the conservative, religious faction is that the Socred government never supported these 'abnormal' lifestyles. The perspective of the people that actually *know* is that 'Well, yeah. There was support coming.' The perspective of the general public is probably that it was never supported. In other words, the public face of the Socred government was 'We do not agree with this lifestyle. This is abnormal. This is not good for our kids or for society and we're not going to put up with it.' On the other hand, for those on the inside, it was clear that there was a lot more support than was ever admitted to."

More recently (and coinciding with a change in provincial government), city and provincial bureaucracies have interlocked with Vancouver's shadow state through numerous relationships (often contracting) and shared mandates. The province offers anonymous testing but locates sites in community facilities. It hires street nurses and community workers to do AIDS outreach and testing in the inner city and West End, as well as running its own successful "Condomania" campaign. The City Health Department funds a needle exchange staffed by provincial nurses but administrated by a nonprofit service center. The city also has an AIDS education coordinator whose campaigns advocate condom use. St. Paul's Hospital houses the Infectious Disease Clinic, which specifically treats people living with AIDS and HIV. These state-centered initiatives aside, the bulk of the education, prevention, and support work around AIDS and HIV in Vancouver is done in or by the gay community's shadow state.

CONCLUSION

This chapter has described the historical development of AIDS politics in Vancouver. It has shown the development of radical democratic citizenship through gay identity as AIDS grew to be a major political issue during the 1980s. With a somewhat tolerant urban political culture, the West End grew into a comfortable (some might say self-satisfied) gay enclave. When AIDS hit the city in the early part of the decade, the gay community lacked any coherent history of political mobilization on which to draw. Responses started from scratch, and gay identity politics and AIDS issues became tightly—and quite self-consciously—interwoven. At the same time, the Social Credit government grew especially vocal in its denial of support for people—typically gay men—living with AIDS. By rhetoric and explicit policy, the British Columbia government sought to exclude gay men from considering themselves as full-fledged citizens. It denied them membership in the political community of the province by saying they were beyond the boundaries of the political community, and therefore not eligible to claim rights relating to education, support, and welfare. To a large extent they were placed beyond the government's mandate to promote the welfare and well-being of its citizens. And while Socred rhetoric was never matched in its negative intensity by street-level bureaucratic policy—in fact, it was much to the contrary!—still, the gay community realized that it could not rely on the state to provide education, prevention, and support services to any appreciable degree.

Gay men and their allies thus realized their own obligations as citizens to "do something" and began to respond to the developing crisis through organizations of their own. The rumblings of radical democracy, then, were clearly evident in Vancouver's emerging response to AIDS issues. As Mouffe defines politics based on an antagonistic distinction between friends and enemies, the gay solidarity in opposition to the state clearly marks that division. Additionally, the gay community's efforts at providing education, support, and prevention services on its own embody the agonistic politics that are a principle feature of radical democracy. Through this history, then, we can see how Vancouver has become what Mouffe would call a "new space" of radical democracy, in Vancouver's case, a place where a political struggle over the relationship between sexual identity and citizenship has occurred.

The historical geography of AIDS in Vancouver also highlights how abstract political processes—from homophobia to welfare state retrenchment—are always geographically mediated in place. This is especially true of the ways that political identity came to inform sexual identity in the city. Furthermore, the volume and wide variety of responses to AIDS suggest that a micro-geographic scale is needed to examine the emergence of radical democracy *within* the city. Thus, in the chapters to follow we examine new and old spaces of citizenship within the city itself across civil society, the state, and the family and home.

Chapter 3

RADICAL CITIZENSHIP IN CIVIL SOCIETY?
ACTing UP in Vancouver

RADICAL CITIZENSHIP IN CIVIL SOCIETY

With the advent of new social movements, civil society has been designated by scholars as the most likely new site of politics (e.g., Castells, 1983; Offe, 1985).[1] Refocusing scholars' attention away from state-centered politics, the concept captures the public sphere of private individuals engaged in voluntary association. Spaces of civil society, Mouffe has agreed, hold a potential for radical democratic citizenship. When one looks across civil society in AIDS issues, the most visible group likely to be encountered is ACT UP (the AIDS Coalition To Unleash Power). During the AIDS crisis, ACT UP has been touted as the most radical organization dedicated to social change because of its penchant for disruptive public acts of civil disobedience—so much so that when I began my research in January 1992 the first organization I contacted in Vancouver was ACT UP. Years earlier, I had heard about its demonstra-

---

[1]While Castells (1983) has written exhaustively on urban social movements, I have not taken up his work explicitly in this research. He was attempting to escape the economic determinism of structural Marxism; yet, he did not have the poststructural vocabulary in the early 1980s to completely break out of that framework. I find his tendencies to view urban politics as a process of consumption and social movements as struggles over spatial meaning to be limiting.

tions through the local media, and, while I knew that it scheduled
monthly meetings at the Gay and Lesbian Centre in the West End,
I was not aware of any recent ACT UP actions in Vancouver.
Nonetheless, I began my research with ACT UP Vancouver because
it seemed to be precisely the form (radically democratic) and location (in civil society) of radical democracy that Mouffe was chart-
ing.

After 120 interviews, however, my first interviewee remained
the only person who acknowledged membership in ACT UP. Other
members had either died, left the city, or were no longer politically
active.[2] There never was another ACT UP demonstration during
my two years of fieldwork, and the lone ACT UP member himself
hinted at the folding of the organization during my very first interview:

> "I don't know what the problem is these days. ACT UP is go-
> ing through a difficult period where we aren't getting the peo-
> ple turning up. I think actually that ACT UP could be folding
> on a certain level. It just might not be necessary right now."

This activist's suspicions about ACT UP Vancouver's necessity were
reiterated throughout my interviews with other people involved in
AIDS politics in the city (cf. von Hertum, 1993). The emerging
theme was that ACT UP Vancouver had been only modestly successful at focusing public attention on the Social Credit government's neglect of AIDS issues. Voluntary sector groups that were
incorporated into the state apparatus were more effective in getting the needs of people living with AIDS met (see Chapter 4).

How are we to understand the failures (and success) of ACT UP
Vancouver in the context of a quest for *new spaces* of radical citizenship? In a site where theoretically we precisely ought to expect
transformative politics, its transgressive form of civil disobedience
and media spectacle proved inefficacious. The simple answer to
this query is that ACT UP failed in Vancouver because Canadian
cities lack a civil disobedience tradition perhaps more native to
American cities. Indeed, as I illustrate below, many locals drew on

---

[2]Since I used a network sampling strategy in collecting oral histories, members
of ACT UP were made aware of my study. None of them who remained in the city
came forward for an interview.

imagery of Canadians' political quiescence in explaining ACT UP's failures. But the case also raises theoretical questions beyond issues of radical democracy's empirical generalizability. While ACT UP movements incorporate the elements of radical democratic citizenship (which I detail below), ACT UP's failure in Vancouver highlights the need to understand the structuration between citizenship and space. ACT UP Vancouver failed in part because it misunderstood and misrepresented the shifting, increasingly overlapping, relations *between* state and civil society that were already going on in Vancouver. That misunderstanding of spatial arrangements (between locations associated with civil society and the state) may have been, in fact, a reason for ACT UP Vancouver's failure. Unlike Mouffe's spatial metaphors, in Vancouver there was no "pure" space of state or civil society, making ACT UP's oppositional stance in civil society seem oddly out of place. This chapter argues that such a misunderstanding demonstrates how fixed and static notions of space in a radical theory of citizenship may fail to capture the ongoing shifts among actual spaces in state and civil society.

ACT UP AS RADICAL DEMOCRATIC CITIZENSHIP

ACT UP seemed to exemplify Mouffe's notion of citizenship in at least four ways. Foremost, ACT UP has become quite well known for its alternative and transgressive approach to the political (Berlant & Freeman, 1993; Crimp, 1993; Kramer, 1989; Geltmaker, 1992). ACT UP's premiere chapter, in New York, was founded as a result of a March 10, 1987 speech given at the Gay and Lesbian Community Center by noted gay activist and playwright Larry Kramer.[3] More accurately, the speech was part of a stinging critique of the political lassitude of the AIDS community, in which Kramer denounced the lack of progress in drug availability, the profit-mongering of drug companies, and the weakness and bureaucratization of GMHC. Two days after the meeting, ACT UP was formed—specifically with the mandate to accelerate drug release

---

[3]A transcript of the speech can be found in Kramer (1989, pp. 127–139).

in the U.S. Its mandate quickly broadened, as its chapters multiplied.[4] The organization officially defines itself as "a diverse, nonpartisan group united in anger and committed to direct action to end the AIDS crisis" (Crimp & Rolston, 1990, p. 13). ACT UP provided a radicalizing opportunity for many who joined. Kramer's invectives were often directed at the political apathy of gay men. He insisted that they must rethink the power structures surrounding AIDS. Rather than ignoring the disease or viewing it as a form of punishment, gay men must see both AIDS and HIV as savage attacks on their very existence. Crimp and Rolston (1990, p. 22) specifically state that ACT UP is committed to "radical democratic change." ACT UP does not seek to "change the system from within" but rather attacks the very assumptions and premises that underlie the practices of, and actually existing relations between, democracy and capitalism (Callen, Grover, & Maggenti, 1991; Olander, 1991; Saalfield & Navarro, 1991).

Second, like Mouffe's notion of citizenship, ACT UP's goal is to challenge existing hegemonies around AIDS. ACT UP has striven to provide a counterhegemony to the prevailing social understanding of AIDS. For instance, one ACT UP New York member described how this oppositional discourse inspired her toward civil disobedience against the Catholic Church because of its clear logic:

> And Cardinal O'Connor, especially at that time, was telling the general public that monogamy would protect them from HIV infection and that condoms didn't work. As far as I was concerned, those were both major lies. And while people were certainly entitled to make their own decisions about their lives—and far be it from me to tell them what to do—I would not sit by silently while they were being lied to. So when the group decided to target St. Patrick's, it just made absolute perfect sense to because it is an extremely important target in this epidemic. (Northrop, 1992, pp. 484–485)

Similarly, Gamson (1991) has centered ACT UP's purpose on the creation of an alternative way of seeing AIDS, one that uses specta-

---

[4]ACT UP chapters have been formed in, among other cities: Atlanta, Boston, Chicago, Cleveland, Dallas, Denver, Halifax, Kansas City, London, Los Angeles, Milwaukee, Montreal, New Orleans, Paris, Philadelphia, Portland (ME), San Francisco (also Golden Gate), Seattle, St. Louis, Toronto, and Washington. See Sword (1991), Crimp and Rolston (1991), Rayside and Lindquist (1992), and Chew (1993).

cle to resist media, bureaucratic, and scientific tropes attempting to normalize AIDS (see also S. J. Gould, 1991). It is on these grounds that theatrical and cultural activism is used so fervently by ACT UP—namely, in order to *displace* meanings. The media are thus manipulated explicitly by ACT UP for their attraction to spectacle (Browning, 1993).

Third, ACT UP is committed to radical democratic principles (Gamson, 1991; Northrop, 1992). There tends to be no hierarchy in decision making, and the chapters are notoriously lacking in any formal organizational structure, as well. The coalition in Vancouver, for example, operated primarily through a telephone tree of 80 people, any of whom could call a meeting if s/he thought an action was warranted. There are no formal membership requirements, and anyone can attend ACT UP meetings or participate in their rallies.[5] People participate to varying extents. No one is obliged to perform acts of civil disobedience at any given demonstration, and the modes of action are decided upon by consensus.

Given these minimal ground rules, fervent discussion and debate are the rule at ACT UP meetings (clearly reflecting the antagonistic nature of radical democracy). ACT UP also tries to interweave related struggles around AIDS, a key component for the radical democratic project. It is not just a movement by and for gay men. For example, in 1991, ACT UP Seattle used that city's Space Needle as a demonstration site to demand a needle exchange program for intravenous drug users. The widespread ignorance on the subject of women and AIDS has also been a key target for ACT UP campaigns (Banzhat, 1990). The group strives to suture social struggles in order to create a new hegemony. Many otherwise sympathetic critics have derided ACT UP's failure to link AIDS struggles across identities more successfully or thoroughly (Crimp, 1993, pp. 315–316; Gamson, 1991). One exception is Russo (1992), who has been more forgiving in his oral history:

> This is a new kind of activism. It's a coalition that we were never able to achieve in the 1970s. Back then the ideal and the dream were that gay people would come together with other oppressed groups like blacks and Asians and women to form a coalition. That didn't happen because we had too many differences. Les-

---

[5]An ACT UP Seattle member noted that law enforcement officials were not denied access to meetings; they were, however, asked to identify themselves as such.

bians were fighting with gay men, the black community didn't
want to admit that was a gay community in their midst and
blah, blah, blah. Now AIDS has brought us together in ways that
we could not have foreseen. ACT UP is composed of gay people
and straight people, women and men, black and white. And all
these people have one thing in common: They want to put an
end to the AIDS crisis by any means possible. (p. 415)

Finally, ACT UP works to accomplish its aims unquestionably
in the venue of civil society, its organized actions typically being
highly theatrical disruptions of public spaces.[6] These "work"—that
is, receive media attention—by transgressing cultural codes of
what is acceptable behavior in public space (see Cresswell, 1996).
Thus ACT UP, as Berlant and Freeman (1993, p. 224) attest, takes
on heretofore normal spaces. The will to disrupt hegemony draws
a strong parallel with the Situationist International Movement of
the 1960s (Ball, 1987). ACT UP *spatially* hijacks cultural attitudes
(relating to AIDS, disease, welfare, and sexuality) with irony and
places them into heavily coded, unfamiliar contexts.[7] So, for example, the spectacle of dozens of couples kissing in public becomes most transgressive only when done by same-sex couples insisting on accurate safe sex education. Situationists and ACT UP
members both rely heavily on what Kaplan and Ross (1987, p. 24)
call "acts of cultural sabotage" that critique mainstream society.
Gamson has observed that ACT UP (p. 35) "trespassed the bounds
of good taste." Both have taken up symbols used to oppress and
have radically subverted their meanings. In addition to such
graphics, acts of civil disobedience and spectacle have been used to
confront "heterosexed" space (Valentine, 1993) with those over-
riding gay and lesbian realities: that alternative sexualities exist,
and they exist in the context of an epidemic that has been killing
gay men. ACT UP's affronting, provocative graphics (in New York,
these are designed primarily by the artist group Gran Fury) target
numerous issues and public figures that, ACT UP argues, block
progress against AIDS. Examples include: ACT UP New York's "Target City Hall" campaign in March 1989; a purported advertisement
that was part of Gran Fury's "New York Crimes" attack on *The New*

---

[6]Sorkin (1992) would argue that this usurpation is appropriate, given the the-
atricalized spaces of late-twentieth century cities.

[7]The situationists referred to this process as *detournement*.

York Times for its downplaying and ignorance of AIDS; and ACT UP's "Stop the Church" campaign in 1989, aimed at Cardinal O'-Connor's persistent attempts to keep AIDS education and prevention materials out of the New York public school system.

ACT UP's most well known actions illustrate the use of civil society to disrupt hegemony radically. On September 14, 1989, activists posing as traders unfurled a large banner reading "Sell Wellcome"—thereby interrupting for a full five minutes the global shifts of capital on the floor of the New York Stock Exchange in a protest of excessive profits by the manufacturer of AZT. Several months earlier, on April 25, Burroughs Wellcome's headquarters in North Carolina had been infiltrated by four ACT UP members. Dressed as businessmen, the four talked their way past security guards and sealed themselves in the building, demanding reductions in AZT's price—a goal that ACT UP eventually won. The movement's demonstrations appropriated locations in civil society—confronting strangers deliberately—in order to make the AIDS crisis visible to them, to press rights claims, and to demand some form of political obligation on the part of fellow citizens. Indeed, Gamson's (1991, p. 38) insistence that ACT UP be sociologically defined as a "new social movement" hinges exactly on Offe's (1985) definition of the term: a group whose politics occur within civil society. Here, Laclau and Mouffe's (1985) argument that we must look beyond typical locations in the welfare state as sites of politics was substantiated.

THE ORIGINS OF ACT UP VANCOUVER

While ACT UP Vancouver itself did not officially form until July 1990, its disruptive tactics were employed by activists at least three years earlier. According to the member I interviewed, ACT UP Vancouver replaced an informal organization known as the Coalition for Responsible Health Care (CoRHL), which was formed specifically to combat Bill 34, the so-called Quarantine Bill that granted sweeping powers to the state to confine people suspected of transmitting HIV. CoRHL drew heavily from the Vancouver Persons With AIDS Coalition (which later became a formal nonprofit society) that had recently broken away from AIDS Vancouver to be "more political" in 1986. CoHRL also lobbied Victoria for an antiviral testing lab in March 1986, and protested at a Socred fundraiser at the Queen Elizabeth Theatre in downtown Vancouver on December 3, 1987 (Flather, 1987). Vancouver activists joined in the ACT UP protests held at the International AIDS Conference in Montreal in June 1989. My lone ACT UP informant recalled the assault with pride:

> "I have this flag from the Republic of China here. The '89 Montreal AIDS Conference opened on June third. And it was a surprise that we did make international news given that Tiananmen Square happened that day. The flags of all the nations were on the podium, and I was quite incensed that they would have the People's Republic flag up after this massacre had occurred. So I stole it. Right under the gaze of Mulroney.[8] That conference was disrupted by members of ACT UP. We delayed his speech for like an hour and a half. He was quite disturbed by the time he finally did speak. It was a coalition of groups: individual activists as well as ACT UP New York, ACT UP Montreal, and Toronto organizations."

In early September 1989, AIDS activists targeted Premier Vander Zalm, holding an elaborate protest at the Fantasy Gardens theme park in Richmond (an inner suburb of Vancouver), which the Premier and his wife owned (Horwood, 1989). There were die-ins held, with mock graves, coffins, and tombstones reading "He Died on a Placebo Study" and "I Died in Poverty Paying for AZT." Protesters demonstrated at Fantasy Gardens, which was at the time sponsoring a fund-raiser for the Lions Club Timmy Telethon, with signs reading "HIV Is NOT a Gay Disease" and "Homophobia Is a Sickness." Not surprisingly, there were many members of the PWA Society on hand. Indeed, a PWA spokesperson was quoted in *The Vancouver Sun*'s story on the Fantasy-AIDS rally (Rebalski, 1989, p. D-12).

With the notoriety and success of groups in other cities around the world, and the growing links between AIDS organizations and the state, an ACT UP group officially coalesced almost a year later (see Wilson, 1990, p. A-8, for a discussion). On July 21,

---

[8]At the time, Brian Mulroney was Prime Minister of Canada.

1990, ACT UP Vancouver officially formed (Shariff, 1990). The group's first meeting attracted 35 people, most between the ages of 18 and 25, and was largely dominated by a gay lawyer, Kevin Robb, and David Lewis, an outspoken former leader of the PWA Society. At the meeting, the chapter was officially designated, and a mission statement was drafted. In part, it read: "We demonstrate and protest; we challenge and demand governments and health institutions take positive action; we research, act on, and make available the latest medical information" (quoted in Buttle, 1990, p. A-17). Apparently there were people there from several other AIDS groups in the city. One former AIDS Vancouver employee recalls the meeting, stressing the tensions between social action and civil society and personal employment in the state apparatus:

"I was at the meeting that David Lewis called. He called a meeting of people that would be interested in the formation of ACT UP. That would have been four or five [weeks] before he died. That would have been the summer of 1990. And we had it in the back yard at his place. It was quite interesting, you know. This would have been before the [*Les Miserables*] episode. I was working at AIDS Vancouver at the time. So a coworker and I went to this thing. We were curious and had heard about ACT UP and read about ACT UP and seen things in the media and so on. And thought, well maybe this is something we can be involved with. But we were sort of walking a fine line because we were also employees of AIDS Vancouver. And so we have to be careful about—you know we were really caught between a rock and a hard place at that point because some things that would reflect negatively on the organization."

ACT UP Vancouver's first official action attracted media attention across Canada. Some 150 people held a die-in during rush hour at Robson Square (see Figure 1-3, p. 21) less than a month after the group's inception (Wilson, 1990, p. A-1). At a Socred fundraiser (ironically, a performance of *Les Miserables*) at the Queen Elizabeth Theatre on August 24, 1990, Premier Vander Zalm was spat on, and his wife Lillian was knocked to the ground by ACT UP protesters ("AIDS protesters . . . ," 1990). Five protesters were arrested and later released.

After the confrontational summer of 1990, however, ACT UP began to wane on Vancouver's political scene. The only other recorded action of that year took place in December, when ACT UP occupied then Provincial Health Minister John Jansen's Vancouver office to demand that British Columbia provide better AIDS services and funding ("Seven AIDS protesters arrested," 1990, p. A-2). During 1991 the group had only three press-recorded actions. In the most notable one, on January 29, an ACT UP member was arrested for allegedly spilling ketchup on and denting Premier Vander Zalm's limousine in front of the U-TV television studio, where he was scheduled to give the State-of-the-Province address. A moving die-in was held along Vancouver's upscale-retail Robson Street during AIDS Awareness Week in October. Another "0" was added by ACT UP to the city's centennial monument, a cement "100" at the south foot of the Cambie Street Bridge at West 6th Avenue, denoting the 1,000th case of AIDS in British Columbia. It then took its demands to Progressive Conservative MP Kim Campbell's local office (Buttle, 1991). By early 1992, its bimonthly meetings at the Gay and Lesbian Centre were drawing no one. ACT UP never held another media event afterward.

ACT UP Vancouver's purpose was always to attack the Socreds, taking a much narrower tack than some of its counterpart chapters elsewhere. Providing information about drugs remained the mandate of the Persons With AIDS Society's Treatments Committee. Lobbying was done by PWA's Advocacy Committee, or occasionally by the Intake Department at AIDS Vancouver. This left ACT UP only staging protests, specifically against the provincial government. As the ACT UP member put it explicitly:

> "In ACT UP's history most of the actions have been taken against the provincial government because of, well, who they were: the Socreds, who had ignored AIDS . . . I feel that ACT UP Vancouver was a localized response to what was happening here. We were dealing with the Social Credit government. There was Bill 34. I mean, we were dealing with local issues."

Evidence from Vancouver fueled my expectations that ACT UP was an accurate expression of radical citizenship, primarily because of its geography. Seven out of nine recorded demonstrations in Vancouver took place in spaces of civil society (see Figure 3-1).

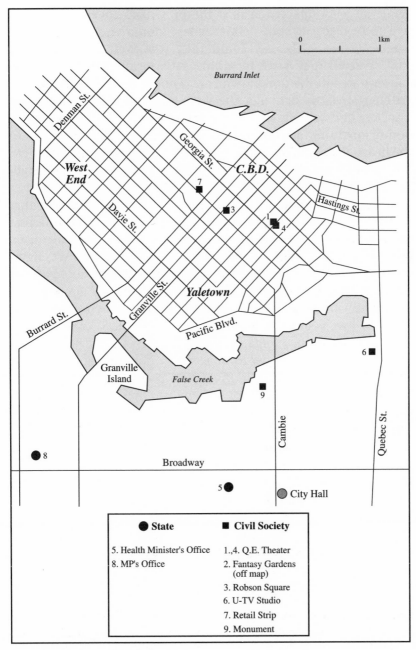

FIGURE 3-1. ACT UP's Vancouver protests, in chronological order.

While all were directed against the provincial government, only two took place at state-defined sites. Moreover, none of these spaces lay inside the gay community (the West End, Yaletown, etc.); instead, they were in visible yet neutral spaces, especially concentrated in the downtown core. Thus, when ACT UP directed action against the state (i.e., the Socreds), it did so in spaces of civil society, for example in front of the Queen Elizabeth Theatre, or during lunchtime at Robson Square (a concrete open space right in the heart of Vancouver's busy downtown retail and office district). If the state was ACT UP Vancouver's target, civil society was its audience.

What are we to make of this geography? One might argue that ACT UP was attempting to educate the public. Yet, that function was already being carried out quite effectively by AIDS Vancouver. Alternatively, one might suggest that ACT UP Vancouver was fighting for the rights of persons living with AIDS. But, as noted above, the Vancouver Persons With AIDS Society (PWA) had already been doing this with considerable success. One might then suggest that ACT UP was voicing a dissatisfaction with AIDS Vancouver or PWA, but, again, these organizations were never criticized, nor was St. Paul's Hospital or other local agencies. The state, however, was always ACT UP's target. The theoretical point I would draw from this narrative is that ACT UP's strategy was premised on a distinction between civil society and the state, which was expressed geographically. The state was rarely engaged on its own turf; rather, it was challenged in disruptive public spectacles. I demonstrate this point below by discussing how the presumed distinction between state and civil society worked through ACT UP's (limited) successes and its (broader) failures.

THE SUCCESSES OF ACT UP

Anger

Perhaps the most effective function ACT UP served was as a very public outlet for people's anger, directed against the virus and the Socreds, enemies to be sure. Civil society (as a space) enabled ACT UP members to vent publicly their enormous anger over the amount of death and government inaction vis-à-vis AIDS (see

Kubler-Ross, 1970, on this point). That function of public spaces helps to explain the location of its protests within civil society rather than in more state-centered sites. By drawing the attention of fellow citizens in the public space of Robson Square, ACT UP Vancouver offered up a very public, cathartic exercise of activists' anger over the tremendous losses they had suffered, as well as protesting the broader context of homophobia and indifference. At several points, Larry Kramer's bitter bill of particulars, discussed earlier, was substantiated in Vancouver. One local writer's description of the group in a local paper defined the group precisely by its anger:

> To join ACT UP, you don't have to be gay or have HIV (the virus widely believed to cause AIDS). You just have to be angry—full of bilious rage in fact—about the government's response to the AIDS epidemic, and be ready for countless bouts of civil disobedience. (Shariff, 1990, p. A-11)

One of the founders of ACT UP here, recalling his participation at a demonstration, illustrated ACT UP's angry release of emotion:

> Nothing else has worked. We've been dealing with this for ten years and people are still dying . . . What goes on in the backs of the minds (of protesters) is the face of a friend we have lost. That's what happened to me—it was a peaceful demonstration until I saw those smug Socreds. Then I saw Billy's (Vander Zalm's) face and I saw red. (Buttle, 1990, p. A-17)

Several people were quite critical of ACT UP's tactics, but acknowledged its need of an emotional outlet, given the context of Socred indifference:

> "And I've never been interested in the politics. It's just hot air. . . . I mean, knocking down the Premier's wife and spitting on the Premier and so on. Well, they both deserve to be strung up. My fantasy would be to see Bill and Lillian strapped to the windmill, spinning around.[9] But we can't all have our fantasy. But, I mean, that doesn't play well."

---

[9] Fantasy Gardens houses a replica of a windmill, evoking Premier Vander Zalm's Dutch heritage.

One man living with AIDS tried to describe the context of anger in his life at the fate of having a terminal illness:

> "Sometimes you can get very frustrated and very angry. You've got to be able to let that out. It's always been very difficult to explain to people that this is a very-high-stress lifestyle. You cannot walk away from it. If [an HIV negative person] starts to get burned out, you go take a vacation and sit on a beach. I can't do that! No matter where I go, or whatever, I *have* this thing and, you know, it's the first thing I think of in the morning and the last thing I think of at night. And I'm immersed in it. Constantly."[10]

Later, he was more specific about how ACT UP serves as a tactic to vent the incredible anger people feel about AIDS: "It also serves as an outlet for those people who have gone beyond anger—who are not just frustrated, who are not just irritated. These people are *damn Goddamn angry!"*

It is important to note that, by the summer of 1990, when ACT UP Vancouver exploded onto the local scene, Bill 34 had been passed, and at the time British Columbia was the only province in Canada not to fully reimburse people for AZT (Mason & Baldrey, 1989). These policies, combined with the callous public remarks made by Social Credit ministers a year earlier and the government's ongoing neglect of AIDS, go some distance in explaining the anger some activists felt, beyond coping with the disease itself.

If ACT UP successfully vented anger, we begin to see the importance of the distinction between state and civil society that ACT UP Vancouver presumed. Recall that, for instance, many members of ACT UP were also involved in the Vancouver Persons With AIDS Society (PWA) or AIDS Vancouver. Yet, because of the emerging links between these community organizations and the state, they could not "be political"; they could not *as the PWA Society* express anger with the Socreds. Once it began to receive state funding, the society had to remain careful not to engage in political activities. Indeed, it began to work *with* the state to augment services, quietly and outside the public space of civil society. The

---

[10]This person died in 1992.

importance of this apolitical stance cannot be overemphasized, as it is a persistent concern throughout the society.[11] As ACT UP was distinctly located within civil society, individual PWA members (and their allies) under the banner of "ACT UP," however, could angrily agitate the state to press for better funding and services without jeopardizing PWA's state funding. Here we see how Mouffe's quest for a de-centered subjectivity among radical citizens is further enabled by the "new spaces" of politics. In this way, ACT UP broadened the tactics that could be employed by citizens on various AIDS issues in Vancouver. As the executive director of AIDS Vancouver explained:

> "I would say that probably AIDS organizations don't feel that they are completely represented by ACT UP either. That said, I think that that kind of activism is very important. And it's not necessarily something that AIDS Vancouver, as an organization, might get involved in. But I think it's important that there be that, sort of, radical-activist element out there to rabble-rouse. I mean, I think it's very important because it makes it easier for us (as a mainstream group) to then develop our programs because people are concerned. People are scared of ACT UP. It's quite ironic. I'm not scared by them. And I really understand why that organization needs to exist. And, I mean, we all know each other. It's not that big a group of people that you don't know each other."

In the press, another former director of AIDS Vancouver was very careful to distance his organization from ACT UP, saying:

> AIDS Vancouver completely understands the frustrations and the anger that was expressed (at the Socred protest). We welcome an organization that gives vent to those feelings of frustra-

---

[11]It was especially pertinent during the summer that ACT UP Vancouver was formed since one of the founding members of ACT UP (and a former director of the PWA Society) announced that he would kill himself in late August. His death coincided with an ACT UP demonstration, in fact (see Kines, 1990). His suicide created an acute and very political problem for PWA, since it was feared that his action would be interpreted as the society's condoning of euthanasia. In other words, fear hinged on the confusion over whether he was acting as an individual or as a member of PWA.

tion and anger. Beyond that, we'll take a look at each political
action they take. (Buttle, 1990, p. A-17)

The member of ACT UP, who was also a member of the PWA Society, reiterated the theme that ACT UP could take the radical position that AIDS organizations partially funded by the state could
not:

> "We already had groups like AIDS Vancouver and PWA Soci-
> ety. At that stage, PWA could not take drastic actions because
> of their funding. They would feel repercussions. Their aims are
> to meet the needs of the infected. And that's what they have
> been doing. I mean they've been working very hard. They can
> go to the proper agency or department and request that needs
> be met, although they can't demand them. ACT UP can de-
> mand them. And it's obvious that if PWA isn't going to be lis-
> tened to, the next stop will be an AIDS activist organization
> taking that responsibility on. That means that there is a posi-
> tion for ACT UP to take a more radical stand. I mean, most
> people you talk to individually at AV or PWA will agree that
> there's a place for us: when, you know, polite glad-handing
> doesn't work any more, then there is a need to take action.
> We're all working on the same issues. I think the institutions
> see this relationship existing. If they're not going to deal with
> PWA on a polite level, right, actually sitting across the table
> and discussing issues and having those needs met that way,
> then I think they recognize that there will be activism because
> the needs still exist and if they're not dealt with, then there's
> only one option we have."[12]

ACT UP Vancouver As a Disciplinary Force

A second theme underscoring the utility of ACT UP also highlights
the significance of the presumed state–civil society distinction on
which the group hinged. It was used as a potential, imminent
threat against the state, or medical authority, from the gay community—even when the actual local chapter had little efficacy!
ACT UP was credited for its ability to bring important ethical and

---

[12]This person died in August 1994.

moral issues to civil society in a very public and immediate way. That threat, it seemed, could be enough to challenge the medical authority around HIV and AIDS. The man quoted above also explained the need for ACT UP by the utility of its potential threat: "It's like having the IRA on your doorstep. If somebody gives us a hard time and we're not getting through by talking, then we sic ACT UP on them."

Here, it seems, ACT UP Vancouver's cultural capital in civil society is emphasized. Located within civil society, with strong roots in the gay community, ACT UP could be used to threaten the state apparatus without the fear of hurting existing funding or service delivery arrangements. ACT UP signaled that it could strike at any time, should some future injustice warrant retaliation. One HIV positive person who dealt with St. Paul's Hospital often recalled an instance where the threat of ACT UP was enough to change a hospital policy[13] almost immediately:

"And they have to listen to us. An example: the hospital board of directors was being a bunch of jerks, so ACT UP had said that they were considering picketing the individual doctors— not only at the hospital but at their homes. Well, they freaked out all over the place. The knee-jerk response/reaction was to say that if that happens they wouldn't treat any more AIDS patients. And I went and saw them and said, 'Guys, you are living on the edge of a gay ghetto! There are gay people stacked up one on the other in this neighborhood. You want to do a scene from *Frankenstein* where you're in the castle and the mob's out front? You're going to tell these people that you're not going to deal with their brothers and sisters? Don't be a goddamn bunch of assholes!'"

This role as a potential, imminent threat of escalating political force enabled ACT UP Vancouver, in effect, to discipline institutions like the state and medical authorities. Here ACT UP's assumption of a clear-cut distinction between state and civil society was crucial to its effectiveness. It enabled ACT UP to work as a disciplinary exerciser of power in the local response to AIDS.

---

[13]The interviewee did not specify the policy in question. He merely indicated that the issue was resolved with the threat of a demonstration.

THE FAILURES OF ACT UP VANCOUVER

Misunderstanding Political Culture

If ACT UP Vancouver's successes pivoted on an assumed state–civil society distinction, its failures rested there too. People familiar with AIDS issues in the city argued that ACT UP's demise could be traced to two broad and related factors: it did not fit the local political culture, and the Vancouver Persons With AIDS Society did a better job at advocating for AIDS issues. For instance, many members of the gay community saw ACT UP as no more than the AIDS front of the Gay and Lesbian Centre and *Angles,* which have been criticized by gays for being too left-wing and antagonistic than need be in Vancouver. Even the Vancouver media did not take to ACT UP the way it did in other cities. For instance, at least two of the demonstrations held in Vancouver were not reported locally, but only in Toronto and Winnipeg papers (Wilson, 1990; "AIDS protesters . . . ," 1990). Coverage of ACT UP demonstrations remained sparse when written up in the local press. The city's tabloid, known for its attraction to sensational media events, even chastised the group's tactics as unproductive: "The violence at the theatre was not justified and did nothing to elevate the AIDS cause the way a more reasoned and intelligent approach would. ACT UP should smarten up before it acts again" ("Acting stupid," 1990).

During my interviews the issue of political culture was described in a number of ways, at a variety of geographic levels, from the nation to western Canada to the city. Some people drew a strong national distinction, with Canada being described as a much more quiescent place than the United States, where ACT UP originated.[14] This alleged culture of complacency was often tied to the different entitlements or rights available in Canada, universal health care being paramount. The greater accessibility of drugs, for instance, was noted even by ACT UP's lone member, who offered the example of cross-border smuggling to illustrate plainly the political-cultural differences between the U.S. and Canada:

> "There's a glut of AZT in Vancouver. There's a huge surplus of it. And there are a lot of individuals in the United States who

---

[14]On measures of difference between the U.S. and Canada, see Goldberg and Mercer (1986).

are forced to pay for their AZT. So what's happening is that it's being shipped across the border from Canada illegally and being given to people who have made the decision to take it."

A more generous welfare state, combined with a political culture that allegedly lacks an activist flavor, meant that ACT UP was awkwardly transplanted from a U.S. model into a Canadian urban context. As one woman half-jokingly asserted:

"I mean, the relatively small role ACT UP played here: this is Canada! There's your answer! There's nothing else to say [laughs]. I'm being a little sarcastic. . . . I mean, think of the Lion's Gate Bridge.[15] If that were New York, do you think people would politely braid [yield to one another] one car at a time? They do that here! [In the States it's] 'shoot out the tires! Me first!'"

Later, she acknowledged the limited, state-centered targets the Vancouver group could aim for, noting that the availability of universal health care in Canada left Socred homophobia as the only legitimate target: "Other than getting rid of Vander Zalm, what would ACT UP here do? That was basically its moment. Basically here it was just people who wanted to be radical and copy what was happening in the States."

A member of the Advocacy Committee at PWA also drew on the distinction in political cultures between the U.S. and Canada in his explanation of why ACT UP seemed so out of place in a Canadian context. He drew the distinction over the better protected private sphere for gays and lesbians in Canada. Being from Toronto originally, he also emphasized that ACT UP was especially out of place in western Canada:

"There's always been a sort of Canadian complacency, I think. You know, when Trudeau uttered those historic words about the government having no rights in the bedrooms of the nation, or whatever. Everybody took it to mean—and incorrectly so—that in Canada it's legal to be gay. Well, it is slowly in that

---

[15]The Lion's Gate Bridge is an often congested bridge linking Vancouver with its northern suburbs.

all the old laws have been repealed. But there's always been this complacency in this country for most people. They haven't had to get out there and fight. . . . I think the problem with ACT UP here was that they tried to use the same strategies that had been used in other places, and while it's appropriate in New York for everyone to chain themselves to some building, or in Washington, or go to the Center for Disease Control in Atlanta and pour red paint over everything, it's appropriate there, but it isn't here, in Canada, especially in the West it's not. That's not how you do things."

Another member of the PWA Advocacy Committee concurred:

"ACT UP—well, it doesn't exist. There is an ACT UP Vancouver, but there is a completely different political dynamic in Canada than in the United States. I don't believe ACT UP ever had been or ever will be successful in Canada because Canadians find that type of political activism to be 'not appropriate.' And this sort of extends to how you lobby in Canada, which is entirely different than in the United States. Canadians do not generally like public outbursts or messy-type confrontations. And if they're presented with that they tend to tune out the issue and the people involved. That's why by and large environmental activism has not had the same effect in Canada as it has elsewhere. The same with ACT UP: it has not had the same effect. We have had demonstrations. We have had die-ins. We have had the appropriate stopping of political figures. And it has had little or no effect on the political dynamic of this country. British sensibilities sort of play a very big role in our structure of government. And in order to get to square one, you have to walk the walk, talk the talk, look the look, and as you walk across that threshold you may be incredibly radical. You may have an ACT UP heart, but to get to square one, you have to present yourself in an appropriate fashion to the political dynamo that you're talking to. Once you're there, you can effect change."

Seeing the cultural politics in ACT UP, one reflective AIDS Vancouver volunteer emphasized that AIDS events need to be safe and inclusive to effect significant change. He cited very inclusive popular events like the annual Walk for AIDS, Dr. Peter's CBC Diaries, or Joe Average's local artwork as examples of cultural politics that have been successful because they do not use confrontational tactics.[16] Hence, he claimed that ACT UP Vancouver only served to alienate the public. Below he contrasts the success of other political-cultural events in the city with ACT UP's failure by stressing how out of place it was. His comments anticipate my treatment (in Chapter 6) of the Quilt as an (alternately) successful site of political engagement in civil society:[17]

"Things like the Walk for AIDS, AIDS Awareness Week, Joe Average: they're a lot softer, basically [than ACT UP]. . . . And I think that the Walk for AIDS is very effective, but it's also very generic. And they make a big deal of inviting the whole political spectrum, which I think is wise politically. But for more radical cultural institutions like ACT UP to be effective there has to be—you can't just impose ACT UP in Vancouver. For those kinds of organizations to be effective they have to grow *out* of a community that's already quite sophisticated and quite diverse, and quite politicized. I just don't think there's a whole lot of interest in radical analysis, or more fundamental analysis of power structures around gay issues in Vancouver."

As a tactic of resistance, ACT UP did not work because of its lack of fit with the local political context of Vancouver, and Canada more generally, according to locals. This point was emphasized further by interviewees who would contrast ACT UP Vancouver with the Vancouver Persons With AIDS Society. Their point, dis-

---

[16]Dr. Peter Jepson-Young (who died in November 1992 at 35) held a weekly series of public education "diaries" broadcast on the CBC evening news in British Columbia from 1990 through 1992 about his life with HIV and AIDS (see Gawthrop, 1994). Through this intensely personal and riveting series, viewers could watch the progression of illnesses and his ability to cope with them. He received far more press than ACT UP ever did locally. See, for instance, Wigwood (1992b), Fraser (1992), Easton (1992), and Parton (1993). Joe Average is a popular Vancouver artist living with HIV, whose colorful art is locally associated with AIDS issues and charities (see Smith, 1993b).

[17]In fact, later on this respondent compared the cultural politics of the Quilt with ACT UP explicitly by saying, "You know what I think? I think the Quilt is the smartest piece of art that's ever happened."

cussed below, shows how ACT UP was out of step with the city's political structure, while PWA has come to articulate with it.

Misunderstanding Political Structure

If ACT UP Vancouver failed to grasp the cultural sensibilities of civil society, it also misinterpreted and *misrepresented* the structural relations between civil society and the state. For example, recall from Chapter 2 that the provincial government was secretly funding AIDS Vancouver and the Persons With AIDS Society. In other words, by attacking the state from civil society, ACT UP failed to acknowledge the Byzantine financial arrangement the province had with the city, which was common knowledge in AIDS circles.

As well, ACT UP never seemed to acknowledge the quite effective advocacy work done by the Vancouver Persons With AIDS Society. By 1990, PWA had a large membership of HIV positive individuals and had developed successful programs and advocacy work with the government and medical system. Several members of the society stressed the overlap of function between the two groups, all the while favoring PWA:

> "ACT UP has not been the force of change in Vancouver. I mean, we used those kinds of tactics for a while. We used to do demonstrations at Fantasy Gardens, and we'd generate a lot of public opinion through the media. Certain people in our organization have always been eloquent spokespeople, so we've always given those people that rein for as long as the group was satisfied. But then you have the issue of accountable representation. In some sense, PWA *was* ACT UP at that time, but we were everything to everybody. We've been quite militant in the past."

Another PWA affiliate member drew the contrast between PWA and ACT UP as follows:

> "To get back to the issue of ACT UP and the PWA Society, the activism is different here between the two. I don't think that that's universally true. I don't think ACT UP here is a movement. I think ACT UP came out of a number of very well in-

tentioned people who wanted to hit the streets more than it was prudent for the PWA Society to do at that point. I think that's really laudable, and I'm not sure it won't resurface at some point. But I think the particular group that got together . . . didn't know their stuff. . . . And whereas I think ACT UP in the states has a very strong advocacy arm that stayed with the society in Vancouver, and it has never left the society here. So without that strong, fundamental base, ACT UP Vancouver just ended up being kind of demonstrations. I mean, if you look at AIDS Action Now! in Toronto, for example, where AAN is a strong force, AIDS Action Now! is very much along the lines of advocacy that the Vancouver PWA Society does—with more of an activist overtone. The Toronto PWA Foundation is like the service arm of the PWA Society here. So the organizational structures are different here."

Another member of PWA noted that the society used to be radical but has changed the definition of radical by its very existence in the city:

"And the PWA Coalition [which preceded the society] was a group of men who said, 'No! I'm not going to take *your* opinion and *your* bent on what's happening, because you have no idea how it is to be me. I am a person with AIDS. I'm taking your drug. I'm doing your treatment. And I have a right to the same things as every other Canadian, even though I am a person with AIDS.' So that was what was radical; that was the thing that started it all. And as the years progressed, those ideas didn't seem so radical anymore. That was the difference. We have evolved beyond thinking that's so radical, because things have changed in our medical system. Things have changed in our social services structure. And those are directly attributable to people with AIDS speaking up for their rights. So that's how it was perceived by the gay community. But it hasn't been anymore. That's why you had ACT UP creating that thing here, thinking that PWA had become less political and less advocating."

These examples highlight ACT UP's failure to grasp the shifting relations between state and civil society in Vancouver, evinced by shadow-state organizations like PWA.[18] Instead, its relentless public attacks on the Socreds in spaces of civil society erroneously assumed a clear structural distinction that highlighted civil society as the favored site for radical citizenship.

ACT UP's agonism in Vancouver was due to its capacity to vent anger in public, as well as to serve as a potential threat to powerful social institutions. It failed, however, to grasp the changes in (shadow-)state structure and culture that blurred the distinctions between state and civil society. It could effect little actual change, as compared to the shadow state. It also threatened to jeopardize the tenuous links that were being forged between the state and the voluntary sector. For these reasons the Vancouver case highlights the significance of political and cultural contexts for locating new spaces of citizenship. It shows how places combine sets of social relations such that citizenship may be simultaneously both enabled and constrained in differing ways. Concomitantly, it also illustrates that terms like "state" and "civil society" may be used uncritically in static, dualistic ways in political theory, and that revisiting them with a geographic perspective enables us to witness radical democracy at the spatial overlaps.

ACT UP VANCOUVER'S IMPLICATIONS FOR POSTSTRUCTURAL CITIZENSHIP IN CIVIL SOCIETY

One might argue that ACT UP Vancouver was at least radical in that it refused to be incorporated. Unlike the city's AIDS organization, it stayed squarely within civil society. Admittedly, many members of the shadow state lament the increasing ties with the state in local AIDS organizations. Overall, though, I am not sympathetic to this critique because ACT UP failed to achieve any of the

---

[18]Here again we see the importance in stressing Mouffe's decentered subjectivity for citizens. Contradictory processes were going on that allowed some PWA members to see themselves as opposed to the state (especially drawing on PWA's grassroots, gay-community heritage), while organizationally the society was moving towards a closer relation to the state. Members could thus position themselves in a number of ways. As well, bear in mind that individual PWA members would have varying levels of commitment and allegiance to the organization at any given time.

cultural or material gains made by the shadow state. We must be wary of committing exactly the error that Laclau and Mouffe try to resist: insisting on an a priori form or location for what counts as "radical citizenship." As Laclau and Mouffe (1985) argue:

> This has led to a failure to understand the constant displacement of the nodal points structuring a social formation, and to an organization of discourse in terms of a logic of "a priori privileged points" which seriously limits the Left's capacity for action and political analysis. This logic of privileged points has operated in a variety of different directions. From the point of view of the determining of fundamental antagonisms, the basic obstacle, as we have seen, has been *classism.* . . . From the point of view of *social levels* at which the possibility of implementing changes is concentrated, the fundamental obstacles have been *statism*—the idea that the expansion of the role of the state is the panacea for all problems. (p. 177)

AIDS politics in Vancouver cannot be judged solely or primarily as exercises in theoretical consistency; they were about educating the public and meeting people's needs in very immediate, tangible ways during a crisis. Thus one PWA Advocacy volunteer concedes:

> "I know that PWA had to publicly distance itself from ACT UP out here. . . . It was when [ACT UP] was at the height of [its] disruptiveness, shall we say. And they had to distance themselves because people were starting to question PWA and our sponsor dollars were being affected by that. And in a way it was a bit of a sellout, but I think it was the correct sellout, because ACT UP had antagonized *everybody.*"

We might further question ACT UP's radical potential by its misplaced and exclusive focus on the state. Mohr (1993), for instance, has recently argued that ACT UP does not challenge the modern state, but actually *worships* its power and reproduces it, by demanding the state extend its responsibility through right claims. ACT UP Vancouver's failure, compared with the PWA Society's success, substantiates this point. It worked from the anachronistic assumption that state action alone would solve or abate problems. One may counter that the state was not guaranteeing "claims to rights" that already existed; in other words, that there was no *extension* of rights being pressed by ACT UP Vancouver. Clearly, the state could have done (and eventually did) more in relation to AIDS issues. However, because the provincial government was ACT UP's *only* target, it failed in the context of a relatively effective shadow state that was providing (at least at some minimal level) for the needs of people living with AIDS. In turn, ACT UP's tactics led not to the augmentation of state services but rather to increased strains between the state and the local ASOs. A deputy minister of health under the Socreds asserted that ACT UP only alienated the Socreds further into indifference. Many ASO employees and volunteers acknowledged ACT UP's utility as an outlet for anger, but wondered about potential negative fallout for the already tenuous links between state and shadow state. Here, again, ACT UP Vancouver's misreading of the state–civil society distinction was significant.

CONCLUSION

ACT UP Vancouver certainly had a unique origin and trajectory, and imposing the radical successes of its chapters in other cities onto this local context is fraught with difficulties. But I think the more interesting point is a warning against radical democracy's tendency to hold state and civil society apart from each other, as it leaves the former to pinpoint the latter as a "new space of citizenship." When we consider the geographies of such (potentially) political locations, we find Mouffe's characterization ironically static and fixed. In focusing more on the radically de-centered subject positions of citizens, Mouffe has ironically essentialized the spaces where these new citizens can be found. She does not seem to take on board the implications of the restructurings of state and civil society that at times enabled a successful politics of AIDS (through the shadow state) to emerge while at other times prevented its success. Canel (1992) has leveled just such a criticism:

> Laclau and Mouffe . . . insist that every social conflict is political, as politics expand to civil society, but they fail to discuss the institutional aspects of politics, the relationship between new social movements and political parties through which the democratization of the state can be achieved. Such a separation between social movements and the political system can potentially

> contribute to a depoliticization of social movements. This is
> most ironic given that the purpose of the argument is to demon-
> strate the expansion of the political. (p. 37)

ACT UP Vancouver directed its actions against the state from civil
society. Like Laclau and Mouffe, it presumed a rather clear-cut distinction between the two sets of social relations. Its failure to recognize that state and civil society overlapped in actual locations
like PWA and AIDS Vancouver, however, limited its efficacy as a
mode of radical citizenship. ACT UP Vancouver was out of place
because the division between state and civil society that it assumed had been remapped—both culturally and structurally—by a
different political culture and an effective shadow state.

There is a theoretical lesson to be learned about the effects of
political spaces on citizens' struggles. Poststructuralism's quest for
new locations of political engagement should not blind us to
changes in the ways that "old" and "new" locations relate to each
other and in turn resituate citizenship. Here, the geographic context of these sites becomes crucial to political theory's often all too
abstract spatial categories. ACT UP Vancouver members assumed
that the state was a rather singular, whole, and unified institution,
and that civil society was a pure position from which to attack the
state (cf. Kirby, 1993). As the following chapter points out (and as
many local commentators in this chapter indicate), there was considerable spatial overlap between these heuristically fixed categories. Politics contained within the state or civil society were far
less effective than those that redefined relations *between* state and
civil society. Consequently, I began to look closely at the ways
Vancouver's two central AIDS volunteer organizations negotiated
this amorphous location between state and civil society. Chapter 4
details those cartographies.

Chapter 4

———•———

FROM CIVIL SOCIETY TO STATE APPARATUS
Shifting Spaces in the Voluntary Sector

INTRODUCTION

Reorienting scholars' attention away from narrow state-centered politics, civil society points to the public sphere of private citizens engaged in voluntary association to meet their own ends. As the boundaries of the political have shifted to include issues of identity and sexuality, locations far afield from city hall have now found themselves at the center of a new urban political geography.[1] So, for instance, despite the fact that the election of Harvey Milk[2] to the San Francisco Board of Supervisors meant that finally gay politics would have formal political representation and recognition at city hall, Castells (1983) discusses the rise of gay and lesbian grassroots in San Francisco's Castro district more broadly as a challenge to the meaning of urban space. Pursuing these lines, radical democratic thought has encouraged the exploration of civil society as a

---

[1]Though issues of sex and sexuality do occur at city hall. See, for instance, Shilts (1982), Geltmaker (1992), and Cooper (1994).

[2]Harvey Milk was the first openly gay city supervisor in San Francisco. He was assassinated along with Mayor George Moscone in November 1978 by fellow supervisor Dan White. See Shilts (1982).

new space for politics. And to be sure, the gay grassroots is precisely where the local response to AIDS originated (Whitehead, 1989). AIDS organizations, at first glance then, would seem to conform easily to radical democracy's normative cartography. By looking away from the state (which dragged its heels on AIDS in British Columbia) and toward civil society (where gay men came together and formed voluntary associations to combat the epidemic), Vancouver's AIDS service organizations are readily explained by radical democracy.

Yet, such an explanation is not entirely accurate—precisely because it ignores the spatiality of social relations. "State" and "civil society" do not exist in any pure abstract sense, but are bundles of social relations that are always located somewhere. Their structuration is always placed in the messy and ever changing landscapes of the city (cf. Lineberry & Sharkansky, 1978; Lipsky, 1980). The social identities that inhabit and structure these relations are subject to historical changes within place, for example. And, for that reason, arguments encouraging us to look away from the state toward civil society imply a dualism between these spheres of life that is out of step with their changing forms. New spaces of citizenship, therefore, might also imply new spatial *interactions* between state and civil society. The purpose of this chapter is to explore such interactions at Vancouver's AIDS organizations.

One of the most important issues confronting political scholars has been the ways that citizenship is reduced to a mere client status through the power of modern state bureaucracy (Ferguson, 1984; Fraser, 1989). Bureaucratization and clientization remain constant threats to the critical potential of radical democratic citizenship. These processes strip citizens of their equal standing before the state and one another, leaving them in a position of inequality and dependency. Yet, in arguing for more formative democratic bearings in city politics, such a sketch itself can obscure citizenship by reproducing rather stationary categorical distinctions among the citizen, the client, and the bureaucrat. Their identities rest on familiar, well-defined characterizations. In the citizens that we imagine the voters, grassroots volunteers, and clients are recipients of urban services, while the bureaucrats are the paid employees, professionals, and experts inside of, and embodying, the state. Further, each identity is typically located dualistically in and around the state, as bureaucrats deliver urban public services to citizens. Changes in the capitalist state and grassroots service delivery systems, however, demand a rethinking of the positions and orientations within city politics.

The overlapping positions of the bureaucrat and the client in Vancouver's AIDS politics are navigated in this chapter through geographies of citizenship across the city's principal volunteer AIDS organizations. As part of the shadow state (see Wolch, 1990), these organizations lie between the state and civil society. Their position (both metaphorically and geographically) reflects the retrenchment of the welfare state as well as the subsequent rise of voluntary-sector service provision (Arno, 1986; Whitehead, 1989). It thereby makes problematic any clear-cut geography of radical democracy. Understanding these organizations as sites of city politics themselves suggests that "new spaces" of citizenship can be found by remapping the edges of conventional locations around the state.[3] Thus, it is not so much that AIDS politics has moved citizens away from the state and toward social movements in civil society (though this is certainly part of the process), but more interestingly that AIDS organizations have come to be spaces where relations of state and civil society weave together.

Toward that point, this chapter details the spatial overlap between state and civil society at these organizations by showing their to-and-fro tack between grassroots community coalitions and large, formal state bureaucracies. Moving from institution to citizens' identities through the next two sections, I offer two takes on how citizens have become empowered[4] at AIDS organizations, where there is a confluence of state and civil society. I show how this overlap can both enable and constrain radical citizenship. For many, working in what amounts to the state apparatus is an effective means of citizenship. For others, these organizations provide important ramparts against state bureaucracy's clientization of them. But these remappings of AIDS organizations do not always empower citizens who work in them. In the fourth section of this chapter, then, I illustrate how AIDS organizations' rather fuzzy geography can also produce relations of bureaucratization and clien-

---

[3]For another example of geographers' conceptualization of the workplace as a site of politics, see McDowell (1995).

[4]I am grateful to Lynn Staeheli (1994b) for helping me conceptualize citizenship this way.

tization, which are anathema to radical democracy. My point is not to argue that these organizations completely inhibit citizens' radical democratic potential. Rather, it is to show the importance of not treating state and civil society as dichotomized spaces in local politics. Organizations like AIDS Vancouver and the PWA Society have evolved in contradictory ways because of their awkward position, pushed and pulled between the state and civil society (see Figures 4-1 and 4-2).

EMPOWERING CITIZENS I:
PAID EMPLOYMENT IN THE SHADOW STATE

In her thorough account of the American and British shadow states, Wolch (1989) acknowledged the critical potential for voluntary-sector service provision. De-centering service delivery is thought to counter the large-scale bureaucratization endemic to

FIGURE 4-1. AIDS Vancouver's rather concealed office on Richards Street (1990–1993). Photo by author.

FIGURE 4-2. Former PWA office (second floor) on Hornby Street (1990–1993). Photo by author.

modern state social service and welfare offices. By moving the point of service delivery away from the state and toward civil society, or the community in which service users exist, it is argued that the needs of the clients are better understood, services can be fine-tuned to meet those needs or more quickly adapted, should needs change. Similarly, such moves toward decentralization also can involve service recipients in the actual delivery of services. By drawing the client into the delivery mechanism, the argument goes, the clientization resulting from modern state welfare provision so often critiqued (e.g., Ferguson, 1984; Fraser, 1989) can be countered. The hierarchy of the bureaucrat-client relationship, with its unequal power relations, control over information, and intrusion into private lives, is undercut by voluntary-sector service provision.

The pattern that emerged in Vancouver fits this theoretical template well, though perhaps for different, locally specific reasons. As the state bureaucracies were hampered in providing support and education services because of provincial politics as well as the very newness and rapidity of the epidemic, the gay community began to form volunteer organizations throughout the 1980s—principally AIDS Vancouver and the Vancouver Persons With AIDS

Society (PWA)—to provide what we would otherwise expect to be services delivered by the state. As demand continued to grow, these organizations successfully drew funding, policy, and often staff from the state itself. They became part of the shadow state: staffed by and located almost exclusively in the gay community, but with increasingly complex ties to the broader state apparatus. What follows, then, is the story of citizenship caught amidst these poles.

I will begin with workers—that is, paid employees—in the shadow state (principally AIDS Vancouver). Outside the realm of class we tend to draw a sharp distinction between political engagement and paid employment (e.g., Katznelson, 1981). We also often draw a sharp distinction between the deliverer of a public service (the bureaucrat) and its recipient (the citizen) (e.g., Pinch, 1985; Stone, Whelan, & Murin, 1986; Svara, 1990). Yet, in Vancouver's AIDS politics such distinctions were not always helpful. Through my interviews with both paid and unpaid members of ASOs, and my observations in their workplaces, I quickly came to question the categorical distinction between citizen and bureaucrat, noting the ambiguous position AIDS organizations hold between state and civil society. Below I trace four themes that convey the ways citizenship gets expressed through people's paid work in AIDS service delivery: identity politics through service delivery; ambiguities in citizens' lives between paid and unpaid work; work as an efficient or viable means to citizenship for some people; and changing orientations toward work that occurred as the epidemic became more prominent.

Identity Politics Through Service Delivery

There is a striking, self-conscious reflexivity between gay politics and AIDS service delivery in Vancouver. The very location of the services, clustered around the West End and Yaletown, bears out that mutual relation. This geography reflects and reinforces the point that many people working within the state or shadow state on AIDS issues are gay or lesbian. For example, there is a gay man who is a provincial outreach nurse to the gay community—and who particularly targets male sex-trade workers. The province pays his salary and rents space for a testing facility in the Gay and Lesbian Centre. The duality of identities and cultures he draws on (state bureaucrat versus member of the gay community) is meant to calibrate the quality of service the state provides through him. For instance, he confided:

> "My fear is that in gay men next year we're going to start to go up [in HIV infection rates] again because the gay population has been inundated with information and considers itself well educated. Again, we watched our friends drop like flies and we're tired of it. It's not logical or reasonable—it's a rationalization and it's risk-taking. And people *are* taking risks again, which is frightening."

Positioning himself as part of both the state and civil society, he also confronts the state with inequities in service delivery to different kinds of citizens (see Wolch, 1990):

> "My anger hasn't gone away. It's been modified. Redirected. I still get really angry from time to time about the injustices and the things I see. Nobody is perfect. No facility is perfect. There's a bad apple wherever you go. I've stood and screeched at the top of my lungs in emergency rooms bringing in an HIV-infected youth who's sick. And they're sitting in the waiting room for two hours when they need to be on a stretcher and on oxygen. Because it's a street kid or an IV drug user they'll triage them. That's when I really let loose with my anger. And it tends to be helpful. I can tack on my nametag too. 'Look! I have a nametag too!' "

A lesbian who also works with street-involved gay youth in Yaletown mirrored the nurse's position between state and community:

> "I work on a contract with the Ministry of Health. The place that we're in is rented by Family Services of Greater Vancouver. The mandate of Street Youth Services is to connect with new kids on the street and basically get them to more traditional services: social workers, medical attention, etc."

She is employed on a contract from the province and is located in a drop-in center along a busy Yaletown street. Besides identifying as a lesbian, she has had strong ties to the gay community and in her own youth had dealt with social services. Her concurrent position among these identities allows her to do her job and advocate for gay youth. This came up when she noted her dissonance with the Yaletown punkers who are less street-involved than her clients (young gay homeless men, many of whom are HIV positive or have AIDS):

> "I shouldn't say too much about [the punkers] because I really don't know much about them. But the young people I see here are—they're reflective on their experience. Their circumstances are different. I suppose I just have more empathy. I don't work down here by some kind of accident. I have history here. And they're gay. I'm gay. They're softer somehow. I don't know. They—touch me. They're my kids. I find the punkers amusing, but I can't take them seriously, really."

Likewise, St. Paul's Hospital is an intense locus of identity politics and service delivery. Located on the edge of the West End, it has been deluged by people living with HIV and AIDS. Many members of the staff had to deal rapidly with their own issues of homophobia or heterosexism in order to provide proper care. One nurse recalled her own realization of this overlap between identity politics and service delivery when she was troubled and confused by a married man (who was bisexual) with AIDS:

> "But when I saw the patients I could not understand. I just could not put together from my life experience this upcountry businessman and his teenage children and the evangelical Christian outlook, and this guy had AIDS. There was absolutely no question. Then it became, if I couldn't understand it, how could I help my nurses nurse my patients? Nothing in nursing taught us anything about this that would help us put it together."

But these issues were not merely centered around anonymous patients. As a major neighborhood employer, many of St. Paul's staff were also HIV positive and eventually died of AIDS. Colleagues who were quietly suspected of being gay by homophobic coworkers suddenly became gay patients with AIDS who needed care and service from their fellow employees. Additionally, gay doctors at the hospital had to come to the fore of treatment as well as advocacy.

The mixing of identity politics with service delivery does not simply improve accessibility. In many ways it is absolutely crucial to successfully carrying out the service. People have to see HIV as a risk to *themselves* before they can access education and modify their behavior accordingly (Osborn, 1991; King, 1993). To make that link less threatening, education is typically imparted along lines of identity. For example, AIDS Vancouver's Man-to-Man Program aims education and prevention directly at gay men through outreach programs in bars, bath houses, private homes, and cruising areas in Stanley Park. Similarly, the Women and AIDS Project (of AIDS Vancouver) attempts to educate women precisely along the lines of their gender identity because AIDS has been stereotyped in North America as a threat only to gay men (Shaw, 1991; Banzhat, 1990). The complexities of identity and position in city politics were underscored by a Project employee who noted that she spoke at the Ministry of Social Services not merely because of its many women clients but also because of the large number of female employees.

> "Usually when people want us to come in for a speak[5] then they're really clear that this information is for the women in the room. But what they're not clear about is the way they, too, need that information because they are women, too, usually. I went in and did a speak at the Ministry of Social Services (mainly women there). And they wanted this information for their clients. These women were very clear about that. But when we start doing the work or the exercises and they start talking, they talk from personal places. Many of them do. Or they'll say something happened to a friend of theirs. Well, that's a lot closer than a client that they're *paid* to service. So we work from the premise that the personal is the political. You need to personalize this, and explore your own attitudes and values and know where you are about it before you can share the information."

---

[5]A "speak" is an education seminar on AIDS and HIV for a specific group of people conducted by AIDS Vancouver volunteers. It is also sometimes referred to as an "AIDS 101."

There appear to be limits to effective service delivery, however, that reflect the limits of identity politics (Phelan, 1989; Cohen, 1991; Annetts & Thompson, 1992). The reduction of AIDS Vancouver to a gay identity and political agenda in city culture had sensitized its gay complement to presenting more diverse identities—especially during its early years. One woman's job in the early eighties involved doing AIDS education seminars in settings that were not gay-specific or friendly. She recalled the ironic role her gender played against gay identity politics in favor of service delivery to "the general population":

"My sense of what was going on when I was hired at AIDS Vancouver is that when people called AIDS Vancouver for more information and they wanted a speaker, they were very concerned that that speaker was going to be a gay man. And that the people who would be attending that speak would not want to come if they knew a gay man was there because he would be perceived as having AIDS and people were afraid that somehow this person would make them sick. I think that that was a valid perception for AIDS Vancouver to make at the time. The perception at the time, by not just the straight population but also a lot of gay men, was that anybody who was perceived to have AIDS was a threat. Anyone who was gay was perceived to have AIDS at that time. But I don't particularly agree with the way that was dealt with, in other words, feeding into that fear, so you give them a woman."

Ambiguities Between Volunteer and Paid Work

People's own work and volunteer commitments have changed over time while they themselves remain in place. Simultaneously, Vancouver ASOs have grown rapidly in the past decade. These two processes locally reinforce each other to produce an often blurry distinction in the shadow state between paid and volunteer work, and this is a second theme that illustrated the nexus of state and civil society at AIDS organizations.[6] The ambiguities are found in the context of individuals' own histories, as well as the more gen-

---

[6]Attempts are persistently made to sharpen the distinction, however, as ASOs continue to bureaucratize (see Patton, 1989).

eral local culture of AIDS work. For instance, at least half of the 20–25 employees at AIDS Vancouver began as volunteers or maintain a volunteer commitment to the organization. Similarly, most people who work directly on AIDS issues in the state itself had previously worked or volunteered at AIDS Vancouver. Many factors explain these connections. People acquire skills or specialized information while volunteering that make them appropriate candidates to hire. Often by volunteering they more readily hear about job openings. The increasing willingness of the state to fund projects or contracts means more people *can* be paid to do work that either had not been done before or had been done by volunteers. Most importantly, there is an increasing demand for shadow-state services, which has translated (in Vancouver) into calls for greater consistency and reliability of paid positions. Finally, it is common for people to speak of a personal need to "do more" about AIDS (Fernandez, 1991). They fulfill this need by either working and volunteering simultaneously, or at different points in their lives.

The complementary attraction and tension between paid employment and volunteering in people's own lives were noted in a number of different ways.

> "My work at AIDS Vancouver is pretty distinct from my being a buddy,[7] because my buddy is like my friend, right? I mean, to speak quite honestly, he's not someone I would have chosen to be my friend. He's not someone I would ordinarily hang out with. But when we do spend time together, we're like friends. So I don't talk to him about [my job at AIDS Vancouver]. It's pretty separate because I don't see my time with my buddy as a job. I see him as someone who's like a family member, you know?"

Thus, some people stress a need to bracket work relations from volunteer relations in their own minds along a public-private divide. Discrepancies between motivations for volunteering and working are sometimes marked in this way. The work has to get done to

---

[7]A buddy is a volunteer position at AIDS Vancouver, common to most ASOs. It is a one-on-one personal relationship between a volunteer and a person who is HIV positive or has AIDS. It is an undefined relationship that can entail both practical and emotional support. Buddies are discussed at length in the next chapter.

meet needs, it is thought, but volunteering is necessary for people to participate, to heal. Frustrated, a man who both works and volunteers at AIDS Vancouver reflected:

> "[Volunteering] creates a nice balance between my anger at the paper-pushing and my wanting to know that what I'm doing is making a difference. . . . I want to be doing work that matters to me, to other people. This week I don't feel that at all on the work side. Not at all."

He went on to describe a recent scene in his organization:

> "There are a lot of times that I don't make a distinction between the work side and the volunteer side. For time sheet purposes, I guess I have to. But like I took all of yesterday off and I'm trying to take Mondays off throughout the summer to maintain a 30-hour workweek. And I came in for a meeting last night at 5:30. [My boss] saw me and looked really surprised, as though he wanted to give me this whole long list of things to do. And I said, 'Hi! I'm here as a volunteer, for the meeting.' And he just shut right up. Because I didn't even want to get into work mode. I didn't even check my message box."

Nonetheless, he maintains both forms of commitment because the paid work allows him to do more overall, whereas the volunteer work gives him a greater sense of personal efficacy.

People also emphasize the sense of virtue and feelings of efficacy to be gained by volunteering, which is thought to be lacking in most work for wages.[8] This point was made by a variety of sources. One volunteer declared: "I get a feeling of satisfaction from volunteering. You're not getting paid for it. You're doing it because you want to do it."

One provincial bureaucrat struck the same distinction, but resented the pretense of superiority that volunteering had over paid work in AIDS issues:

---

[8]For a discussion of the "moral narcissism" associated with being a citizen, see Ignatieff (1989).

"So this has always been a sore point for my people that are out there burning out and working their tails off and getting no real acknowledgment from [the community]. If you collect a salary for what you do, you ain't worth it. You ain't committed. And you ain't doing the job as well as if you're a volunteer. . . . Volunteers are always better than people working in the area."

Ambiguities were detailed not only through individuals' lives but in local political culture and structure. The rapidly changing form of organizations is most recently an issue. People lament the growth in service organizations (from small, grassroots offices to large bureaucracies) that shifts work away from volunteers (Patton, 1989; Arno, 1991). Reliance on paid staff to complete tasks can mean greater continuity and reliability. It nevertheless challenges the history and spirit of voluntarism and self-help around HIV and AIDS. One man who both works and volunteers noted a trend away from volunteers toward employees:

"I see the role of volunteers as doing the *work*. And the staff members should be delegating the work and, in conjunction with volunteers, deciding on the directions that the organization should go. The paid staff should be the coordinators of the volunteers. But I see volunteers as the people doing the actual work: speaking, buddying, answering the phones. I'm seeing a move away from that here and I'm really, really worried about that. . . . If there's too much work to be done, why don't we call in more volunteers instead of creating another half-time position?"

In a single place over time, as personal commitments change and the shadow state grows, tensions between different kinds of responses to AIDS erupt. These tensions appear structurally in Vancouver's shadow state and are located between volunteers and bureaucrats, in bureaucrats who used to be volunteers, and in people who are both volunteers and employees.

Work As a Means to Citizenship

While I have discussed the ways that identity and position are being negotiated amid shifting relations of state and civil society in

Vancouver's ASOs, it is important to underscore the shifting perception of paid positions themselves. Waged work sometimes can be the only, or the best, way for some individuals to respond to the AIDS crisis locally—that is, to be a good citizen. One woman described her work in deeply political tones, emphasizing her own responsibility as a citizen to others:

> "It's something about working in AIDS. You get this information and you realize that—it's quite a process to be able to find your voice to be able to talk about this stuff. I had this information and I felt like there was no turning back. Somehow I had this responsibility that I wanted to pursue."

Work further becomes a means to citizenship as a greater amount of time can be spent working rather than volunteering in AIDS organizations. The need to "do something" is mediated with the need to earn a wage. Working "in AIDS" helps ameliorate this tension in people's lives. For instance, one man whose partner was HIV positive chose to work in an ASO for the understanding environment as well as his own desire to effect change:

> "I moved to Vancouver to join my late partner who I met while I was living in Manitoba. And when I moved here it was important to me to do something tangible. And this job was offered to me. And I took it because I knew that if my partner were to become ill—and he wasn't ill at the time. But I knew that when he would get ill this job would give me the time I needed to be with him. And that was the single most significant reason why I actually got involved in the paid-work end of things. It was something very tangible to do in the face of not being able to do very much for him."

Still others stressed their ability to offer much-needed professional skills in the context of a crisis that politicizes service delivery:

> "I didn't just take the job because it was a job. It was very much the issue at the time and there was a personal sense that I had a lot to bring to that work, having both experience in sexuality education and—you might think this is odd but— the threat of nuclear war, because that work was around issues

of death and dying. So the two really came together in my work in AIDS education."

Shklar (1991) argues that citizenship is a matter of social status actually premised on the right to vote and to earn a decent wage. The latter condition manifests itself interestingly in the Vancouver case study. The capacity of work to be purposeful, meaningful, *and* offer a living wage is often affected structurally by class location. Note that the response to AIDS in Vancouver has largely come from the middle class (see also Patton, 1989). The secure economic position many of these individuals enjoy enable them to be employed in situations where they literally *can* work for social change. As I have noted above, this process is partially subverted by the virtue bestowed on volunteers, yet, I would maintain that the point demonstrates the contradictory ways that citizenship is being structured in Vancouver. One man reflected that his employment flexibility freed him to use work to explore his efficacy in society, and acknowledged this privilege:

> "I've been pretty fortunate. To earn my way I had to find things I could do that did not demand long-term commitment from me. . . . I guess what I'm saying is that I've always been really lucky in the sense that I've always been able to pick things that I wanted to do. And when I picked something I really tried to pick something that was going to keep me whole. In other words I did not want to see, 'This is my work. And this is my life.' I really wanted something integrated. [The work around AIDS] is intense and engaging but also quite fulfilling. [Jobs where I did not feel like that have made me say], 'If I'm going to do something, I want to be—to some degree— in control over it.' And I realize I'm really fortunate. Truly, I've been very fortunate."

Changing Orientations Toward Work

AIDS has changed the meaning and nature of work that people have always done toward more poststructural understandings of citizenship. As one nurse at St. Paul's summed up her job since AIDS, "I have been known to say it's a shitty way to get your life enriched." A common theme—not just in Vancouver—has been the rise of a culture of obsession around AIDS work because the crisis is so constantly at hand (Fernandez, 1991; Grover, 1992). Through their work, people come into immediate contact for the first time with gay men and people who are living with HIV and AIDS. That closeness can resignify an otherwise ordinary job in the state apparatus and link it squarely to identity politics. A straight person working as a librarian for an AIDS organization spoke about the politicization that her work has brought to her life:

> "My attitude's changed since I've been here. I mean, I went from knowing nothing to knowing quite a bit. And being very moved by—oh, you go through so many emotions. I am moved by the people that I work with, their dedication. I'm moved by the people who are HIV positive and some of their concerns. I could always imagine, but I couldn't really empathize quite as well with them as I do now. And the frustrations of being a small community organization. Watching where some of the money goes, well, you feel the inequities of a lot of things, and the prejudices. You get frustrated by people for their ignorance, who don't understand or accept or try to learn. Sometimes you get irritated and other times you feel hopeful. . . . I like the freedom I have here, where I can develop my own ideas and people let me go with it. But I find I have to take a lot of time and stop and be with some of the people who come in here. It's that that gives me more satisfaction than other jobs might. I've always liked working with people, but I mean, I take it slower with them now, which is nice. Because that's what it's all about for me now. And stuff comes back to me better. I think I give a little more than I used to. There's a certain sincerity around this work that I've noticed. Maybe it's my own growth and I just haven't noticed it before, but it's very prevalent around here."

She went on to discuss how she has become an advocate in her personal life, not merely for people with AIDS but also for gay men, because of her work situation:

> "I seem to have become an AIDS educator in my own way—and actually a 'gay community' educator. I mean, educating people who are somewhat homophobic. I'm amazed at how

little a lot of people know about the gay community. And the statement, 'I don't care what people do. I just don't want to hear about it.' And so, of course, I have to take that one on. I tell them that people have to show who they are so that a lot of the inequities that they've experienced are wiped away. And so they're not trying to flaunt something to offend you, they're just trying to be accepted, to live a life that in my mind is just as normal as our lives. 'Oh no! You can't say that!' You know, that kind of thing in response. So you go into the whole thing about sexuality and all that. And I find I spend more time on those issues than on AIDS issues, but that could just be the people I know. My father has learned a lot and he's a far better man for it! [laughs] He's changed."

By taking up each of these four themes, we have seen the limitations superimposed on radical citizenship through a series of mutually reinforcing dualisms: work and politics, citizen and bureaucrat, state and civil society. The discussions above explain the political dimensions of paid employment in AIDS issues. For many people, their workplace has become the space that enables radical democratic practice, and it is certainly clear to see their agonistic citizenships are making a difference. But in a sense, this is only part of the citizen's struggle, having to do with the obligations toward other members of the political community. The other side to the identity is an equal standing before the state, secured by rights and entitlements. The embodiment of this aspect of citizenship, however, was also expressed in Vancouver through the state–civil society nexus in Vancouver.

EMPOWERING CITIZENS II:
RESISTANCE TO CLIENTIZATION

One of the most important facets of the AIDS movement has been the demand by people living with AIDS that they themselves should have a voice, and claim a certain expertise, in relation to state and medical authorities (Callen, 1992; Altman, 1988; Patton, 1989; Crimp, 1989). In so doing, they overwhelmingly reject the label "AIDS victims," and seek to empower themselves in the context of a terminal illness and often overpowering medical and po-

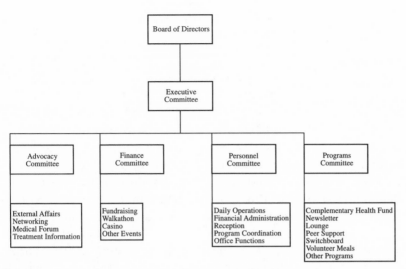

FIGURE 4-3. Vancouver Persons With AIDS Society: organizational structure.

litical discourse. In Vancouver the first self-help group for HIV positive people began in October 1984, with the meetings rotating among people's homes. Over the next two years, the coalition grew and became the Vancouver Persons With AIDS Society. In November 1986, it officially opened its office at the Gay and Lesbian Centre on Bute Street (see Figure 1-4, p. 22) and later moved to a small office above a garage on Hornby Street (Figure 4-2). The society grew out of people's frustrations that AIDS Vancouver's nonprofit status prevented it from taking a more explicitly political stance against the provincial government. It also developed out of a frustration with AIDS Vancouver's lack of a politically assertive voice. During my fieldwork, PWA had approximately 1,200 members. While no member is required to participate, the society is run by volunteers, with continuity provided by a small paid staff.[9] There are four standing committees (apart from the Executive Committee), each in charge of a specific portfolio designed to empower people living with HIV and AIDS (see Figure 4-3).

---

[9]Continuity is a recurrent structural problem in organizations of people living with AIDS not merely because of the voluntary nature of the (unpaid) work, but more importantly because the frequency of illness and death means that a reliable participation is impossible.

Citizenship and Self-Empowerment

It has long been recognized that the process of *clientization* is a distinctly modern form of state power that has threatened the citizen's position. Clientization refers to the processes whereby bureaucrats' claims to expertise and control over information and resources place citizens in positions of dependency and need vis-à-vis the state. Since in liberal theory citizens are defined as being in a position of equality relative to one another, and rather autonomous from the state, clientization processes have challenged liberals' de facto characterizations of citizenship in modern democracies. Weber (1968) was perhaps the first theorist to note the relation between bureaucrats' knowledge claims and state power over the citizen, and Habermas (1984, 1991) has drawn heavily on his analysis to trace the disempowerment of the citizen through bureaucratization and juridification of the state apparatus (see White, 1988). Feminists like Wilson (1977), Ferguson (1984), and Fraser (1989) have paid particular attention to the way clientization has been effectively gendered through policies of the welfare state, thereby placing women who receive state aid in the unequal, disempowered position of clients of the state.

In Vancouver the PWA Society is explicitly mandated to resist the clientization of people living with HIV and hence to promote their citizenship. Its mission statement expresses this goal clearly:

> The Vancouver Persons With AIDS Society exists to enable persons living with Acquired Immune Deficiency Syndrome and Human Immunodeficiency Virus to empower themselves through mutual support and collective action. From our personal struggles and challenges come our courage and strength.

PWA members resist clientization in two ways. The first is through greater self-empowerment in dealing with external organizations, such as hospitals, the Ministry of Social Services, and insurance companies. Ferguson (1984, p. 143) notes that a key strategy in creating dependency among clients is bureaucrats' exclusive control over the information most immediately relevant to the citizen. PWA challenges this type of monopoly in several ways. With its Treatment Information Project, the society provides up to date information on drug treatments and therapies (both conventional and alternative) to its members. It keeps tabs on experimental drug trials, as well. In these ways, patients are placed on a more equal footing with doctors when it comes to managing their care. Here, the traditional paternalism of Western medicine is explicitly challenged. For instance, one man recounted his first contact with PWA:

> ". . . the self-empowerment mandate really worked for me. Heavens, yes! I didn't know a thing about self-help organizations before I came here. I came in, and a [member] read the riot act to me. Told me that I had to go and get my blood tested. Here was this passionately speaking, really hunky 40 year old man talking to a total stranger. I'd never experienced that before! And there was my doctor: 'No. You've only been HIV positive for six months. There's no reason in the world to test your blood!' I yelled at him, 'I want it tested!' [laughs] I'd never yelled at my doctor before in my life! He started muttering something about patients' rights and so on. But it didn't change the test results. I should have been on prophylaxis for PCP, and I should have been on AZT. He had been neglecting my treatment! So that was my first taste of this organization."

The PWA's providing its members with information enables them, in turn, to "speak for themselves" and to resist depending on others as authorities about their very own well-being.

The Citizen As Advocate

Clientization is further resisted through what has come to be known locally as "advocacy." PWA's Advocacy Committee works against clientization on both collective and individual bases. On a collective level, it lobbies government to protect the rights of people living with AIDS and HIV (Gates, 1992). One Advocacy member detailed recent lobbying efforts:

> "I write a lot of letters and send a lot of faxes to the federal government. We have an ongoing dialogue—sort of—with Kim Campbell[10] and her administrative assistants. An example is that we met with Kim Campbell about three weeks ago now.

---

[10]At the time Kim Campbell was the Prime Minister of Canada.

And we spent an hour and a half and we were talking about
funding of the National AIDS Strategy and how the government has yet to make a commitment. So we go to Ottawa.
[One member] just got back from Ottawa. He was there for
five days at the national income security thing. And that's the
kind of thing we do. We travel more. We go to Victoria. We go
and bug them."

By way of contrast, another Advocacy volunteer sketched out the
individual advocacy work:

"We do the pick-up-the-phone-to-the-social-worker-and-say,
'You can't cut this guy off of his benefits!' With the landlord
we do the 'You can't throw this person out of their home because it's against the law!' We advocate for people to get their
Canada Pension Plan benefits, or their UIC [unemployment
insurance compensation] benefits, or their disability insurance."

Advocating for members not only empowers them, it is argued, but also empowers the advocate (Katz & Bender, 1990). By
becoming a resource to other people living with AIDS, volunteers
at PWA themselves gain a significant measure of control over their
lives. One member put it as follows:

"We do not have a client/service-provider relationship. We are
members helping each other, sort of, cope in the world with
AIDS right now. And by that I mean, we use our collective
skills to help each other, to have the ability to advocate for
ourselves. We provide each other with the information to
manage our treatment by having the treatment information
here; by managing our Canada Pension Plans by checking it
out for each other, providing that information *here*. So, in
essence, we are advocating for ourselves and we are taking
control of our lives. And the old adage 'knowledge equals
power,' that's the center of the way it is here. But it's mutual
support here."

Clearly, then, PWA empowers citizens and resists their client status. The self-help philosophy links individual health and welfare

with a collective resistance to disempowerment (Powell, 1990; Katz, 1993). Thus, in their reader on the subject, Katz and Bender (1990) introduce that kind of resistance as a defining feature of the self-help movement:

> As professionals and other human service workers become involved with self-help groups, they must undergo (and many do) a role change, shifting from that of the impersonal expert, assumed by self and others to know best, to that of listener, teacher and guide. Both governmental departments and voluntary human service agencies with programs targeted towards specific human needs have an interest in adapting philosophy and practices to the concept that people should help themselves to the greatest extent possible. (pp. 5–6)

Another emerging theme in social work texts is the concession of authority to clients (Chesler, 1990; Adams, 1990). Certainly the Vancouver PWA Society has forced bureaucratic authority to shift its authoritative stance toward people living with AIDS. For instance, a woman whose infant son was HIV positive recounted how PWA helped her resist the dependency on medical authority she felt:

> "And that first phone call with [the peer counselor], he was just wonderful. He was very supportive, gave me very practical information to go to the hospital with, what to ask about, that sort of thing. He really, really helped me with the hospital. I didn't feel so victimized, because if you don't know even what to ask then you're totally dependent on the medical people to explain everything to you, and you just feel powerless. They're in total control and you're in no control, and especially when there's such an internal fear that you feel totally out of control of."

This challenge to the traditional medical authority has even been conceded by doctors themselves in Vancouver. Locally, for example, during a discussion with a doctor at St. Paul's Hospital, the doctor noted the change in his own profession:

> ". . . but there's no question that when you look at the activist groups that they've had a *profound* effect on us, questioning almost everything we do in this disease and other diseases. Par-

ticularly, the issue of what is the right of the individual, and
what is the individual's debt to society? And those cut across
many diseases. Quite clearly mandatory testing may have
some important social benefits. On the other hand, there's no
question it compromises individuals' rights because of the
prejudice. Access to drugs: surely it should be everybody's
right to take anything they want—particularly if they're dying. Yet if every individual chose that, then that compromises
the individual's responsibility to society to be an experimental
animal. So the issue of the balance between individual rights
and the responsibility of the individual to society in patient
care has been a predominant one. And it's attacked the traditional paternalism of medicine."

As they occupy a new space of citizenship between the state
and civil society, AIDS organizations foster radical democracy by
institutionalizing citizens' obligations toward one another and by
affirming the equality and rights to which all members of a given
political community are entitled. But it is important to point out
that this ambiguous position between state and civil society can
also work against radical democratic ideals. Without wishing to
negate the affirmations of citizenship in the preceding discussions,
I next want to explore the ways in which this spatial mixture of social relations can effectively *disempower* citizens.

DISEMPOWERING CITIZENS:
REPRODUCING BUREAUCRATS AND CLIENTS

Service Provision

In spite of these strong resistances to clientization and dependency, the structures and practices within AIDS organizations
nonetheless reproduce relations of inequality that threaten citizenship. Since all ASOs in the city provide some manner of service,
the potential for clientization and bureaucratization are always
present. For instance, a restructuring of AIDS Vancouver's intake
department to make it more efficient, and "statelike,"[11] led to a

---

[11]Volunteers and staff who had worked in state welfare agencies voiced support for moves toward more efficient and professional models of service delivery.

handful of volunteers quitting because these changes altered the tone of service delivery at the organization, making service recipients seem less than equal to volunteers. One former intake volunteer voiced her frustrations as follows:

"They changed the whole format. They changed so many things about it, that it was coming out of their heads, and I work out of my heart. And I just said no way! When I did it, Intake was [a group of us] on Fridays. And the fellows came in and there was real need. Sure, some of it you had to sift through maybe. Some were on drugs. Well, it was very seldom that somebody went out of there that didn't get some kind of money. I mean, many times I had a check to go and pay somebody's rent. You wouldn't give them the money, but they still got the need met. And I'd go over to Granville Street and pay it to the St. Helen's Hotel or whatever. I'd take food to people rather than giving them the money. I don't know how to explain it really. [The former coordinator] worked out of the heart. And we did too. He's a wonderful man. And then staff changed, and [he] was no longer in that area, and it [became] all paperwork, paperwork, paperwork. And you have to know this. And you have to know that. Well, I just couldn't go up to one of these guys that I'd gotten to know and they're really in need for some reason or other, and say, 'Well, you know John, you just got to do this. You've got to give me this paper and that paper. And I'm sorry but until this is all done I can't do anything.' I can't work like that. So I left. I told them. I told them why. I just can't work that way."

Perhaps most ironically, the Vancouver Persons With AIDS Society also reproduces clientization in a number of different ways. Foremost, the organization does deliver services to its membership. Consequently, despite the explicit self-help philosophy an inherent structure of service-provider and client-recipient is inevitably structured through PWA. In other words, its members become de facto clients. Services include: personal advocacy work; housing subsidies; personal referrals; a complementary health fund for medicines not covered by B.C. Medical; hospital visits; free haircuts; a tax consultant; a lending library; a drop-in lounge; a monthly newsletter; free lunches to members on site. While certainly some of these services seem trivial to people's lives, others can be valuable enough to structure a significant degree of dependency. Moreover, we can see how the organizations' position as part of the state apparatus might exacerbate this sort of disempowerment.

A case in point is the housing subsidies. The PWA Society is under contract from the B.C. Housing Management Commission to grant approximately 60 housing subsidy vouchers to deserving members, who are decided on by the Housing Committee.[12] This arrangement is more than just an exercise in decentralization. These subsidies can be vital to a PWA living on a handicap pension or long-term disability. Monthly income on GAIN[13] would approximate $755 (Can.). Moreover, consider the PWA's housing market. Many PWAs try to locate in the West End, as close as possible to St. Paul's Hospital, B.C.'s "Centre for Excellence" in AIDS-treatment. Given the high West End rents, access to care might very well *depend* on a member's getting a housing subsidy to live close to AIDS resources.

> "I resigned from the Housing Committee just because I was getting phone calls late at night. In fact, our whole board quit at the same time because we felt that we were making decisions and they were being overturned by these people. And we were getting extremely harassed, on the basis of, 'My friend needs one. And I want him to have one. And I'm a board member and he's going to get one.' Right, even if he doesn't qualify. And I was going nuts."

The move toward clientization was acknowledged frequently—and often with resignation—by members I interviewed. The increasing size of the organization, they felt, made a culture of clientization nearly inevitable at PWA. One man made the point explicitly:

> "I think right now the society is in a transition mode from the brokerage paradigm to the client paradigm. The client

---

[12]The subsidy ensures that recipients will not spend more than 30% of their income on housing.

[13]The handicap welfare program from the B.C. Ministry of Social Services.

paradigm says, 'We're going to do this for you. And we're going to tell you to do this.' The brokerage model says, 'Here are the tools. You do it.' The brokerage model is the self-help paradigm. That's the other problem, the increase in bureaucracy, getting things done. The epitome of the client model in the AIDS community is AIDS Vancouver. We run on the brokerage thing—the self-help mandate—although that is changing. We send out a demographic survey to the voting membership, the results of which are in our current newsletter. One of the questions was, 'service or support?' The vote was fairly evenly split. Part of that was I think people didn't understand the question. But there's also an ambivalence. We're at a focus point where it can go either way. There are some who think we should be doing more in the way of services; there are some who think we should be doing less in the way of services. It's one of these things where time is going to work it out."

Growth

Whenever I asked interviewees to describe how things had changed since they'd been involved in AIDS issues in Vancouver, consistently they mentioned how much their organizations had grown. Concomitantly, the spread of bureaucratization was acknowledged, along with the increase in paid staff and volunteers at organizations. During my fieldwork, for instance, the number of paid staff at AIDS Vancouver doubled from 12 to roughly 24. The move from small, cramped offices by AV and PWA together into the bright, refurbished Pacific AIDS Resource Centre also signaled a certain maturity of AIDS organizations in the city. The increased need and demand for services, of course, logically explain this growth. Its costs, however, can be readily seen in the loss of—or at least the persistent threat to—the ASO's grassroots atmosphere and spirit. Repeatedly—at both AIDS Vancouver and the Persons With AIDS Society—I was told that the camaraderie, the family atmosphere, and the informality were vanishing. These shifts have made PWA seem more like an arm of the shadow state than a community-based organization in civil society, or a surrogate family. For instance, one former employee described the changes he had seen since the mid-1980s:

"The thing that I think I notice most is that the interpersonal relations amongst the guys that work here doesn't seem to be like it was before. I mean there was always slamming and crap like that going on in the past, but I mean they'd hug each other at the end of the meeting. And then they'd come back and do the same thing the next day, but at least they'd hug each other at the end of the meeting. And now, I don't see that kind of personal concern anymore. The organization has gotten too big. And people don't know each other well enough, and they're not prepared to put that much emotion out and all this sort of stuff. And the result is that I think we've lost a lot of the sort of moral leadership quality that existed in the past. I think in part that's just due to the growth of the organization."

While I was not able to obtain membership figures, the enormous growth of the organization is not difficult to believe. In 1986 there were just 15 members, and their principal fund-raiser, the Walk for AIDS, raised a mere $8,000 (Can). Eight years later there were just over 1,200 members who now work with a million dollar budget drawn from a variety of sources including the state (see the growth through 1990 in Figure 4-4). The society has had no choice

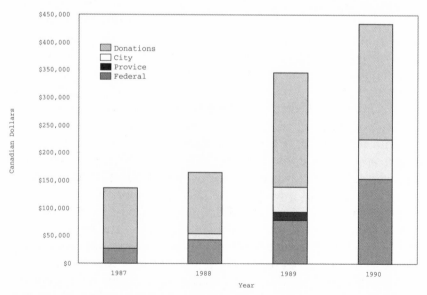

FIGURE 4-4. Vancouver Persons With AIDS Society: revenues by source, 1987–1990.

but to bureaucratize. The spirit of participation is difficult to inculcate across such an enormous organization. Inevitably, members fall into two camps: those who provide the services and those who only take them. Most often, this division was described resentfully:

> "Ideally the situation in this society should be 'each according to their needs, from each according to their talents.' The problem is there are many, many people out there who just want to take, take, take rather than give something back. I mean, so goes the way of the world in general."

So, in a telling slip, an Advocacy volunteer surreptitiously placed fellow members as clients while describing the necessity to agitate the state bureaucracy:

> "I'm here to be adversarial, because I'm not the one being denied benefits. I'm not the one who's going to get penalized. I can just sit back and be a real bitch. And the client—I hate to use that term—but the member who's come to me for help— so then I perceive them as a client (but that's my own social work background partially)—doesn't have to deal with the results of me being a real bitch. Social services either deals with this mess or we go to the media."

Several long-term members noted the decline in a family-like atmosphere, which corresponded with the society's two moves to larger offices over the past four years:

> "By like '89–'90 . . . the small, family atmosphere was breaking down—not breaking down, that sounds negative. But it was disappearing. I don't mean that in a negative way. But there were more strange faces coming in. People didn't know each other so much."

> "But anyway, the old office was really fun [in the Gay and Lesbian Centre]. You used to walk in and everybody, eventually you knew *everybody* who came in. And you'd sit around and

joke and carry on, cavort around. You name it. Give each other a hard time. We used to sit around in the afternoons and
play games. Scattergories and crap like that. And people
brought their lovers and friends and parents to the office. I
can't recall how many hundreds of brothers and sisters and
mothers and aunts and uncles and grandmas and everything
else that I'd meet. Yeah, sure. Kevin Brown's mom would come
trotting in there. She was just like a member of the family. You
know, come in the door and smile and the eyes would light up
and the big smile and the big hug. It was more—people cared
more for each other. It was more intimate. There was less people, you know."

PWA is also witnessing a shift in its membership that con-
tributes to its internal clientization. Members noted the rise in the
number of street-involved or IV drug using members, and claimed
there had been a change in the social class of the membership generally. Consequently, to many new members PWA has become just
another local service organization to which members presented
themselves as clients because the self-help model was *so* foreign to
them:

"I think the definition of support has changed. I think now
'support' is more basic needs like food, shelter. I mean, if we
even thought about giving out food bags in 1988 people
would have been offended that came to the door. There was
no way they were going to leave with a food bag. And now
AIDS Vancouver runs a food bank. So food is an issue. Housing: people needed help paying their rent in those days, but
they didn't need help finding housing if they could present
themselves to a landlord. Now we have families on welfare
with children, so that's changed a lot. Sometimes I feel like a
financial aid worker. Sometimes I feel like a social worker. A lot
of the people I see probably see me as another service provider
that they probably have been dealing with their entire adult
life. Sometimes I feel that way."

One of the most ironic outcomes of this dichotomy is that
many persons living with AIDS in the city stay away from the
shadow-state organizations that were meant to be so attuned to

their needs. Typically, they cite the "internal power politics" and disorganization for the reluctance to be active in the society. As one person reflected:

"For me, I would rather make use of an institution or a society like PWA *as* a client. I would rather make intelligent choices, do my research, say they can do *this* for me; I will go in and get *that*. If I don't know enough about something, I'll go in and investigate it. I would rather do it that way than sort of be co-opted by the whole thing."

In other words, to resist dependency and the internal politics of the organization, some persons living with AIDS find a certain degree of empowerment by acting as occasional clients.

ASOs Disciplining Clients

Vancouver's shadow state not only facilitates bureaucratic structures and clientization itself, it also "cerns" clients for the central state as well.[14] Bear in mind that, despite both organizations' gay grassroots ties, AIDS Vancouver and PWA both are linked to the state through financial and contract ties (see Figures 4-4 and 4-5). These linkages facilitate clientization, as the organizations become just another social welfare line in which to stand. AIDS Vancouver, for instance, has developed increasingly close ties with the Ministry of Social Services. During its intake process, AV makes it easier for clients to present themselves to the Ministry in order to access benefits more rapidly. While the intake process at AIDS Vancouver enables clients to get more of what they deserve from the welfare state, it does this by clientizing them before they even get to the state itself. One AIDS Vancouver intake worker put it this way:

"I think the Ministry is starting to recognize that AV is certainly a help to them as opposed to a hindrance. I think in the past they've always considered us as being, you know, 'Get out of our way! *We're* here to look after these people!' Now the

---

[14]"Cerned" is a term coined by Paul Smith (1988) to denote how individuals are constituted by multiple social relations simultaneously. The word highlights the lack of fixity and often contradictory makeup of social subjects' identities.

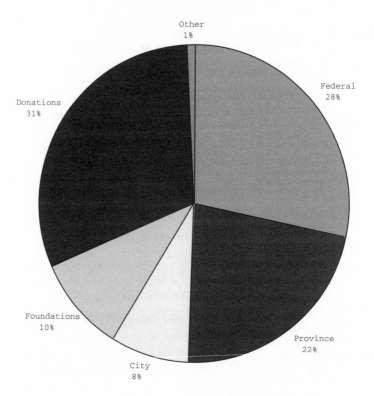

FIGURE 4-5. AIDS Vancouver 1992 revenues by source.

Ministry is phoning *us* when they're finding out about a client who's ill. They will phone us and find out if we've had any contact with the individual. It's certainly becoming a two-way street."

Ironically, the Persons With AIDS Society often reproduces state clientization in spite of its explicit mandate to the contrary. This point was made clearly to me by a peer counselor at PWA. He asked me what I was specifically interested in, and I described the clientization process and how it often made the democratic citizen unequal and dependent. He nodded knowingly. Tweaking on my theoretical ruminations, he told the following story. I quote him at length because it illustrates the difficult position *between* citizen and client that a member of the Vancouver Person With AIDS Society faces to maintain an adequate standard of living:

"You talk about citizenship. I guess every day I talk to at least one person who is struggling to make decisions between his responsibilities as a citizen and his ability to demand rights, which perhaps he doesn't feel quite right demanding. And I have to say to him, 'You have a life-threatening illness. You must survive. Will you be able to survive without this help?' This is a major problem for our members. And I would never, in my wildest dreams, have thought that a major part of my life was talking about that question. I can sure give you an example. But I want to be somewhat noncommittal. How can I express it? I guess the easiest one to talk about is this form here. It gives you a tax advantage. It's called the 'disability certificate' [disability tax-credit certificate]. And if a doctor signs it, it means that you pay about $1,200 less in income tax than if he hasn't signed it. Now, in order to sign that, the doctor has to say that you have a severe, marked, permanent disability. Look at me. Do I? 'Severe'? 'Marked'? 'Permanent'? Those are strong words. I ride a motorcycle. I go skiing. I can work in this office reasonably long hours and still be mostly with it [laughs]—this is the end of a long day for me. I can do 40 push-ups. I go jogging. What's the doctor supposed to say to me? My T-4 count has been hovering around the 110 level for over a year now. My immune system is severely compromised. I cannot stand stress. I can't hold a job. It's totally out of the question. People wonder about whether or not I have a severe disability? I asked my doctor to sign that form and he did, on the basis of the amount of fatigue that I feel, and on the basis of the fact that my ability to deal with life-threatening situations has been severely compromised. But people have problems with that. We've got doctors who have problems with signing the form for people that should have it, because they don't have to sign it. What is one's responsibility as a citizen *and* to pay that $1,200 in taxes because this illness has progressed? I think that's probably a good example you can use. There are other examples, but they're not as nice. That's a classic. I was going up the chairlift. The guy beside me said, 'What do you do for a living?' I said, 'I don't. I'm disabled.' He just about threw me off the chair. He wasn't upset that I was disabled, just didn't believe me. This illness is not *like* other illnesses. I mean, if I were blind, there would be no problem getting that form signed, even though I would be capable of holding down a full-time job, having a wife and a house full of kids. I guess I couldn't coach the baseball team, but I could sure coach something or other. This example with the form, it's one of the great layers of this onion. Where you *sign* that you are disabled, and that you're no longer to be a functioning member of society that you've been. You are talking about a huge decision-making process, and it's affecting men who are relatively young in large numbers. Their concept of themselves as givers and providers changes to one who must take. And we all loathe the thought of the day where all we can do is lie in our hospital bed and have our tubes fed and our messes cleaned up. Yeah. We face quite a citizenship problem, all right! I hand out those disability forms by the dozen. I went into the tax office the other day and told the woman I needed 60 more."

This volunteer demonstrates the paradox of the shadow state that has so worried critics like Wolch. If AIDS organizations had remained steadfastly placed in civil society (in this case, the gay grassroots), would they be able to deliver the amount and variety of services that citizens require? Does it make sense to retain an image of a gay organization when the populations being affected by AIDS are shifting in the city? And yet what are the costs of growth and expansion? Increasing ties to the state, with their attendant mandates, policies, and procedures that can trump equality in favor of efficiency? Just as the state–civil society intersection at AIDS Vancouver and PWA can empower citizens, it can disempower them too.

CONCLUSION

What are the implications of this shift from civil society to the state—from citizenship to bureaucracy and clientization—for radical democracy? As a geographer, I would stress the need to recognize the shifting social space on which Vancouver's shadow state rests. The meaningfulness of places like the Pacific AIDS Resource Centre is being constantly redrawn by changes in the relations between state and civil society/community. Organizations like PWA and AIDS Vancouver denote the ongoing restructuring of the capitalist welfare state. They provide services for the state, derive portions of their funds from the state, and maintain lines of communications with it. Yet, they are also a highly visible part of the gay community that spawned them (e.g., Figure 4-6 and 4-7). They derive great portions of their funds from grassroots fund-raising within the gay community too. They recruit their staff and volunteers through the gay community. And, as noted in Chapter 2, a large proportion of the people who use their services are gay. The spatial duality at Vancouver's ASOs enables citizens' struggles to succeed. By drawing on their grassroots origins, volunteer organizations can better identify with the needs that the state had failed to acknowledge; yet, by drawing on their statelike qualities, they can better accommodate the heightened levels of demand for services that inevitably accompany increased needs.

To illustrate this overlapping of state and civil society I have tried to convey the impacts of these restructurings on the actual expression of citizenship as it relates to AIDS issues. The concept of citizenship was derived not from its original definition in liberal democratic theory, nor from the virtues of civic republicanism, but rather it was arrived at poststructurally via the issues it points up, namely, the rights, duties, and responsibilities implied by member-

FIGURE 4-6. AIDS Vancouver at 1993 Gay Pride Parade. Photo by author.

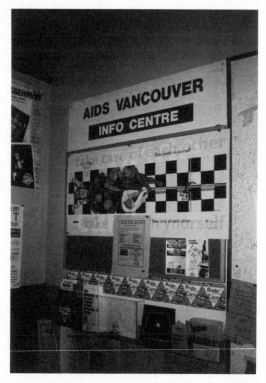

FIGURE 4-7. AIDS Vancouver Information Centre, Little Sister's Book Store, West End. Photo by author.

ship in a political community. By relaying how these issues were defined (and by whom) at AIDS Vancouver and PWA, it was argued that the categorical distinction between citizen and bureaucrat proved unhelpful in the political context of AIDS issues. This point was understood through the rise of a shadow state, an effective state bureaucracy, and a mobilized gay community's politics that worked through those structures. I have attempted to show that one's calling, or profession, may entail aspects of citizenship—not merely because of its results but also because of attitudes toward work itself that have politicized it.

Citizens have also been disempowered, however, by this melding of dichotomized social relations. Increases in the size and demand for ASOs' services, along with increasing relationships with the state, cause a certain amount of clientization that can be detrimental to a full expression of radical citizenship. By framing the quest for new spaces of citizenship geographically (by which I do not just mean "empirically"), we can better appreciate the potentials and the pitfalls of politics that gravitate toward radical democratic ideals. New spaces of politics should be fully investigated because they do hold such promise and because the restructurings of social relations (like the decline of the welfare state) have made it necessary to retheorize them. But they are not necessarily assured arenas for new forms of radical democratic citizenship. Thoroughgoing exploration of them must continue. As certain recent offerings in the AIDS literature have shown, AIDS has challenged city politics fundamentally (Shilts, 1987; Kramer, 1989; Perrow & Guillen, 1990; Fernandez, 1991). I would insist that the categories through which we capture those politics must adapt in turn. That adaptation must take the form of constantly rethinking where citizenship really *occurs* rather than automatically jettisoning state-centered spaces for those associated with "civil society." With this in mind, I continue my exploration of citizenship in the next chapter, where the social relations of the state and those of the family or home intertwine.

———•———

Chapter 5

FROM THE HOME
TO THE STATE
"Just Being There"
As a Buddy

CHANGES IN AND BETWEEN
THE STATE AND THE HOME

The preceding chapter demonstrated how organizations like AIDS Vancouver have shifted from exhibiting relations of civil society toward being wings of the state apparatus, marking new spaces of radical citizenship. These sorts of blurred boundaries can also be found between the state apparatus and the home. In these barely visible spaces, citizens are empowered through social relations of state service delivery and familial support. At their junctures the shifting morphology of the state and changes in the family collide. From the private sphere, the statistical and hegemonic decline of the traditional nuclear family and the rise of "postmodern families" point up the lack of a uniform model of family structure (Stacey, 1991). Presently there is far less agreement on the structure of the home—and consequently its geography—than society admits (Koontz, 1992; Mack, 1993; Massey, 1994; Sarup, 1994). Gay, lesbian, and queer identities, as well as their intimate relationships, reflect and reinforce this variance. We can see the tensions explicitly when "family values" are claimed to be threatened by the very existence of gays and lesbians (Hunter, 1995; Varnell, 1996). Reinterpreting that tension, many texts abound with meditations on the extremely painful struggles of growing up gay *and* as part of a heterosexual home (Monette, 1992; Nardi, Sanders, & Marmour, 1994; Gay Men's Oral History Group, 1989; Preston, 1991, 1992). Within gay and lesbian life there has been an ongoing experimentation with and forging of what Weston (1991) calls "families we choose" (see also Hunter, 1995; Andrews, 1994; Benkov, 1994). Her argument is that, far from being antithetical to the family, gay people's relationships should be viewed as an alternate form of kinship in contemporary life. Like the state, the family and home are experiencing quite a restructuring lately, which complicates any static geography of citizenship.

Furthermore, shifts in family structure and ideology are reflected and reinforced through a number of contradictions and tensions *between* the public sphere of the state and the private sphere of gay men's homes. Consider the two following examples.

First, in a number of locations across Canada and the U.S. the (local) state grants domestic partnership benefits to same-sex couples. In certain places couples can even register their relationships with the (local) state. Repeatedly (and most recently in Canada in 1996), however, the nation-state has refused to condone gay marriages, which would place gay households on an equal legal footing with traditional heterosexual ones.

Second, the liberal democratic state is meant to avoid involvement in the private sphere wherever possible, theoretically speaking. The home, and certainly the bedroom, are off limits to the state—unless the body politic is threatened by what goes on there. Gays and lesbians, however, have experienced blatant intrusions on that front. In the 1986 *Bowers* v. *Hardwick* decision (McKenzie, 1991; Halley, 1993; Hunter, 1993) the American Supreme Court endorsed the right of the state to outlaw particular sexual practices—which were taking place between consenting adult men in the bedroom—that contravened the prevailing morality of the wider political community. In Canada, two gay bookstores (Little Sisters in Vancouver and Glad Day in Toronto) took Canada Customs to court for blocking their materials on the grounds that they were obscene (Fuller & Blackley, 1995; Calfia & Fuller, 1995). Ironically, the same titles destined for nongay bookstores passed across the border and into the homes of Canadian readers without contravention. The plaintiffs were largely unsuccessful in challenging Canada Customs' mandate.

Amidst all this confusion, the stigma of AIDS has played no small role in the renegotiation of state and family responsibility for support. Some individuals with AIDS have chosen not to tell their families about their antibody status, out of shame or fear of rejection. They rely instead on alternate forms of kinship for support. For many gay men, their seropositivity creates or exacerbates tensions between themselves and their partners or their biological families at the very time when support is needed most. Furthermore, gay, HIV positive couples have to face the reality of both partners having to care for each other while ill themselves. For still others, the distinction between kinship and biological families is not necessarily so sharply drawn. Often some mixture of both is drawn upon in building support networks. While some relatives might be resentful at the extension of the HIV positive person's private sphere, others welcome the relief, finding the burden of supporting a person living with AIDS to be overwhelming at times. These strategies raise pressing political questions. What happens when the family does not support a person living with AIDS, or when that support collapses? In those circumstances, what rights do PWAs have to support from members of their political community? What obligations do fellow citizens have to provide that support—especially when the state does not? What happens when support, family, and home do not (precisely) geographically coincide? The starting point in answering these difficult questions, at least in Vancouver, is that the AIDS voluntary sector—as part of the state apparatus—intervenes.

Between these shifting spaces of state and home, we find the fascinating position of the buddy. A buddy is either a volunteer at AIDS Vancouver or the client who requires his/her service.[1] Buddy-volunteers provide one-on-one practical and emotional support to a person living with AIDS or HIV. Their wide, comprehensive mandate and links to both the state apparatus and the family complicate any static geography of the citizen. They occupy spaces of *both* the home and the (shadow-)state. This fuzzy geography reflects the multiple social relations characteristic of radical citizen-

---

[1]The roles are typically referred to as "the buddy-volunteer" and "the buddy-client" for the sake of clarity.

ship. It also empowers citizen-volunteers to meet their obligations, as well as citizen-clients who are entitled to support as members of the political community. The buddy-volunteer may be the only family a person with AIDS has, while at the same time becoming a form of state surveillance into a client's private life. I demonstrate that duality in this chapter by considering the myriad ways that "support" gets defined in buddy relations, while making the case that buddying is a form of citizenship defined through locations where elements of family, home, and state relations are combined in places across the city. This redefinition of buddy relations toward the state apparatus, however, is not entirely empowering for clients living with AIDS, and the potential for disempowerment in this hybrid space of home and state is also discussed below.

PUBLIC VERSUS PRIVATE: STATE VERSUS FAMILY

Since the seventeenth century the public-private division has been an influential structural force in liberal democratic theory, partitioning out social institutions as separate and often unequal spheres of life. Recently, however, scholars have demonstrated just how universal that well-worn dichotomy actually is. A recurrent theme hones in on the public-private cuts being made at both institutional and individual scales of analysis.[2] Both liberal defenders (Held, 1987; Kymlicka, 1990) and feminist critics (Okin, 1991; Fraser, 1989; Pateman, 1989) agree on the presence of a twofold dichotomy in liberal democratic praxis: public versus private institutions and public versus private dimensions of individual lives (see Figure 5-1). Often the split comes down to where the theorist places "civil society" on the conceptual map, and these thinkers disagree about the normative implications of the dichotomies.

Their cartographies remain remarkably consistent nonetheless. Pateman (1989), for instance, argues that nested within the institutionally framed private sphere of civil society institutions is another public-private dichotomy that segregates women and "domestic life" away from the public life of civil society. Similarly,

---

[2]My discussions with Phil Howell, Don Mitchell, and Susan Ruddick have been particularly helpful to me in considering this issue, and I am grateful to them.

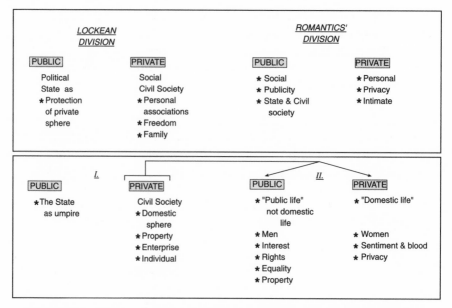

FIGURE 5-1. Public and private spheres in political theory. Top: based on Kymlicka (1990), pp. 247–262. Bottom: based on Pateman (1989), pp. 121–133.

Kymlicka (1990) insists on preserving the liberal notion of privacy in individuals' life, even within the family, which he theorizes as a component of the more broadly private world of civil society. Bearing in mind that radical democracy transgresses public-private binaries (whatever their axis), the point to take from these discussions is that when we spatialize relations of the family, we must not merely consider the fixed domestic location of the home. We must also consider "private" locations where intimate relations are lived. The family (and the support it gives) is typically located within the home, and so that site is discussed below as enabling citizenship through the buddy relationship. Kinship relations, however, need not only be confined to the domicile. They can also take place privately in public spaces, yet still be understood as "familial" and private. Buddy relations, it will be shown, empower citizenship by fostering support in these venues as well. Consequently, these sorts of familial locations are also highlighted in this chapter. After offering a brief history of buddies in the AIDS crisis generally, and in Vancouver specifically, I will show how these relationships worked in locations of home and family. The locations exhibited hybrid relations of kinship and state service delivery. They empowered volunteers to become supportive members of clients' families while also permitting some degree of state surveillance of the private needs of people living with AIDS.

THE BUDDIES

Origins

Buddying was started at the Gay Men's Health Crisis in New York (Kuklin, 1989) and the Shanti Project in San Francisco in the early 1980s. In Vancouver, these innovative programs served as direct models for the buddy program. The open-ended definition of support stems from the variegated and diverse needs any particular person living with AIDS might have at any given stage of the illness's progression. That open-endedness also denotes the widespread failures of both state and family structures to provide adequate support immediately during early years of the crisis. One of AIDS Vancouver's earliest buddy coordinators recalled the program circa 1984:

> "The needs in those days were in some respects pretty comprehensive. And there's been various attempts over time to combine and to separate the various aspects of need. The buddy program initially covered everything and anything. And then we tried to get a little more specific where the buddy program was more emotional support, under particular guidelines; and practical support, transportation, food, financial assistance, information about medication, being separated from the emotional support but still being handled by AIDS Vancouver but by different volunteers. You know, there are some volunteers who'd be very happy to drive a person with AIDS to and from doctors' appointments, but not being so confident or willing to get involved at an emotional level and be there for them on an ongoing basis."

Chapter 2 detailed the province's negligence in supporting people living with AIDS. Recall that in his public refusal to fund

AIDS Vancouver, the provincial Health Minister was quoted in 1987 as saying AIDS Vancouver could "take care of their own kind." The claim was popularly interpreted as homophobic: gays were not citizens, and thus beyond the entitlement to care and welfare that is a fundamental feature provided to the citizen by the state or political community. Neoconservative ideals legitimized the state's sluggish response to AIDS: the state could not afford, nor was it really its job to provide for, the needs of HIV positive people.

According to conservative political thought, of course, the family is the favored or "natural" site for the provision of care for the individual in a democratic capitalist state (Gardinier, 1992; cf. Elshtain, 1983); so the state might have been drawing an ideological link between the gay community and the family early on in the crisis. Whatever the logic, the provision of support to HIV positive gay men was beyond the public, institutional sphere of the state. Support was to be isolated in the private sphere. Yet, as Chapter 2 discussed, the state was rhetorically insisting that a subpopulation that was disproportionately suffering from the epidemic be rallied to support its own terminally ill members. The sick, the dying, and even those "at risk" were being forced to provide support—in a sense *to one another.* It is this spirit of informal mutual aid and friendship in a crisis that underscored the formation of a buddy program at AIDS Vancouver.

As I have already suggested, the situation in the city showed that very often gay men's biological families could not have been more separate from "their own kind" in the West End. In nearly every interview with buddy-volunteers, and in innumerable discussions with others, stories abounded about the schisms between people with AIDS and their biological families. For many gay men, coming out to their families had produced an alienation that meant they had not spoken with each other in years. They were reluctant to make contact with news of a terminal illness that was bound up with their sexual relations. Sexuality was not always the issue, however. Some gay men recalled how, when they had told their lovers or partners about their status, they had been thrown out on the street. Others told tales of coming to Vancouver not just because of the quality of care there but also because families and hometowns across Canada rejecting people living with AIDS out of distress, fear, and ignorance. A few gay men living with AIDS even recounted how they had left Vancouver to "go home to die," only to return to the city because their families could not cope with their illness and/or their sexuality. These painful alienations and tensions often exacerbated the distance between gay men and their families, and thereby generated buddying (e.g., Preston, 1992).

To trace out further the origins of the need for buddies, we must recall that AIDS has long been a holocaust for gay men's social worlds within gay neighborhoods. The literature on AIDS is replete with stories of friend after friend becoming sick and then dying—all out of the public's sight (Shilts, 1987; Kramer, 1989; Russo, 1990; Monette, 1990; J. Brown, 1992). Longtime AIDS activist Vito Russo (1991) described this hidden nature of the disaster well:

> Living with AIDS in this country is like living in the Twilight Zone. Living with AIDS is living through a war which is happening only for those people who are in the trenches. Every time a shell explodes you look around to discover you've lost more friends. But nobody else notices—it isn't happening to them. They're walking the streets as though we weren't living through a nightmare. . . . [I]t's worse than wartime because during a war people are united in a shared experience. This war has not united us—it's divided us. It's separated those of us with AIDS and those of us who fight for people with AIDS from the rest of the population. (p. 299)

The tragic political-cultural geography he describes was confirmed in Vancouver by one activist who died shortly after our interview:

> "The whole thing is a sort of smoldering powder keg of people who are just so angry at having *lost*. You know, you're not talking about losing one friend. You're talking about losing dozens. Here in Vancouver, in the West End, there's nobody I could meet that doesn't know somebody who's got it or who hasn't had somebody die of it. Everybody's been touched by this thing. And it's a goddamn nightmare that people want to turn away from, but there's nowhere to run!"

In other words, it is likely that, even if gay men turned to their own social networks for help, to their own "families we choose," their gay friends or partners might also be sick, dying, or already dead. One volunteer, for instance, insisted that he had only one buddy, when in fact, as our interview progressed, he acceded that he really had two—but that they were partners. Another volunteer related that, after his first buddy-client died, that client's partner became ill and requested that this individual become his buddy, as well; with his partner dead, he had no one else to care for him. For all these reasons, then, buddies—as formal volunteers—stepped in and began to offer support.

Buddying at AIDS Vancouver

The actual number of buddies can vary at any given time, due to ebbs and flows of volunteers, but there were roughly 93 during my research. Across that time period AIDS Vancouver's client base ranged from about 1,150 to 1,200 (not every client needs or requests a buddy). The buddy relationship typically lasts about a year, and ends with the client's death, although the buddy coordinator estimated that about 10% of her matches did not work out. As Figure 5-2 indicates, buddies usually have only one or two

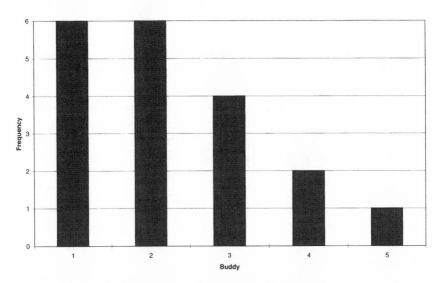

FIGURE 5-2. Number of clients per buddy.

clients over their volunteer career.[3] There are no firm statistics on who buddies. In discussions with employees in Support Services, the estimates were fairly reliable: at any given time about half of the buddy-volunteers are self-identified gay men and half are straight women. There is a wide range of ages, but, modally, most buddies are in their thirties. Most are "middle-class" and white. This rough sketch is confirmed by a quantitative study by Letts (1992, p. 27) in Vancouver.

The Buddy As a Radical Citizen

Buddying can be interpreted through Mouffe's outline of radical citizenship in at least three broad ways in Vancouver. First, the antagonism between people living with AIDS and their traditional families and the state would seem to define the political dimension of buddying. Buddies exist, in a sense, because that antagonism exists. Buddy relationships were both structured and experienced though the friends-versus-enemy polarities described by both Russo (1990) and the Vancouver activist earlier (see page 127). Buddy-volunteers compensate for the strained relations between people living with AIDS and their biological families, as well as the state. Often they help the person deal with anger over this neglect.

Buddies embody a truly de-centered subjectivity, a second way in which they are radical citizens. The volunteer positions are filled largely by gay men and straight women. Clients include, among others, gay men, IV drug users, and women. In classical liberal theory—as so many critics have argued—these are hardly the identities that "citizens" have inhabited in the past. Furthermore, these identities themselves are neither static nor comprehensive to the buddy-citizen. Part of what makes buddying so fascinating is that it defies fixed definition. This variability of the basic job definition shows that the position works not just through the wide variety of social relations that it embodies. The people that I interviewed had a difficult time trying to give an overarching or comprehensive definition. Likewise, I stammered at first upon trying to conceptualize buddying *as* citizenship. My categories told me

---

[3]This sample is not necessarily random. It is developed from the buddies who were willing to speak with me.

that a buddy-volunteer was something of a social worker—the welfare function of traditional city politics being appropriated by the emerging shadow state (Krefetz, 1977). And, to be sure, this characterization is hardly inaccurate, as we shall see presently. Yet, almost immediately I had to rethink (and eventually leave open) my ideas about what buddying was, which leads to a fourth characteristic of radical citizenship. Helping to clarify matters a buddy coordinator gave a concise introductory definition of a buddy:

> "A buddy[-volunteer]'s role can be any number of things. It's a very difficult role to define because it has so many aspects. There's a practical aspect in terms of, if someone needs a buddy to go in and change the cat litter because they need to stay away from it because of toxo,[4] or just someone who needs someone to walk their dog or drive them to a doctor's appointment or around the park, or help them negotiate the system to get their needs met. Or, do they need someone to talk to who's outside their realm of friends, or perhaps there are no friends, and they're isolated. So it's a fairly difficult role to define and each situation is different."

The multifaceted, often shifting nature of support underlies this chapter's argument: that citizenship can be located in both public and private spheres (since it can be a component of any social relation)—but, more precisely, its actual locations (that is, where buddying takes place) empower citizenships that inhabit both the state and familial relationships. So, third, the broad definition of support makes buddying precisely the kind of agonistic politics that Mouffe champions. Buddies strive to make a difference in their clients' lives by offering "support." Typically, however, support falls into two categories: emotional and practical. It is important to emphasize that these are not mutually exclusive categories, but rather they almost always overlap. One volunteer recalled her client in such a way that this overlap was made all too clear:

> "For my first buddy[-client], it started out while she was healthy, she wanted somebody with the same interests to be social with. She did need some physical support, in that she

---

[4]It is a disease of the central nervous system.

tired easily. She didn't drive. So she wanted somebody to be social with, that also understood the disease, her physical limitations, and also she was a recovering alcoholic, so she wanted somebody that understood a 12-step program and was comfortable with that and the jargon. So when we first started we would go out for a lunch, a walk on the beach, a couple of plays, that type of thing. As she got more ill, I would visit her. She had family as well, but as a support, what I would do is that when there was nobody available I would visit. I took over food. I made sure the apartment was clean, made sure she was okay. I would check in by phone. And when she went to the hospital, I took a fairly regular shift at the hospital. I was there almost every morning to make sure she ate, because before she—whatever they call it when they stick the feeding tube into your stomach. . . . While she was still on solids she wasn't able to eat, or chose not to (there was a little bit of both there). So I was there for psychological and physical support, in that I fed her. I gave her back rubs and leg rubs. I trimmed her nails, that kind of thing. I helped keep her clean. When she got very, very ill and the tube was inserted I just spent time there, just a physical presence: so her family could get a rest, and her friends. I was just one of the people *there.*"

Practical support can involve anything from shopping for the client, driving her/him to the hospital, or dealing with social services if the client is too weak. It often entails taking over domestic responsibilities in the client's home: cooking, cleaning, changing diapers, or doing laundry. Most recently, these domestic chores are more systematically taken care of by the City Health Department's Long-term Care team, or other departments at AIDS Vancouver. Nevertheless, volunteers will do these tasks if requested.

Emotional support tends to be very basic. Volunteer training stresses listening skills, for example. Thus talking, listening, spending time with the client, helping them cope with the various illnesses all fall under the rubric of emotional support. One buddy alluded to the significance of emotional support as he summarized his relationships with all five of his clients:

"So I've had five buddies in five years, sort of thing. They've all been great in their own ways. Some you get closer to than others, which is only natural. You have friends, you know, and sometimes you feel some of your friends are closer than others. And there's reasons, of course, for that. I felt that in practically all instances their needs were completely different. And I think that, on the whole I was able to fulfill these needs and change as it was required. In most cases, I would say that they really wanted—and I'll use the word "spiritual support," and I'm not indicating by that that any of them were particularly overreligious. Some believed stronger than others. But they all wanted—I think the main thing was to learn and listen and not be judgmental. And it taught me a great, great deal."

The refrain of "just being there" clearly underscores the emotional support component of the buddy relationship. One very experienced volunteer, for instance, noted the significance of her own physical presence to the well-being of her aphasic client in the hospital. Being there as an emotional support, however, takes on even more significance when buddies acknowledge that they may well have to be there for their clients' deaths. The buddy-volunteer quoted immediately above went on to recount a particularly special instance of his "just being there":

"It'll be two years on the nineteenth of this month that he died. And again, I was fortunate enough to be with him. Again, it was sort of a funny thing because I was going out for dinner that evening and the day before I had said to one of the nurses . . . , 'Here's the phone number. If there are any drastic changes, please call me.' And all evening long we were sitting there and I thought, 'Oh isn't this nice, no phone calls.' And I got home and there was a message from the nurse. I phoned and he said, 'You better come.' And I got there and he'd been comatose for hours. His family and friends were around. And [the nurse] said to me, 'He needs changing.' And I would help the nurses if they asked me. So we shooed everybody out, and I spoke to [my buddy]. And I said, '[The nurse] and I are going to change you.' And he opened his eyes and he sort of squeezed my hand and he said, 'You're here!' He shut his eyes and he died. And I don't know if this is true or not, of course, and I never will, but I have a feeling he was waiting until I got there."

The clients' needs seem to be the defining element of the buddy relationship. Those needs dictate the form that support takes. And since those needs are often acutely located in the home, buddy-volunteers can be understood as citizens in the private sphere. Somewhat conversely, the buddy-clients should also be understood as radical citizens. The support they most need is provided to them on the grounds that they are entitled to this support as fellow members of the political community. As Fraser (1989) argues, welfare policies directed by human needs rather than by bureaucratic structures offer a more satisfactory form of politics—one that need not be entirely hemmed in by the public-private divides in liberal democracies. From the accounts and description above, it appears that new forms of citizenship complicate a solely public reading of political obligation—either at the institutional or individual level. When we begin to consider the importance of where those needs are being met, and how context makes meeting those needs quite a political act, this point becomes all the more clear. To substantiate it, I will sketch out how buddying is found in the private spheres of home and family in the following section.

MODES OF CITIZENSHIP IN THE PRIVATE SPHERES

Because of the twofold dimensions of the public-private divide, we must recognize that buddying can also take place wherever support and care transpire in public or private spaces. To demonstrate this point, I have culled the locations specifically discussed in the buddy interviews and have plotted them in Figure 5-3. While by no means a representative sample, the histogram demonstrates a mix of public and private spaces where relations of intimacy and privacy were struck. It shows that, while both volunteers' and clients' homes are reported with frequency, public urban spaces (e.g., "out for a walk") are also listed. When volunteers discussed the geography of their buddying, their cartographies reflected a full span of public and private spaces available for meetings.

Buddy-Volunteers: In the Home, Part of the Family

"And my very first meeting with him was very awkward because my first buddy was very healthy [and this one was not].

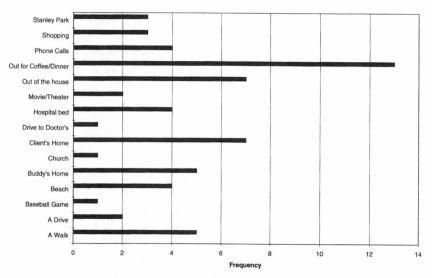

FIGURE 5-3. Locations for buddying.

But I went to meet him at this scuzzy little East Side hotel. It was disgusting: this little, tiny room. And I walked in, trying not to act disgusted, and he sat down with me, and we had some coffee. And then he said, 'Will you help me make out my will?' And I was like, 'Okay, nice to meet you, too.' And we worked out his will because he was going through chemotherapy at the time for skin cancer."

The private nature of buddying, associated with domestic support, is evident when we consider the actual locations of interactions between buddy and client. Buddying does *not* take place at AIDS Vancouver, but often at the client's home. Volunteers are encouraged to interact in the client's lifeworld. Here we can see how radical democratic citizenship cannot be understood as a mere shift toward civil society, as the private sphere of the home must also be mapped as a new space of citizenship. This point was made repeatedly by buddy-volunteers, who confessed that they were unable to follow the latest AIDS Vancouver scuttlebutt—since they hardly ever came into the office! Their volunteering took them elsewhere. Buddying occurs throughout the city, but most often in private spaces like the home of the client (or the volunteer).

Similarly, clients were also mapped—often quite directly—into volunteers' own homes and families. Many buddy-volunteers insisted that they had to step into the vacuum left by the absence of biological kin. Repeatedly they described the extreme tension and alienation between clients and their biological families:

"And that was where I found out that people turn their backs on their children. I don't care if your child is gay or lesbian. I don't care whatever they are—they are *your* child! How can you turn your back? I just couldn't understand that. I was absolutely horrified."

"[My most recent buddy's] mom and father had a great deal of difficulty over his illness. So the illness was a great source of friction there. I think it's fair to say that of all those four guys I've buddied, the one thing that they did have in common was that none of them—*none of them*—wanted to go home. So even the ones who knew nobody in Vancouver, preferred Vancouver to home. Home was always somewhere else."

"When he got really sick, he decided to move back to Port Alberni from Toronto to live with his family. And that didn't work out too well. He stayed there for a few months but part of the reason he wanted to be with them was that they had never gotten along really well, and he thought that they could come to some better relationship. But it didn't happen. It got a lot worse. And he basically got thrown out on his head when he was extremely sick during that cold weather that we had just around Christmas time. He had to find an apartment then. He was on his own: he had no furniture, no money. He was sleeping on the floor and, like he's—you know how they get thin, eh—unusually thin, even for a person with AIDS. They just tipped him out. They brought him over here to Vancouver. Dumped him. And then his family went on vacation for a month."

Usually the fact that the client both was gay and had AIDS served to compound the distance between him and his family. Furthermore, with adulthood, the links of care between some people and their families just largely disappear. Geographic distance also played a crucial role. Where is home? It is typical for gay men across Canada to migrate to larger urban centers. Thus, in many client cases, biological family was literally elsewhere, making ongoing support difficult. As well, it is important to note the negotiated, constructed nature of "family" in gay and lesbian life. As a number of authors have shown, new patterns of kinship ties are being formed in gay subculture that do not necessarily mimic the traditional heterosexual family (Weston, 1991; Preston, 1991; Andrews, 1994; Benkov, 1994). Current and former partners, friends, and coworkers can all be considered family. From all these points we must situate the buddy-client in a web of familial relationships that reinforce and reflect new forms of family, and reject any static or singular geography of "home." One volunteer made this point especially well, I think:

> "You have death, but you also have life, you know. When my [buddy-client] died—that's the one I'm having trouble getting over—he died on February 24th. And the funny thing was that in the Fall, before he got dementia, he sent me into his bedroom to pick up something. And there's this big dozen, long stemmed red roses for *me*. So I said, 'Well, what have I *done*?', you know. And he says, 'Well I might not be here when you become a grandmother.' (I just found out I was going to be a grandmother.) 'I might not be here,' he says. So he gave me these flowers. And we used to talk about it and everything. Anyway, he died on the 24th of February. And on the 25th my little grandson was born in Edmonton. And they named him [after my buddy-client]. You know, that was just wonderful."

For another volunteer, it was helpful to draw on her own family and friends to build up an emotional support network for her buddy-client:

> "I guess I've introduced my buddy to, like, my kids and their friends. I have two sort of late teenage girls. And their friends, their boyfriends, the people I work with, my relatives—I've in-

troduced him to them all. He just has a really strong taste for lots and lots of new people. He's just a very outgoing person. It's difficult for him, physically, to get around, so it's just easier if somebody can bring all these people to him. Even if I don't physically bring them to him, I get, like, my sister to write him letters."

Still another volunteer drew her buddy-client into her family and home more explicitly:

"And I had a little blanket that somebody had made me, which was *his* blanket. He knew where it was [in my apartment]. And he used to put the blanket over him. And he used to put his head on my lap. And he used to lie there and sleep for about two hours before it was time to go back again. But I think I was just—an anchor—was all I could say I really was. I was a haven he could go to, even if it was just on the telephone. *He was like family with me.*"

A gay man who is a buddy-volunteer noted the pliancy of the term "family" for him and his client (who's also gay) with particular acumen:

"My buddy doesn't really have a family. When I mean 'family' I mean mother, father, brothers and sisters. He does have a foster sister who lives in the city here that he keeps in touch with. And she's a lot of support to him when he's in the hospital. His parents he's never met before. His father, I believe, is in prison and his mother's in a mental institution. And he does have his foster parents in another province, but they never write to him or anything. So there's really not a lot of communication happening there. And that could probably be his fault too, of not keeping in touch with them. But as for his family and friends, there's myself and his foster sister, and then there's another friend who's moving in in a few days, and probably one other person. We are his family, really. We care a lot for him. We're there for him. We're not like his other friends who sort of disappear when he's in the hospital or whatever. Like many gay people, that's really their family— not their blood family—but friends. And I think probably in the last two years he knows about this now. He knows that he does have this family and friends that he can trust, and he knows that they'll be there for him."

Besides becoming part of a renegotiated family structure, the buddy-volunteer also augments the client's private sphere alternately by supporting the existing family *in situ*. One buddy coordinator emphasized this point to me during her interview:

> "I can think of one buddy right now who is much more support to the partner than the person who is quite ill right now. In that, he'll go and hang out at the house when his client is asleep, so the partner can leave. You know? He may not even have that much contact with the person, but it's really important in the whole scheme of things. If you think about it, the client's getting supported because his partner's being helped out, you know. The partner is more able to be there."

Rather conversely, the client's existing private sphere can also be sustained by the buddy relationship because the volunteer is emotionally close, but yet still maintains a certain structural distance (as a volunteer). The volunteer can do things for the client that the family simply cannot. One veteran buddy recalled this point with tragic poignancy:

> "In another buddy-client's case what happened was that—this was the one whose mom used to come out once a month and stay for basically a week. The last time she came, he didn't recognize her. And she couldn't face it. So she never came back, which I understand. I mean, I'm not judging her for that. But it is simply a fact. And it's why, in the end, I did end up being a sole support for him. So I'm the person he said good-bye to when he died. Actually, when people ask me, 'What do you do? What can you do that nobody else can do?' the answer I usually come up with is that it's often easier for a buddy to tell the person that it's okay to die. And I've done that for a number of my buddies. It's a very important part of the process. And it's one that many, many family members, and even close friends, find very difficult. And I've known some who did do

it. But there were others who there was no way that could be forthcoming from those people who were close to them."

Buddies: Private Support in Public Space

In the section above I have argued that buddying shows how citizenship can be a component of kinship or familial relations.[5] It takes place in private locations like the homes of the volunteers or clients, extending the actual geography of where we ought to look for citizenship. The social geography of radical citizenship, however, must also be widened. Buddying takes place not only in the private (institutional) sphere, but also through relations of privacy and intimacy, which are often best situated in public spaces across the city. Support is sometimes best given through the privacy that those spaces afford the client to talk freely and share emotions. Alternatively, buddies use public spaces to compensate for their clients' lack of relations in their private sphere, where they may be constantly alone. In a fascinating article Wilton (1996) has shown the "diminished lifeworlds" of people living with AIDS, for instance. While not all HIV positive people experience it, this constriction can often mean being confined to the home or hospital, to be imprisoned in private space. In such a context, emotional and practical support would seem best achieved by buddying in public space. Here we can see the dual distinctions embedded within the public-private dichotomy in effect geographically. Moreover, we can see how citizenship is enabled and empowered through these locations, as they encourage and enable domestic and emotional support to people struggling with a terminal illness.

Repeatedly the importance of this variable geography lay in the locations' capacity to provide settings of intimacy where emotional support could be practiced (Figure 5-4). Consider, for instance, the following samples of buddies' geographies:

"We walk *miles!* Just miles and miles and miles. I have walked from Spanish Banks over the Burrard Bridge *back* to Stanley Park. And we went to Lighthouse Park . . . And oh, man did we

---

[5]One might argue that citizenship has no bearing on the intimate relations between buddy and client. The following section challenges that criticism indirectly, and I take it up explicitly at the close of this chapter.

FIGURE 5-4. Geographies of buddying. (a) Helmcken House for people with AIDS. (b) Sea Wall, Stanley Park, West End. (c) Out for coffee, West End. Photos by author.

climb! We found a nice, quiet little cove and we talked. . . . And if he's extra tired, we just stay home and talk or watch videos. Once in a while—I don't know what it is—but I say something and it triggers a very large disclosure. I mean, I feel very privileged that he talks to me about these things. He is one of these people who has absolutely no family support. He has only told one other person that he tested positive. And he no longer sees that person after telling them—after knowing them 20 years. Personally I think that's bloody shameful."

"We go to the beach. We talk. We sit around and have coffee."

"So I would drive him to his doctors' appointments. I drove him to his treatments at the hospital. I drove him for his blood work. He loved gardens, of course, with all his plants. And of course I met him in the June of that year, so we visited practically every garden in Vancouver, sort of thing. We went out to Vander Zalm's place. And we were over in North Vancouver. He was a very good photographer. Actually there's a picture that he took on one of our trips that he had enlarged and framed for me, which is over there. So we did that. And we socialized also. He was here [in my home] quite a bit of the time."

"And he was out at UBC Hospital, and he and his lover lived in the West End, and his lover had a full-time job and it was very hard for him to take time off. So he would end up only seeing him in the evenings and on weekends. And all his friends worked. So he felt really isolated. And, as I said, at the time I was doing shift work so I had a lot of hours. I could go out during the day and do lunch or get together in mid-afternoon. At a certain point he was able to go out for a day pass. I'd borrow a friend's car and we'd go out for a drive to Spanish Banks and walk along the sand or we'd go to the Dairy Queen if he had a craving for ice cream. So a lot of it was just a matter of being a companion."

The settings, however public, provided private space to talk or (again) "just be there." So, buddying takes place in private spaces (like the buddy's or the client's home, or the hospital room), or it can take place privately in public space (like taking a walk through Stanley Park or dining together at a restaurant).

The ineffable quality of buddying often led volunteers to talk about their relationships through more common social relations that we socially structure as private. It was common for them to draw upon the discourses of friendship or family in numerous ways to capture the relationship they had with their client. While it is important to emphasize that these are only partial readings (direct challenges will be detailed in the following section), there remains a fair degree of accuracy in these very private characterizations. Volunteers often spoke of their clients as being in the private sphere of their lives. Compare the following quotes that equate buddying with friendship. This level of intimacy empowers the client by providing her or him with reliable emotional support:

> "The term 'buddy,' I think, is just sort of synonymous with 'friend' in that you have a commitment with that person to, well, be there for them."

> "I see that the volunteering is almost a private part of my life. I don't really even think about it. I don't even submit hours. So it's like my buddy is one of my friends. He might drop by the office and we might go out for a coffee together. And so the whole thing is—it's really difficult to see it now as 'volunteering.' It's more like friendship, even though it's not like my other friendships."

> "The relationship is sort of a combination of everything—of *just being there* for them. I mean, I know too you have to act as a resource person, because you're probably going to see needs

that they have (like home care or extra help with meals). And as a resource person you can come back here and arrange for a lot of the things they may need. But it is a friendship, if you're lucky. Like, I guess everybody's relationship is different, but it's a friendship also, hopefully."

Several volunteers at AIDS Vancouver have also "buddied" informally for friends and relatives living with AIDS. The fluidity of public-private divides in buddying were made all too clear to me when I would ask respondents how many times they buddied. Six respondents interjected, "That depends on how you count." They had done exactly the same tasks for longtime friends with AIDS that they did for their clients. In other words, their public role as volunteers in the shadow state became somewhat blurred in their own minds with their private roles of support for friends and family members.

The sheer intimacy of these relationships, I think, cannot be downplayed because it truly emphasizes new forms of kinship. The intense emotions buddy-volunteers felt when they talked about their clients is, unfortunately, impossible to convey in written text, yet, it cannot be ignored. The buddy quoted immediately above went on to describe another client, choking back tears:

"Asking me how to define support makes for a rather impossible question to answer. And this case is a very good example of why because the CNS [central nervous system] involvement started very early in that one. Dementia is the unkind word; the hard word. And there came a point when that, together with the morphine, which was for internal KS[6] lesions, 'support' in its conventional sense was no longer possible. He ended up in palliative care at St. Paul's. Most of the time he was aphasic and unresponsive, because of the dementia. So what that meant was that at that point "support" becomes very, very difficult. I mean, there were times when I would go to the hospital and go away without going in. We all did that at points—just couldn't cope."

---

[6]Kaposi's sarcoma is a cancer that causes purple-black lesions on the skin. It is a common AIDS-related condition for gay men.

Volunteers, as I have noted earlier, must often deal directly with the client's death. They grieve; it is part of the volunteer work. Death and grief, however, are culturally quite private experiences (Kubler-Ross, 1970). That privacy and intimacy can be intensified for people surrounded by AIDS, such as gay men in Vancouver. While it is not common for buddy-volunteers themselves to be self-disclosed as HIV positive, one man I spoke to was. Like the interviewee above, he also underscored the intensely private, emotional bonds that buddying forged for him. Confronting his client's death from AIDS necessarily meant anticipating his own:

"I'll stay as a buddy certainly as long as my buddy will have me, and as long as he's alive. And I'll really have to see. It's going to be very important if my buddy were to die that I be there for him and take a break after. But then I really don't know. A lot of people take breaks because it's their first or second time that they experience someone dying with AIDS, but I've experienced it so much it's become a bit of a routine. And death to me is not an ending; it's a beginning, a freedom that we all need in our lives. So I really don't know what will happen. But I think it's important, too, that I consider my own health at the time."

A final mode through which we can see the relationship between privacy and buddying is by its concealed and confidential nature. Buddy-volunteers operates under strict confidentiality guidelines from AIDS Vancouver. They cannot divulge their clients' names or describe them in such a way as to identify them. The clandestine character of buddies' politics underscored the observation that it is a form of citizenship that must be difficult to see from the public sphere of shadow-state service delivery. I interviewed a former AIDS Vancouver volunteer who, though not a buddy herself, wrote a master's thesis on buddying. She concluded that one of her most interesting findings was that she was profusely thanked for her interviews. The exercise had given the volunteers a chance to discuss the relationships with their clients openly—yet still confidentially. A certain emotional release or catharsis was gained by the volunteers, whose own feelings can be erased or overwritten by the stigmas and need for confidentiality endemic to AIDS work. As her quote below demonstrates, buddying can often be so private and concealed as to frustrate the volunteer:

" . . . at the end of these interviews people were very gratified, and very thankful that I did it, because it was—for many of them—the first time anybody has ever asked them about their experiences, and had some concern about them as human beings. And for a couple of them, at least, it was like this big weight had been lifted off of them. And one of them actually said that doing the interview sort of brought him back to his commitment to the organization, because he'd been thinking about quitting. He'd felt unsupported. So for him to sit down and talk about his feelings, his buddy, or the organization—or life in general—it sort of refocused him and gave him a sense of recommitment."

My own research experiences (Brown, 1995a) substantiate this viewpoint. Both volunteers and staff across all facets of the local response to AIDS thanked me too for bearing witness to their citizenship.[7] The concealed nature of AIDS beguiled them.

Buddies As Arms of the (Shadow-)State Apparatus[8]

The explanation of buddies' empowerment, however, cannot end with the emotional or home support volunteers give clients. As intensely private as buddy relations can be, they *simultaneously* exhibit quite public institutional dimensions that position them within the context of an increasingly bureaucratic system of shadow-state service delivery. As with the more general shift toward some degree of statization in ASOs, the public dimensions of bud-

---

[7]"Bearing witness" is a recurring theme in the writing on AIDS (e.g., Whitmore, 1991; Chambre, 1991). Bearing witness derives from Quaker philosophy and imparts the feeling that, even if one cannot readily solve the injustice at hand, one acknowledges it publicly so that it does not go completely unnoticed or ignored. The persistent stigma and secrecy surrounding AIDS makes the concept pertinent here.

[8]As Ursel (1992) has demonstrated, the reach of the state into the Canadian family is hardly new. I would suggest, however, that with buddies the reach is more concealed and subtle since it is via the shadow state, which retains components of the gay grassroots milieu, as well as private social relations of kinship.

dying can be both empowering and disempowering for the citizen-client. Following Wolch (1989, 1990), *statization* is the increasing penetration of the state in people's lives. Indeed, the term "client" is the most blatant example of this structuring, as it denotes being the formal recipient of a service. In other words, it is one side of a bureaucratic relationship. Citizens become clients when a relationship of public dependency is struck between them and the bureaucracy (Ferguson, 1984; Elkin, 1987; Fraser, 1989). While not every buddy-volunteer referred to their match as "my client," the changes in AIDS organizations discussed in earlier chapters clearly signal a bureaucratization in the shadow state that perpetuates the clientization of service recipients, including buddy-clients. Buddy relationships, therefore, are not immune to the structurings of modern state bureaucracy.

One structural way the public institutional sphere invades the private realm is in the fact that buddy relationships are by definition relationships between private individuals contrived by an arm of the state apparatus. People at AIDS Vancouver often insisted that buddying entailed a formal, well-structured responsibility, likening it to employment. One volunteer made this point—in contrast to the more "friendly" buddies quoted earlier—by distinguishing buddying from friendship explicitly. He shows how buddy relationships differ depending on the mix of people, personalities, and so on. More to the point, however, his message highlights the shifting social relations through which buddying is practiced. That shift seems to be taking place between the private relations of home/family and the more public relations of the state apparatus:

> " . . . but it's hard to explain the nature of the relationship be-
> cause, like I said before, it's not pals. I mean, it's called the
> buddy program but it is quite a specific kind of thing. It is
> structured and there's an element of duty to it. And that's for-
> eign to real social friendship. And there's that element of duty
> to it because it is a volunteer-work commitment. Most clearly,
> it's a duty in that I don't really allow myself the luxury of, 'Do
> I feel like calling my buddy this week?' I call my buddy this
> week."

Similarly, an AIDS Vancouver buddy coordinator substantiated this perspective as she described her own orientation toward the program, reminding us that support can take a variety of forms and can occur in a variety of locations that political theory does not readily identify as spaces of citizenship:

> "A lot of people have the idea that being a buddy is being a friend. And I really shy away from that. And I try to stay away from that for a lot of reasons. Specifically, because it would set up expectations and there'd be a lot of room for failure. If you're not good friends with someone, are you not a buddy? 'Am I doing a bad job?' [In some cases being a buddy is about practical support, so] if a friendship develops from that, fine. So what I try and really stress is that, yes, you are an emotional support as much as the person wants or needs you. But you're not a failure if you're not listening all the time, or if you don't click. We're still playing a really, really important role in someone's life if we're running to the grocery store and picking up prescriptions for them because they may not have anyone else to do that for them."[9]

Recall the comment earlier to the effect that buddies could often do things that family members could not—like giving one "permission to die." While that function can sustain the client's private sphere, it *works* because the buddy relationship originates as one between complete strangers brought together by an arm of the state. One buddy went so far as to say that being strangers who lacked a common history was precisely what made the support relationship successful:

> " . . . I think I disagree with a lot of buddies. I think the thing that makes a buddy relationship work is that there is no history. So the buddy comes unencumbered. There are things that when you are [already] in a relationship you can't let pass, that you can just let kind of roll off your back when you're a buddy. So you come without whatever the encumbrances of

---

[9]One reviewer questioned whether this quote implied a sense of duty or obligation on the buddy-volunteer's identity as a citizen instead of an example of the state apparatus structuring of social relations. The dichotomy implicit in his query misses Mouffe's fundamental point about her idea of citizenship, namely, that it can be a part of *any* social relations (including, presumably, state relations, too).

the past are. And there's a certain kind of freedom in that, which I don't think exists in other kinds of relationships. And, you know, with my friends I will have a history. And in my sense, the absence of a history is quite important. That's where many buddies would disagree with me. They say, 'Well, we make our history as we go,' to which I would say, 'It's not the same thing.'"

As well, there are limits and conditions—placed by AIDS Vancouver or the buddies themselves—bracketing the buddy relationship explicitly that denote the state-defined dimensions of the relationship. For example, AIDS Vancouver insists that money not be exchanged between buddy and client. Should a client need money on short notice, s/he can make a formal application to AIDS Vancouver's Emergency Assistance Fund (another branch of the Support Services Department). One of the first buddy coordinators recalled that he would insist that there be no sex between volunteer and client, since it would complicate the relationship and make it "less professional." Further, the volunteers themselves often had their own limits that suggested state institutional overtones. One client begged to move in with his buddy, into her apartment, because his home life was so abusive. His family would say things like "This is what God has done to you!" or "Are you going to die in my fucking bed?" While this buddy regarded her client as "family" and acknowledged that his home life exacerbated his illness, she would not allow him to move in. That level of support simply went beyond the call of duty. Another example was noted by a coordinator who recalled a volunteer working with a severe drug addict. She noted ironically that the relationship worked because of the buddy's *limited* support role. He was not there to get his client into recovery; he was not there to rescue him, as it were. *As defined by AIDS Vancouver,* his role was to accept the client as he was and provide support to him in that limited context.

The constraints placed on buddies by the public institutional sphere also came up when volunteers discussed how unique their relationships with their clients were. Buddying was just not like any other relationship they had ever experienced. A common theme that emerged was that the coupling of volunteer and client is basically (at least at first) a relationship between two complete strangers. Volunteers and clients are matched according to interests and the clients' needs, but nonetheless the catalyst between volunteer and client is a public one between two strangers, facilitated by a public service agency.[10] Thus, for example, many buddies confessed that they never would have known someone like their client had it not been for their volunteering. Neither public nor private life would have otherwise brought these two individuals together. Many older straight women, for instance, noted they had never known anyone who was self-identified as gay. Now they had a reliable understanding of the gay subculture, at least as it operated in the West End. Similarly, some gay middle-class men acknowledged that they had never before dealt with working-class people—even if they, too, happened to be gay.

As well, middle-class gay men and straight women are increasingly having to deal with the "dual diagnosed client." This is a person who is HIV positive and also has some form of addiction. As my fieldwork progressed, this type of client became increasingly common in Vancouver as "the face of AIDS" changed, becoming less predominantly middle-class gay men in the West End. Issues of class and gender became much more prominent toward the end of my ethnography, as more and more social identities came to be associated with the shifting demographics of "the AIDS crisis." In other words, social worlds are made to collide because of the public dimension of the buddy relationship. To the extent that these differences are overcome but not suppressed in an effort to build an agonistic, progressive coalition in AIDS politics, the buddy's role can be empowering.

Another example of the state's permeation into buddying is in the manifestation of "support." While at times buddies spoke of their clients in terms of family and friendship, some used social work as a simile to describe their relations. Here, the template for buddying was a state service delivered by professional bureaucrats with some degree of expertise to a needy client for his/her own good. One volunteer in particular recalled a client whose needs were tightly focused on practical issues. And even though the

---

[10]As a voluntary relationship entered into by strangers and as part of a grassroots organization, one might argue that buddies also occupy a position within civil society. I have emphasized the statist dimension of the relation because of the ASOs' movement away from civil society and toward the state, discussed earlier.

client also had an actual social worker, his buddy came to be one as well:

> "Almost always my client was somebody that was very needy. He'd recently moved back from Toronto after having lived here in illness for a length of time. He abruptly left the city for Toronto without telling anybody; whilst in Toronto he got sick (sicker), and out of fear and no income and so forth he moved back to Vancouver. When I met him he was sleeping on the sofa of his only two—what he considered to be— friends. He's just been discharged from St. Paul's. He'd had a bout of PCP.[11] And he needed an apartment, furniture, sheets, towels, food, his bearings: everything. So I helped him set up himself. He was able to negotiate the rent of an apartment where he used to live. That was done through an associate of his and a social worker. I helped him set up his apartment. I got him on Easter's Meals. I helped with the assessment for extended care or home care from the Health Department. I'd go over and make meals. I'd go over and do laundry. Talk with him a bit; watch a lot of TV with him. I contacted people he knew because he had lost contact with all of them on purpose, and helped to reestablish some of that. I just basically helped to facilitate in his life, which at that point was very focused: TV and his bed (that was about the extent of what he wanted to do)."

Later, this volunteer continued:

> "I suppose there was an element of social work in all of that, in terms of access to resources. It was very much resource management: just trying to figure out what is available from where. For example, he was isolated in his apartment. He could not get telephone service because he'd skipped on a significant amount of money owing to B.C. Tel. So, through trying to negotiate with the collection agency, which was quite an experience (I had never had that experience before), and through the assistance of people at AIDS Vancouver and some

---

[11]*Pneumocystis carinii* pneumonia, a common AIDS-related pneumonia.

very helpful people at B.C. Tel we were able to apply an Emergency Assistance grant to pay down his phone bill. And on the basis of there being a toll restriction on his line, they gave him a phone. And that way at least he could use the interphone to let people into his building, because you couldn't get into the building!"

As one interview has already suggested, having a buddy in place also enables AIDS Vancouver to monitor a client's life, to augment or maintain service delivery. By this reading, one of the buddy-volunteer's duties is to engage in a kind of public surveillance on the private lives of clients. Here, of course, geography plays a crucial role in empowering the citizen, as the buddy can reach into private locations to detect needs and support that other modes of citizenship or state welfare cannot. AIDS Vancouver emphasizes this role as an integral part of its support services:

"[A buddy-volunteer] is what's called a resource broker. You walk into the place. You look around. Is there food in the cupboards? Do they need home care? Maybe they don't know about the resources and the services available to them. Because [AIDS Vancouver] doesn't have contact with the client at their home, we don't know what their needs are. . . . It's a point of contact. Buddies are the eyes and ears, very much, of AIDS Vancouver because they are frequently *in* the home."

"I see us as a state-like resource in that we provide services. Intake, in particular, does not want to be a part of someone's friendship network or a part of their family network. We can't get the job done, be objective, and move onto the next client if we start getting involved in the way we were before—in the client's personal networks. And that's the role of the buddy. So I almost see it as this large organism where the buddy is in the network and they are the eyes and the ears for Support Services. And Support Services is almost the brain of the structure. The brain tells the buddy, 'Well, go into the house and have a look.' And the buddy comes back and says, 'The person has no food.' So the brain tells the foodbank people to make up a food bag to take over to this person's house to drop off. Then the foodbank person comes back and says, 'Well, also they can't get around because they need a scooter.' Then the brain. . . . So I see it in that way, as an organism. The buddy is definitely in that unique position where they are part of the person's support network. They may not be a part of the friendship network, or they may. But they are definitely part of the support network. 'Support network' is a term that includes a family network, a friendship network, an enemy network, all the people that are involved in your life in some capacity."

Were buddies positioned solely in either state or family locations, this capacity could not be maintained. Indeed, it is precisely the voluntary sector's concealed form of statization that troubles Wolch (1989, 1990) in her outline of the voluntary sector overall. Because the shadow state mediates between state and family with buddies, its information on its clients can eviscerate personal privacy and further the (shadow) state's role in people's lives. Given the theoretical inequality premised on the bureaucrat–client relationship, we might also envision situations where the bureaucracy rather than the client determines the appropriate level of support needed. In these sorts of scenarios we might hypothetically anticipate some degree of disempowerment of the buddy-client. Buddies' publicly determined role in the state apparatus could also be another example of clients' unequal and dependent positioning vis-à-vis the state apparatus, anathema to the citizenship of the client.

CONCLUSION: BETWEEN HOME AND STATE?

This chapter has argued that, in considering shifts in citizenship away from the state toward "new spaces" in civil society, one cannot ignore the public–private divides that crosscut those spheres. Most importantly, the sphere of home and family is certainly not downplayed or dismissed in new geographies of citizenship that have emerged during the AIDS crisis. They show just how political "private" relations of support ranging from domestic tasks to emotional therapy can be. Not having such supports exacerbates a person's struggle with a terminal illness, and places him/her on an unequal footing with the state and fellow members of the political community. Buddying empowers both the citizen-volunteer and the citizen-client by taking place in the private sphere of the home and privately across public spaces in the city.

The pliancy between state and family aspects of buddying has a geography that *enables* citizenship in these contexts. Mouffe's theory of radical citizenship has not considered the effects of this "new space" on political engagement. Yet, the buddies who inhabit the new spaces can readily be understood as radical citizens. Their existence is premised on the antagonistic relations clients have with already failed support networks. They are typically de-centered subjects: sometimes family, but also acting as a kind of state surveillance agent, or sentry. This duality operates because of buddies' agonistic efforts to support their clients however they can. This hybrid concoction of state/family relations is facilitated by the spaces where buddying actually occurs, in locations that enable volunteers to support their clients in different ways simultaneously. The overlap of state and family relations in particular locations underscores the ongoing restructuring of those institutions, but it also enables the variability in types of "support" that people living with AIDS require. Buddies' interactions with their clients took place where they *needed* to occur. Buddies are very much like state social workers—but also very much like family. "Just being there" is the spatial metaphor used by buddies to explain their role in clients' lives. The actual geography of their citizenship, however, shows the importance of space in enabling their political interventions to succeed, and the limitations of political theory's static and aspatial conceptualizations of "state" and "family."

The potential for disempowerment in buddy relationships is less likely, but it is still possible. The state apparatus uses the buddy-volunteer as its "eyes and ears" into the client's home and private sphere. Ostensibly this mode of surveillance is meant to augment support, but one does not have to be a civil libertarian to recognize the infringements on privacy that buddying can pose. It might open up a person's personal life to a degree of inspection that is unwanted. It might place the volunteer in an awkward position where s/he risks betrayal of the client's trust. It might exacerbate the client's dependent position and ironically eviscerate true support. By drawing on modern bureaucratic domination, buddying may place the client in a position of dependency on the state that might not be wished or warranted. On the volunteer side, citizens may be placed in the awkward position of having to monitor or "spy on" their buddy's lifeworld whether they think it prudent or necessary. I hasten to add that my point in raising the specter of disempowerment is not to cast aspersions on the buddy program at AIDS Vancouver. Rather, it is to show that buddying is not necessarily or structurally a neat solution to the disempowerment caused by modern bureaucratic apparatuses in a democratic society.

Many nongeographers, I suspect, would insist that terms like "home" or "family" or "kinship" are not spatial and that the spaces I have pointed out share no commonality. The diversity of locations where buddies are found, across public and private spheres, suggests that spatial context is irrelevant to this form of citizenship. That objection can be countered on a number of fronts. Foremost, geographers have been insisting for over a decade that *all* social relations are spatial (e.g., Massey, 1984), and the geographies of the home remain insistently multifaceted (e.g., Veness, 1992; Douglas, 1993). Kinship relations, forging new forms of family, occur through buddies in many different locations, but especially in the homes of volunteers and clients. They may also take place in public spaces, but political theorists have asserted that such venues are often appropriate sites for expressions of privacy and intimacy. This point seems especially apposite in terms of people living with AIDS who may need to get out of the home in which illness confines them. By this way of thinking, public and private sites of buddying are not incidental to the practice. They do share a common theme: they take place where the buddy-client needs them to occur. The diversity of buddy locations enable citizenship to emerge in the buddy relationship. Politics may be occurring in a wide variety of new locations, but the implication is not that context is meaningless. On the contrary, these politics take place where they need to in order to be agonistic. For buddies, "just being there" does not mean just being *any*where.

———•———

Chapter 6

FROM FAMILY TO CIVIL SOCIETY
Citizenship at the Quilt Display

The politics of AIDS is inextricably bound up with our grieving.[1]

THE CANADIAN AIDS QUILT DISPLAY, MAY 1993

One of my volunteer tasks was to greet visitors at the entrance of the exhibition hall where the Quilt was on display. I stood and silently watched as the families and friends of people who had died of AIDS walked into the hall. They were strangers to me; and yet, when our eyes did meet, we would exchange such knowing looks! During the display, I watched more forms of grieving and remembering than I had ever seen before in a single place: from howls of laughter, to quiet reflection, to uncontrollable sobbing, to utter shell shock. The connection I felt with all these strangers and their emotional reactions to the Quilt can only be described as understanding. Indeed, the slogan for the Vancouver display was "See It and Understand." The Quilt display was a political space of civil society, where a group of strangers gathered to make the AIDS crisis visible, to share expe-

---

[1]Froman (1992, p. 3).

riences, and to raise funds. But, it was also a space of grief for family and friends, a place for them to remember their dead publicly.

Grieving plays an integral cultural role in informing family and
civil society's discussion of AIDS—despite society's traditional
placement of grief and personal loss in the private sphere alone
(Weinberg, 1992; Crimp, 1989). The quotation that opens this
chapter underscores the need to understand the cultural context of
AIDS citizenship. But this is no straightforward task, and it has important implications for the way radical democracy conceptualizes
politics and space. As the vignette above cautions, we miss an important cultural context of citizenship if we only examine its politics in social relations that are antagonistic, as does Mouffe (as we
will see). This advice is especially pertinent given the task at hand:
to uncover the multiple locations of citizenship in respect to AIDS.
It is simply incomplete to situate radical democratic citizens in the
AIDS crisis without looking at their collective public expressions of
grief and remembrance. These memorials occur in civil society for
several reasons: to raise money for local groups, to educate and
make the crisis visible in the city, and to link different social identities in struggles that always surround AIDS. Yet, as friends and families of the dead come together publicly, these are family spaces as
well. These themes emerged in the most outstanding and powerful
cultural geography of citizenship that I witnessed during my fieldwork, namely, the Vancouver NAMES Project exhibit of the Canadian AIDS Memorial Quilt, in late May 1993.[2]

Radical Democracy in Space: Antagonism?

Recall that Mouffe (1995) uses a philosophical compass to find
radical democracy. She draws a distinction between "politics" and
"the political," arguing that, while *politics* can refer to situations
where people collectively struggle toward a common end, what
makes those situations *political* has to do with the way those struggles occur (e.g., Mouffe, 1995, p. 262). The key for her is an "antag-

---

[2]In Vancouver there are numerous sites that link AIDS politics with grief and
collective memory across civil society: World AIDS Day (December 1), AIDS Awareness Week (in mid-October), and the Walk for AIDS around Stanley Park (in September). The Quilt display, however, had the most powerful impact. These events
are coordinated through the shadow state itself. the NAMES Project (as I argue later)
is further removed from the influence of the institutional shadow state in Vancouver, more reflecting the import of "civil society."

onistic moment" when friends square off against enemies to achieve their collective end. Such an agonistic division obviously captures the spirit of modern politics (Lefort, 1986) and can be found across all manner of social interactions. Mouffe therefore points us toward this friends-versus-enemies polarity when looking for radical democracy because it signals the conflict inherent in modern politics and widens the possible ground where politics might actually take place.

Yet, if we are to follow Massey's (1995) suggestion and "think radical democracy spatially," interesting cultural nuances must qualify Mouffe's political geography. I raise some of these challenges here in describing radical democratic citizenship at the Vancouver display of the Canadian NAMES Project Memorial Quilt. The NAMES Project Quilts are movable national memorials that commemorate people who have died of AIDS-related causes. Toward the end of my ethnographic fieldwork on AIDS issues, in May 1993, I volunteered to help with the display. Drawing on my own experience and interviews with other volunteers, I use the display to show how radical democratic citizenship is currently unfolding in urban public space. I warn against using antagonism or agonism as the key signifiers for this space of citizenship. Focusing on a "friend-versus-enemy" rubric omits the cultural importance of grief and mourning, which makes the display no less political but all the more meaningful to participants. At the Quilt display, political relations were tied to expressions of grief and love that did not immediately hearken back to Schmitt's definition of politics. In fact, imposing such a framework risks an ironically antidemocratic reading of the Quilt display (as someone else's meaning is imposed onto the participants' own experiences).

I do not, however, want to reject Mouffe's cartography of citizenship out of hand, but rather want only to qualify it. The political may certainly be defined by an antagonistic moment, but that *temporal* dimension must be complemented by a neglected *spatial* one (Soja, 1989). Space might not necessarily reproduce agonistic structures at such an immediate, situational scale as aspatial political theory might suggest. Mouffe's reading of politics may work better at a more general spatial scale (and I consider this point later), but it does not seem to capture the immediate significance of the Quilt event itself for its participants. So this chapter warns against a possible danger of deduction in radical democratic thinking, where we see citizenship only in locations where antagonism comes to the fore. The interplay between personal and collective memory made the display meaningful as a political venue for grief and mourning.

Following a description of the display, and the debate between its politics and its mournfulness, I sketch themes of radical democratic citizenship at the Vancouver display (fund-raising, visibility, and solidarity). I then interpret the Quilt display as a space for grief (drawing on the display itself as well as literature on postmodern memorials) to show why it is important to leave the meanings of memorial spaces plural and open. Consequently, I argue that radical democratic theory must develop a keener appreciation for the cultural saliency of politics in particular places and at particular spatial scales.

THE NAMES PROJECT QUILT

Background

The NAMES Project Quilt is a movable memorial that commemorates people who have died from AIDS-related causes. It is not a whole quilt itself; rather, it is a series of 12' by 12' patchworks of 8 individual panels onto which a white border has been sewn and grommets fastened at the corners. The individual panels are each 3' by 6'(Figure 6-1). A panel can be made by anyone: lover, family,

FIGURE 6-1. Panels turned in at the Vancouver display. Above: "The Lord is my Shepherd." Opposite top: "Brian Liggettt and Kelly Ranger." Opposite bottom: "Paul Gallant." Photos © 1993 Judy Weiser. Reprinted with permission.

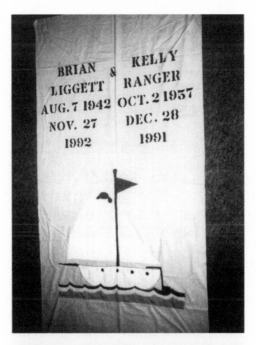

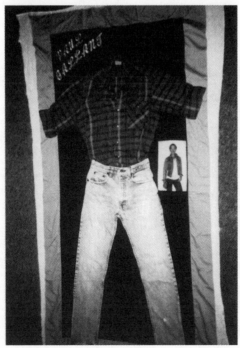

friend, coworker, caregiver, even a complete stranger (J. Brown, 1992). There is no limit to the number of panels that may be dedicated to an individual. Most importantly, however, there are no set rules about how to make a panel (other than to specify the dimensions). Neither is it required that the person's name be explicitly mentioned on the panel (though names are registered when the panels are turned into the Project). An awesome diversity in designs results when they are collectively displayed in public spaces (Figure 6-2). At the Vancouver displays, a blank 12′ by 12′ panel was left in the center of the display, with felt markers attached. This "Signature Square" permitted visitors to remember the dead in their own private-yet-public way. As well, the names of people who have had panels made for them are read aloud by volunteers during the display.

The concept of an AIDS quilt began in San Francisco in 1987. At a tribute to Harvey Milk, placards were publicly displayed listing the names of people who had died of AIDS in the city. A political activist and Quaker, Cleve Jones, was struck by the power of the display's simplicity. Racked with grief, Jones was nevertheless eager to re-create this memorial in order to work through his pain and anger at the AIDS deaths of people he knew. He came up with the

FIGURE 6-2. 12 × 12s displayed in public. Photo © 1993 Judy Weiser. Reprinted with permission.

idea to make a quilt for his friend Marvin Feldman, who had died four months earlier (Ruskin, 1988). That was the first panel. From there, the idea caught on locally, nationally, then internationally. The NAMES project started in Canada in 1988. In the summer of 1989 the NAMES Project Foundation—Canada sponsored a 7-city tour for the display, enabling some 50,000 Canadians to see the Quilt and over $80,000 (Can.) to be raised. To date there are seven local affiliates that have hosted a Quilt display: Halifax, Montreal, Ottawa, Toronto, Winnipeg, Calgary, and Vancouver. Displays have also been hosted in Kingston, London, and Sudbury, Ontario, Edmonton, Alberta, and Victoria, B.C. Several other national affiliates have begun, and in June 1994 the first global display of the national quilts was held in Hyde Park in London. The Canadian AIDS Memorial Quilt was part of that display. The Quilt was shown in Vancouver first in July 1989 at the city's art gallery. Several volunteers at that display, along with others who were involved in the local response to AIDS, created a nine-person steering committee in the fall of 1991 to bring the Quilt back to Vancouver by May 1993. In all, 172 volunteers were recruited through local ASOs, hospitals, and gay community venues to staff the event. The display took place at the British Columbia Enterprise Hall, on the former Expo '86 site, from May 20 through May 23.

Grief or Politics?

Almost since the first 12' by 12' squares were sewn, a debate has emerged around the Quilt about whether or not it is political. Allied against a political reading are two very separate interpretations. Most vocal is the activist stance, which argues that collective memorial events like the Quilt sap important energy that is best directed toward explicit confrontational political action (Kramer, 1989). Along Freudian lines, mourning and melancholia signify a turning away and denial of reality, which activists would argue depoliticizes the AIDS crisis (Crimp, 1989; Freud, 1937). Mourning, then, is seen as antipolitical, at odds with activism, as it saps precious energy into narrow, selfish, and collectively unproductive channels. This criticism rests on an interpretation that stresses the sole function of the Quilt as a venue to express grief and mourning. If one reads letters enclosed with panels when they are turned in, they are not full of political manifestos or arguments for social justice (see J. Brown, 1992). Rather, they are celebrations of the individual memorialized. They explain who that person was and why s/he was important. Their functions as expressions of grief and mourning are certainly impossible to ignore.

Others refuse to locate politics at the display; regarding politics as irrelevant and inappropriate to the Quilt. In Vancouver during World AIDS Day in 1992, a downtown storefront exhibited AIDS prevention art, much of it quite political (Miller, 1992). In the signature book at the exhibit, one person complained bitterly that it seemed strange to be in a room talking about "discourse" while so many of his friends were dying. By this interpretation politics is thought to diminish the personal pain of loss of a loved one because it de-focuses attention from the love that linked these people together. These critics bridle against coding citizenship into the experiences of making or viewing the Quilt. Mohr (1992), for example, argues that a political reading corrupts the celebration of an individual's life taking place in civil society.[3] Politics and grief must be kept segregated. Here, politics *interferes* with mourning as well and is discouraged by mourners, though for very different reasons than those that activists would stress. This argument was stressed during my volunteer training. During the final training session volunteers were told that the NAMES Project had invited representatives from the Ministry of Health to read names at the display. Volunteers loudly booed and sneered at this invitation because, they argued, the Ministry has not been seen as doing enough for people living with AIDS. We were told in extremely uncharacteristic officious tones that "this is *not* a political event."

Others insist that the focus on the individual—inherent in the panels themselves—does not negate the Quilt's political potential. Directly counter to Mohr's liberal individualism, Hawkins (1993) argues that it is through a strong focus on the individual that the politics of the Quilt actually become manifest:

> Contrary to the common NAMES Project disclaimer, "politics" is by no means foreign to the AIDS Quilt. . . . In any event, what characterizes the overt political witness of the NAMES Project is the degree to which social or political statements are not only personalized but actually personified.

---

[3]Mohr is an avid liberal; he draws a sharp spatial distinction between what ought to occur in private and public spheres.

The political nature of the Quilt, proponents argue, stems precisely from the ignorance and denial of mourning and grief that need to be witnessed. This witnessing must take place in a supportive environment because grief cannot be worked through under hostile circumstances spawned by AIDS' stigma. Numerous panels on the Quilt have only first names, nicknames, or initials, because relatives refuse to acknowledge that their loved one died of AIDS. One letter to the American NAMES Project conveys that context poignantly:

> I made this quilt piece for C.J. The Quilt does not bear his name because his family does not want anyone to know their son died of AIDS.
> I met C.J. a month before he died. I visited him every day until he died. He struggled a great deal and knew of his family's struggle to accept him and the fact that he had AIDS. The saying on the quilt piece, "I love you a skyful," is one his mother chose when I told her I wanted to do a piece for the Quilt. It is what she used to say to him from the time he was a little boy.
> It was my hope that seeing this as part of the NAMES Quilt she would be able to grieve openly with others who have had loved ones [who have] died of AIDS.
> This has not happened yet. I have hope it will. Until then, I celebrate the life of this wonderful gay man with this panel sewn in love.
> —Kay. (J. Brown, 1992, p. 211)

This letter contextualizes the need for a space of collective memory and memorial for family and friends, which the Quilt enables (as we shall see). Sturken (1992) has been the most forthright in pressing for an explicitly political reading of the displays:

> Cultural memory generated by this memorial to a controversial epidemic can be seen as inherently political; it defiantly marks the human toll of the epidemic and says: We must mourn these lives lost, challenge the homophobia that worsens the AIDS epidemic, and fight the policies that make prevention and treatment so difficult. Yet cultural memory is by no means a simple, liberatory act of negating official history or creating a 'united front.' The AIDS Quilt is the locus of a clash of identity politics, where issues of race, gender, sexuality, and class are in conflict. The cultural memory generated by the quilt is often subsumed into historical and national narratives, and becomes part of the controversial marketing of the quilt. The quilt raises fundamen-

tal issues around the politics of public commemoration, such as
for whom memorials are created and to whom they belong, and
how a memorial defines who is forgotten. (p. 66)

For her, politics seems to expand and become *the* defining feature
of the Quilt, losing the dead in the process. Perhaps a more bal-
anced perspective is offered by Crimp (1989). In a now classic es-
say, he stresses the need for both mourning *and* militancy in the
AIDS crisis. The implication that he draws for the Quilt is that militancy can occur *through* mourning. It is useful to quote him at
length:

"We look upon any interference with [mourning] as inadvisable
or harmful," warns Freud [1937, p. 125]. But for anyone living
daily with the AIDS crisis, ruthless interference with our bereave-
ment is as ordinary an occurrence as reading the *New York Times*.
The violence we encounter is relentless, the violence of silence
and omission almost as impossible to endure as the violence of
unleashed hatred and outright murder. Because this violence also
desecrates the memories of our dead, we rise in anger to vindicate
them. For many of us, mourning *becomes* militancy. (pp. 8–9)

Certainly for this reading of the Quilt we could adopt Mouffe
and Schmitt's theoretical cartography on which they locate citizenship: the friend-versus-enemy duality. Mouffe draws on
Schmitt to underscore the conflictual nature of modern democracy, against Oakeshott's conservative definition of society as a public cooperative enterprise of citizens (the *res publica*). In Mouffe's
(1993) own words:

Political life concerns collective, public action; it aims at the
construction of a "we" in a context of diversity and conflict. But
to construct a "we" it must be distinguished from a "them," and
that means establishing a frontier, defining an "enemy." Therefore, while politics aims at constructing a political community
and creating a unity, a final unity can never be realized since
there will permanently be a "constitutive outside," an exterior to
the community that makes its existence possible. Antagonistic
forces will never disappear and politics is characterized by conflict and division. (p. 69)

Mouffe finds this definition useful because it is at once open
enough to capture varieties of social relations that would enable

new spaces of citizenship to be recognized as political. Simultaneously, it points to the modern character of democracy: the absence of a common good, producing conflict and division (Lefort, 1986). Schmitt's definition of politics as a friend-or-enemy relation can be applied to the politics of AIDS generally.[4] During the AIDS epidemic, the enemies have included the state, a broader homophobic society, those who do not understand, even the virus itself.[5] Previous chapters have noted antagonisms amid Vancouver's spaces of citizenship. As a space where elements of citizenship are struggled for, however, Quilt displays do not pivot on antagonism, yet are new spaces of citizenship nonetheless. I trace how the elements of citizenship emerged at the Vancouver display below, before taking up the implications of this empirical challenge to Mouffe's theoretical project.

CITIZENSHIP IN CIVIL SOCIETY

Fund-Raising

The most explicit means by which we can see politics at the Quilt display was through its function as a fund-raiser. Some 172 volunteers were recruited through local AIDS service organizations (ASOs), hospitals, and gay community venues to staff the event. From May 20 through 23, 1993, more than 4,200 people saw the Canadian Quilt in Vancouver, and over $5,000 was raised for local organizations that provided direct service to people living with AIDS (Table 6-1). Fifty-four new panels were turned in at the event, bringing the total number of panels to 414 in Canada. The Quilt leaves not only an emotional impression, but the understanding of fund-raising too. This point can be sharpened further. All contributions would go directly to people living with AIDS and HIV. The unifying theme of the recipient programs in Table 6-1 is that they provide *direct* support services to people living with AIDS, rather

---

[4]Indeed, Sturken (1992, p. 77) states explicitly, " . . . one could argue that through its construction of an enemy, the quilt is inevitably an accusation, and hence an object of anger."

[5]Patton's (1990) chapter that contrasts discourses within immunology and virology make the virus-as-enemy reading startlingly clear through their espionage and warfare tropes used to explain the workings of HIV in the body.

TABLE 6-1. Recipients of Funds Raised at the Quilt Display

Program	Organization
Complementary Health Fund	Vancouver Persons With AIDS Society
Emergency Assistance Fund	AIDS Vancouver
Positive Women's Network	Positive Women's Network
Healing Our Spirit	First Nation's AIDS Project
Vancouver Meals Society	Vancouver Meals Society

than education or prevention services aimed at people who are HIV negative. Each organization was given roughly $1,000 (Cdn) from the proceeds. To direct funds toward an already bureaucratizing shadow state is likely to invoke the cynical "PLOA" charge (person living off of AIDS). As a fund-raising venture in civil society, the object of the display was not only to pay tribute to a person who had died, but also financially to assist someone—most, likely a complete stranger—who continues to live with the virus and its effects. That form of citizenship is rendered all the more powerful in the context of attempting to meet the needs of people with AIDS directly.

Visibility

The siting of the Quilt display was hardly a neutral decision politically or culturally.[6] It was chosen to augment the visibility of the AIDS crisis for the city and the nation. The British Columbia Enterprise Hall is a glass-enclosed public area overlooking False Creek on the edge of downtown Vancouver (see Figure 6-3). It was built by the Social Credit Government as part of the 1986 Expo site and remains the only standing complex from that event.[7] The Enterprise Hall, as a symbol of the province's arch conservative political culture, aroused antipathy in the gay community. That animosity took the form of spatial appropriation rather than avoidance of the hall when the director of AIDS Vancouver suggested the Enter-

---

[6]For examples of the ways geographers are analyzing the politics of public spaces, see Mitchell (1996).

[7]Popular local imagery of the Vancouver 1986 World Expo is complicated and contradictory; a straightforward reading of hegemonized mass culture will not do (see Ley and Olds, 1988).

FIGURE 6-3. British Columbia Enterprise Hall. Photo by author.

prise Hall as the site for the display. Because of its association with the Social Credit party, the venue have resonate within the gay community precisely because of heightened visibility.[8] It was not merely gay appropriation of a public space, but of a site that signified homophobic and neoconservative cultural politics in British Columbia during the early years of the AIDS crisis.

Further, the location of the hall itself was culturally significant as a political appropriation of urban space (see Figure 6-4). The hall is at the very edge of the downtown peninsula just the other side of Yaletown from the West End (the city's main gay neighborhood). Yaletown is the location of the Pacific AIDS Resource Centre and many other ASOs. That area has always been a defining boundary or edge of gay culture in the city. Visitors to the Quilt from the West End and downtown would often walk through Yaletown to arrive at the hall. Many were visibly overcome with grief

---

[8]In 1990, for example, the hall and the surrounding Plaza of Nations were rented by the Gay Games Committee and renamed "Celebration Centre" (Metropolitan Vancouver Athletics & Arts Association, 1990). The hall housed an artisans' market by day and parties for athletes and visitors by night. The spatial and organizational connections are more direct than the text implies. The executive director of AIDS Vancouver at the time had been the director of the Gay Games. Interestingly, he is also an urban geographer by training.

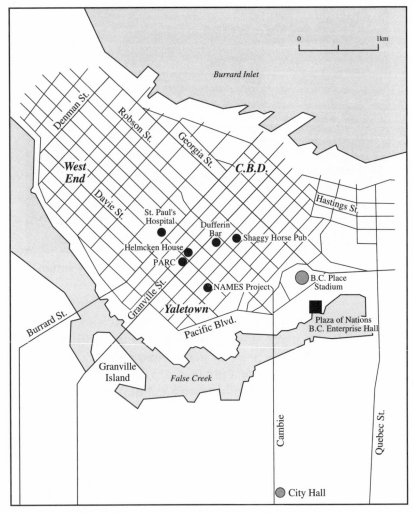

FIGURE 6-4. Location of the Vancouver Quilt display.

and sorrow. To have a Quilt display on the *opposite* side of Yale-town from the West End represents a decided extension of gay vis-ibility in Vancouver, an extension of safe public space for gays and lesbians in the city. Visitors to the Quilt from the West End and downtown would have to walk through Yaletown to get to the dis-play hall. Many were visibly overcome with grief and sorrow. For these reasons the use of the hall was a space of citizenship in city politics. It amounted to a cultural appropriation of a formerly neoconservative space and represented resistance to homophobia in local culture particularly. The stakes of this erasure were made painfully clear in an anecdote an organizer shared with me. I quote it at length because it poignantly illustrates how visibility was a key political function of the Quilt. As she recalled:

"I answered the phone and I got, 'I want to know how somebody's name gets on the Quilt.'

And I gave them this whole speech about how if you want to make a panel, and if you want to do this, and etc. Gave her the whole speech.

And she said, 'No. No. You don't understand. I'm afraid someone's going to put my son's name on a panel.'

And I said, 'Well, did your son die of AIDS?'

'Yes.'

'Well, then, they're perfectly welcome to do that.'

'Well, how do I keep them from doing that?'

And I said, 'Why would you want to?'

And she said, 'Don't give me any lectures!'

And I said, 'Ma'am, I think I'm probably going to completely disagree with you, but let's stay on the phone and let's talk. You don't have to listen to me if you don't want to. You can always hang up. But let's see if we can talk first. Why wouldn't you want your son's name to be on the Quilt?'

'Well, someone will find out that he had AIDS.'

'Well, you just told me that he did.'

And she said, almost in tears, 'There are some very cruel people out there.'

And I said, 'You mean people who would know that your son died of AIDS?'

She said, 'Yes. You have no idea what they could do.'

'No,' I said, 'but I do have an idea what fear can do. And I don't mean to lecture you; and I don't mean to make it sound like your fear isn't real, because you sound very frightened. But what would be the worst that would happen if they knew?'

'I can't begin to tell you,' she said.

'Well, what would be worse than living with what you're living with now?' And it wasn't my place to lecture her, nor to say, 'Lady, you're full of it! There's nothing wrong with dying of AIDS! You should get over it!' . . . But I said, 'Tell me his name. I have the master list. I can tell you if there is already a panel made for him. But I'll also tell you that, if there is, we're showing it.'

'Well, I'll have to get a court order!'

'Well, you go right ahead. This stuff belongs to the NAMES Project Canada. It's on public display on a contract. And if you want to make a scene in the press, you just go right ahead. We'd love it. We could use the publicity. It'd be great.' Well, she told me his name, and I looked, and there was no quilt panel for him then. I had no idea if someone was making one for him though [who would turn it in at the display]. [So I told her there was no panel for him] 'and the people that you're afraid of wouldn't go to a Quilt display anyway! So why don't you come down this weekend and see what the Quilt is, and see if it changes your mind anyway?'

Well, [when I mentioned this story to people on my steering committee] two of the nurses from St. Paul's went, 'Oh yeah. We know her! She's really, really, really rich. And she's really, really, really ashamed.' And there was a collective panel, with like 15 names on it. And his first name was one of those names. So his first name is now registered. And I don't know if his mother saw the display or not. But you talk about phobias and the need for change! And I just thought this story should be taped."

The display's prominent visibility—in a public space of civil society—spotlighted the question of the AIDS community's involvement in the broader political community (the city, the nation). By imploring fellow citizens to take notice, and by providing a context where mourner-citizens themselves could be witnessed, the Quilt forced participants to consider their relationship to others affected more directly by the crisis (see also Miller, 1992).

Solidarity

However adaptive to new circumstances a refashioned concept of citizenship will be, Mouffe argues that to be truly radical it must connect different social identities such that a new "democratic imaginary" might be formed (Laclau & Mouffe, 1985). To be sure, the Quilt display linked different struggles and identities around the epidemic. By 1993 in Vancouver AIDS was becoming more than just a "gay disease." Thus, by then the democratic principle of completely open participation was a strong theme surrounding the Quilt (Weinberg, 1992). The display was open to anyone—regardless of their proximity to or distance from the AIDS crisis. Participation was open-ended, too. One could make a panel for a loved one—or for a complete stranger. One could volunteer to work at the display or simply visit it. Thus, while a sense of community might be gained through participation, the strong theme of differences negated any single criterion as the basis for that sense of community. A multiplicity of social identities was certainly evident at the Quilt. Foremost of all, the *emotions* at the Quilt were varied; in other words, different people had different reactions to it. There were simply no rules on who or how to be at the Quilt:

> Aside from the grommeting together of panels in twelve-foot squares for major displays, there is no larger principle of organization at work: no hierarchy, subordination, or ranking; no "metanarrative" that tells a single story or even settles on a particular tone. The Quilt is the ultimate collage, one that is constantly being reformed, reinvented. Its center is wherever you find it; no one tells the viewer where to start, finish, or pay particular attention. Nor does it require of the viewer anything like an "appropriate" response. (Hawkins, 1993, p. 755)

Another way the Quilt built up solidarity was through its close juxtaposition of so many time-space scales. As Mohr would argue, the Quilt is an intensive celebration of the individual who had died from AIDS. Obviously, people attend the display to remember and memorialize specific loved ones. The discourse of the individual and her/his (lost) contribution to the mourners' lives are what the display is all about. Yet, such a reading is wholly incomplete, for the Quilt is also a *collection* of panels, and is constantly growing. So, literally, differences are sewn together. Another Quilt volunteer brought up this very productive tension between individual and societal loss by speaking about her buddy, who had died the previous winter:

> "It doesn't know any boundaries! And I think that the other thing that gets me so passionate about it is that it's young peo-

ple. We're losing a whole generation. Look at the Quilt! Look at the ages on it! They're all in their early thirties! I'm 36. And my buddy was 35 in November. So, he's just so young! It's just so sad. God, he did everything! He was a world champion figure skater. He was a designer. His stuff sold on Rodeo Drive. And that's lost! And that's not to diminish the other people that have died of AIDS."

In this way, one need only scan across the arena to witness the extent of loss. The dates on early panels—ones chronicling deaths from 1983 and 1984, for example—juxtapose with recent dates on the new panels. Together in place, they show the emerging history of the Quilt. Then, walk over to where the new panels have just been turned in to see it stretch even further into time.

The focus on so many different individuals in one site also fostered solidarity spatially. Names and places from across Canada get sewn together. Here, the loss of grieving family and relatives is spatially bound up with the loss to the nation. The Canadian Quilt constantly calls to mind the American Quilt, and others, as well. In other words, it becomes impossible to only think about one loss, or one person. Rather, that loss is—by the size, spatiality, and temporality of the Quilt—situated in an epidemic of loss. As Sturken (1992, p. 69) has argued, "The tensions between these two levels—the quilt as a massive project versus the quilt as a product of intimate, local communities—is a major part of the quilt's complex effect." Later, her reading is more precise: "While an individual panel carries a particular power in its intimate way of speaking to the dead and the viewer, that same panel carries the weight of a collective message of a community and of a nation when it is part of a vast display" (p. 79).

The display then, was a time-space that functionally brought together a wide variety of social subjects, with no simple axis of community, nor a single, substantive identity for "the citizen." One display volunteer in particular discussed this point at length through the range of emotions she experienced:

"I really liked the people at the Quilt, especially because I didn't know ten billion other people who were working on the Quilt, or even ten! But once, going after the first night, I really felt the rest of the people—and it was a very warm, warm feeling. I liked that a lot. And what else? Oh, I cried a lot. Yeah. It was very sad. I found it very sad. But not always. You know, sometimes I would just be there, and I'd be talking with friends and seeing people, and we'd be laughing [remembering someone they had lost]. Or I'd see funny panels and laugh. Or I'd see really beautiful panels and admire them. It wasn't like there was no sadness at all. It was just that there were times when I wasn't so totally sad. You just think, 'This is so unbelievable!' And also, of course, I thought, none of us would be doing this—none of us would be spending hours and being here and doing all this stuff if it wasn't for all these people that had died. And was just—like in a way it was just sickening, really. Like, the Quilt is a really beautiful thing, but it's such a paradox because this thing has been created that's so beautiful, but it's so fucking unnecessary! You know? And then I saw these people on Sunday, who I don't know very well. I just met them all once. But one of the guys, he and his lover were there. And he was wheeling his lover around in a wheelchair. And he looked really, really, really sick. Most everybody else who was coming, you know, they looked like they were friends or relatives or people who were pretty healthy. But that man in the wheelchair staring at the panels just hit home to me. This is who it is, and here he is looking at panels. And he will—possibly quite soon—be in the position of having a panel for himself. So that was very sad. I had to go home shortly after that. Yeah. . . . The other thing I did like about the Quilt is that it was very—the people who worked on it, you could tell—it was very inclusive in terms of—representational—in terms of who really is affected by AIDS. Like, it wasn't just gay men. I mean, there were lots of gay men, but it was mothers and sisters and friends and brothers. The minister who works at St. Paul's [hospital] was there. It was just—everybody was there! And I liked that a lot, because that's the truth of it. So, I liked that."

Across time and space and with an emphasis on both individuality and differences, the Quilt display brought a wide variety of social subjects—both living and dead—together in one public site in the city.

How are we to reconcile the philosophical cartography of radical democracy with the ethnographic map offered above? I think a sensitivity to scale begins to reconcile the different possibilities. Schmitt's definition might be applied usefully to the politics of AIDS at a much broader scale than the Enterprise Hall itself (Sturken, 1992). Friends were inside the Enterprise Hall, at the event. They were represented in the panels, in the visitors, in the volunteers. "Enemies" (if they had any presence at all during the display) were outside; they were the ones who did not understand. Their (in)actions fueled the need for the Quilt itself; the reason that fund-raising was even necessary was because of state inactivity, for example. During the AIDS epidemic, the enemies have included the state, a broader homophobic society, those who do not understand, even the virus itself (Patton, 1985, 1990; Bull, 1993). The display venue was chosen in bold opposition to an antigay government and its lack of action on AIDS issues. And, as I have shown earlier, other spaces of citizenship across Vancouver certainly exhibited the friend/enemy dualism. But, as a space where elements of citizenship were struggled for, the Quilt display itself did not exhibit a culture of antagonism for its participants.

The danger here is that an ironically antidemocratic reading may be tendered by abstract political theory, which emphasizes new spaces for politics that exhibit antagonistic social relations. That definition does not necessarily fit with the maps of meaning that guided visitors through the display site. It does not speak to their experiences in that space. Theoretically, it may be necessary to define solidarity inside the display by noting the presence of antagonism outside, but does it follow that this antagonism made the display meaningful to visitors? Without a certain degree of empirical sensitivity, radical democratic definitions of the political threaten to impose a rather exogenous, abstract—and ironically fixed—definition onto the display that is probably more accurate at a broader spatial scale. Here, I suspect, is a major failing of political theory's aspatial quality.

Compare the Quilt display to the buddying described earlier (see pp. 125–152). The antagonisms felt by people living with AIDS and their need for support clearly empowered buddy-volunteers to "just be there" for them. Much of their support was directed against this antagonism explicitly. The references to "enemies" or some sort of "constitutive outside" at the Quilt were far less self-evident in that memorial space. Antagonism was not so culturally salient at the Vancouver display itself; grief, mourning, and memories of friends and family *were*. I would argue, therefore, that in order to think of radical democracy spatially, one must be sensitive to the cultural saliency of local politics. I will develop this argument both theoretically and empirically below.

In sum, three themes capture the elements of citizenship at the Quilt display in Vancouver. As a mode of education and visibility, the Quilt made the AIDS crisis understandable and tangible for a wide variety of people. This, in turn, caused a certain pluralism and linking of diverse social identities around the tragedy of the pandemic. As a fund-raiser, the Quilt also provided an opportunity to give to organizations that deal directly with PWA support, rather than education or prevention. These elements of citizenship were empowered by a space of civil society that brought strangers together. But that is only part of the story. It only gets at one side of the Quilt display's importance in empowering people. The display was organized, staffed, and attended by families, friends, and kin of the dead. They were the ones who made the elements of the display. These more plaintive, familial social relations helped empower the politics of the Quilt display, and they too must be witnessed as radical democracy. I therefore trace out their lineaments below in order to better appreciate the cultural geography of citizenship.

CITIZENSHIP IN FAMILIAL SPACE

Multiple Meanings at the Site

I have already noted the openness of the Quilt tradition generally, lacking rules, hierarchy, membership, or style. Volunteers at the Vancouver event, for instance, were given the following advice:

> During the course of this display you will encounter visitors from all walks of life, all ages, races, etc. Many of these visitors will have some personal connection with the Quilt, either because someone they know is represented by a panel, or maybe they or someone they know is dealing with HIV in his/her own life. Viewing the Quilt can have a strong emotional impact, whether it is the first time or the tenth visit to this or other displays. *It is not our role to intrude on visitors' experience of the Quilt, but rather to give them the physical as well as the emotional space*

they may need. (emphasis in original; Vancouver Affiliate of the
NAMES Project, 1993, p. 3)

This flexible and pluralistic orientation to sites of collective
memory has been recently recognized by historians and cultural
critics alike as an important challenge to simplistic political orientations to public memorials. It opens up the need to recognize the
way the meanings placed on such events by family, kin, friends,
and so on, should not be subsumed or replaced by broader theoretical renderings. Bodnar (1992), for instance, has investigated the
intersections of personal, individual meanings and broader hegemonic framings historically in American public memorials. He
concludes with an emphasis on the negotiations that occur at the
site of a memorial:

> Citizens drew upon the past and present to invest public com-
> memorations and memorials in America with meaning. This
> public expression of memory was entirely dependent upon a
> process of symbolic communication that simultaneously al-
> lowed for a diversity of expression and privileged some expres-
> sions over others. To the degree that these expressions were offi-
> cial and abstract, their pluralist dimensions were obscured. On
> the other hand, their multivocal and pluralistic quality tended
> to constrain both their ideal restatements of reality and the po-
> litical objectives of officials. Public memory was never clearly or
> permanently defined but, rather, it was continually constructed
> in a realm where the small- and large-scale structures of society
> intersected. (p. 245)

The Vietnam Veterans Memorial is perhaps the best contemporary expression of the complexities in trying to fix public memory in a monument. Interestingly, parallels between the AIDS
Quilt and the Vietnam Memorial are often made on the basis of
their openness to visitors' interpretations as well as the strength of
the visitors' emotional responses (Blair, Jeppeson, & Pucci, 1991).
Scruggs and Swerdlow's (1985) account of the struggle to build the
wall traces out the multiple meanings (from family and friends)
that collided unexpectedly with the memorial's function, design,
and even its placement. They argue that the design of the monument—in listing the names of the dead (over 58,000 of them),
while simultaneously reflecting the families and friends back to
themselves on the black granite—was politically "neutral" but sig-

nified personal remembrance, education, and the extent of loss. The Quilt works in a similar way. By "naming names," it insists that we never forget people who have died of AIDS (see Figure 6-5); by providing kin the opportunity to contribute to the expansion of the monument (by creating panels, putting on the display, visiting), the participants are reflected in this public memorial as well (see Figure 6-6) (Hawkins, 1993). These strategies have caused the Quilt to be labeled (for better or worse) a "postmodern" memorial for a number of reasons that suggest a break from the heroic monuments of modern architecture. The memorial has "multiple authorship" and explicitly references its textuality, or capacity to convey meanings (Blair et al., 1991; Smith, 1993a). The Quilt rejects a *single* meaning, or metanarrative, away from the display. In-

FIGURE 6-5. Naming names. Top: "Dan Lee Cotton." Bottom: "Craig." Photos © 1993 Judy Weiser. Reprinted with permission.

FIGURE 6-6. Participants reflected in the memorial. Top: Shawn Feeney and friends. Bottom: Man looking at panels. Opposite: Friends embracing. Photos © 1993 Judy Weiser. Reprinted with permission.

stead, multiple and contradictory codings are anticipated and encouraged.[9] The literature on collective memory and postmodern memorials identifies multiple interpretations and resistances to historically singular and wider readings of politics in memorial

---

[9]The distinction is made between "both-and" interpretations and what Blair et al. see as the more modernist "either-or" approach to the possibility for architectural interpretations. For discussions of how multiple authorship, textuality, and contradictory codings signal the postmodern movement in architecture, see Jencks (1986).

spaces (Blair et al., 1991). The point here is that the plurality of meanings at events like the Quilt display make predetermined, antagonistic definitions of the political problematic when they are deployed in material space. I am drawn to this point vis-à-vis the Quilt not merely by the theoretical arguments above but also from my own participation in the display.

A Space of Grief and Mourning

Vignettes from the Vancouver display do not culturally situate the Quilt on some pivot of antagonism between friends and enemies. Consider a sample of the messages left by visitors on the Vancouver display's signature square. They do not highlight an antagonistic or agonistic stances. Rather, like the panels themselves they are expressions of grief, loss, and mourning, whose need for visibility makes them political, makes them citizenship. These private messages are written publicly, in a space full of strangers (Figure 6-7).

FIGURE 6-7. Writing on the Signature Square. Photo © 1993 Judy Weiser. Reprinted with permission.

Notice that they often address the dead directly, as much as pay tribute to them. As bystanders, we are left to wonder about the specifics raised in these messages, but we are always certain of the importance of the messages themselves:[10]

"Dearest Janet Murphy:
We love and miss you dearly and wish you were here.
                    Love from Mom, Dad, and Pat and
                    Tony. 1957–1992"

"Gary:
I miss you. 12 years together just wasn't enough time. I will always love you.
                    Tom xxx"

---

[10]One reviewer has questioned my use of these messages, asking, "Is it entirely appropriate to use the entries [on the signature panel]? While powerful, could it be seen as invasive? Or are these public statements?" This question ignores the reason the Quilt display was held in a public space of civil society and not some more secluded, private location. Its public, voluntary collection of strangers allowed for a visibility of mourning, grief, and remembrance that has been almost impossible during the AIDS crisis. That visibility in public space is the entire point behind "naming names" through the Quilt.

"To my son:
  We had so little time together, but I always loved you.
      Dad"

"Dear Richard:
  You were my beloved brother, but you were so much more, my friend. You taught me to see the beauty in all things. You taught me that we are all created equal. You listened when no one else would. You were my bastion of strength. No one understood me like you did. You gave so much and in the end, left nothing for yourself. You were unselfish to the end. I miss you Rick, sometimes I feel so alone. Remember the things we planned to do together? I did them all, but it wasn't the same without you. I never did get to feel your arms around my waist on my motorcycle. I got the Xmas tree alone this year. God, I miss you. I'm so sorry I couldn't be there for you in the end like you were always there for me. I think of you everyday and want you to know you're the best brother I could ever ask for. I will love you always, Richard. Don't let the bastards get you down!
      Your proud brother, Nathan xoxox"

"Dad:
  I never thought things would be so tough without you. Wish we could have had more time together. You have enriched my life more than I could have ever told you. I am proud to be able to call you my dad. You changed more lives than you'll ever know.
      Love, Steph (Teppy)"

"To Dan Cotton:
  By the time I met you, you were so sick. They had you on so many painkillers that I don't know if you really recognized me. I hope holding your hand helped. You fought so hard. You said you could give your own injections but you could hardly see. You wanted to walk when you couldn't stand up. You were so stubborn—you drove us up the wall—but you were being human—even when we wanted you to be more than human. I love and care for you because you were a real person who wasn't perfect. I could see how much you hurt, how brave you were.
      Love, Rivka"

"To all the many loving friends:
    Godspeed and keep them.
                              Bob"

"Serge:
    I'll never forget the times we flew together. Now you're flying
free! I miss you, so do the people and friends at Air Canada.
                              God bless, Love, Jacqueline."

"Anre:
    I'm sorry I couldn't say goodbye. Did you know we came to
visit you? Always remembered, even across 3,000 miles.
                              Bill"

"Bill:
    I will always love you.
                              Vincent"

"To all my friends:
    I shall let go but never forget.
                              Olivia"

"Uncle Don:
    I loved you ever since I was born. I love you!
                              Ashley"

Politics as some sort of "antagonistic moment" simply does not
convey the cultural saliency of the Quilt display. That does not
mean that politics was totally absent, but merely that citizenship
emerged from social relations of grief, mourning, and love—not
antagonism—at the display.

CONCLUSION

In this chapter I have argued that radical democratic theory needs
a more contextual and scale-sensitive conceptualization of the political. Recognizing the antagonistic, agonistic nature of modern
democracy—that is, how politics are made political—should not
override an appreciation of the different ways that contemporary

struggles over the elements of citizenship—rights, duties, and membership in or exclusion from political community—(literally) take place. At the Vancouver display, citizenship was practiced by raising funds for people living with AIDS, pressing visibility for the AIDS crisis, and linking disparate social identities around the epidemic locally. These efforts can signal broader antagonisms among different groups, but leaving the interpretation there negates an important cultural geography at the event itself. Constructing a "we" might logically entail constructing a "they," but that does not mean it happens within the confines of places that make citizenship so culturally salient.

As a time-space event of citizenship in civil society, the Quilt display enabled a group of strangers to come together to practice radical democratic citizenship. Their orientation at the display itself, however, was hardly antagonistic. As a plaintive space of grief and mourning for family and friends, the Quilt empowered a politics that did not hinge on a friend-or-enemy duality. It was a space where personal memories were revisited and mediated through public memorial. That interweaving of personal and collective memorial made the Quilt display's politics culturally salient to participants. Antagonism can certainly be read at a broader spatial scale, but radical democratic thinking has not as yet realized the subtlety of spatial scale needed to make that argument. Appreciating this point suggests that radical democratic theory must recognize the multiple spatialities of the politics it seeks to nourish. If it does not, it runs the risk of becoming, ironically, a rather antidemocratic body of theory. In the case of the AIDS Quilt display in Vancouver, radical democracy should not come to impose its own rather imprecise meaning of politics onto those who are actually practicing the politics. The broader point, of course, is that radical democracy must, as Massey (1995, p. 283) puts it, be "thought more spatially."

Chapter 7

———•———

CONCLUSION: WHERE HAS THE CITIZEN GONE?

SPACES AND CITIZENSHIP

This research has explored the geographies of radical democracy surrounding the AIDS crisis in a major North American city. Radical democratic citizenship holds the promise for a reinvigorated leftist politics where different political struggles are linked together rather than ordered hierarchically. It seems to transcend the liberal-communitarian debates of conventional democratic theory by emphasizing both the conflictual and rights-oriented character of modern politics, as well as the moral-communal basis for those politics. Radical democratic citizenship insists that political practices must strive to make a difference (agonism). To earn the label *political,* those practices must be antagonistic, exhibiting elements of friends squaring off against enemies. Following this *new* grammar of politics, however, citizenship may be articulated in a wide variety of social relations and de-centered subjects, and we must look toward "new spaces" of politics beyond the traditional state-centered locations to fully appreciate the scope of contemporary politics.

However attractive this new spatial rhetoric may be to radical democratic thought, we must recognize the dangers of spatial metaphors. They can import fixed, essentialized notions of space into the geographical imagination of political theory (to the extent that it actually has one). Radical democratic thinkers (and practitioners) must understand that all social relations are fundamentally spatial (just as they are temporal). Therefore, spatial *metaphors* are not sufficient in themselves to chart these "new spaces" that radical citizens promise to inhabit. These days it is surely insightful and promising to look away from the state as the ultimate or sole container of political processes. It is necessary to look toward relations of civil society and the family, as scholars of new social movements have been insisting for some time. But with this reorientation we must see how these relations are always already spatial, forever taking place in actual locations and specific contexts throughout the city.

The ambiguity of the geographic categories that political theory uses to locate political engagement has been the consistent theme throughout this study. Political theorists distinguish the state, the family, and civil society as distinct arenas of social life, yet fail to consider that these relations are always spatial, associated with distinct locations in the city. However heuristically discrete social relations may at first seem, they do overlap in different parts of the city. The distinctive sets of social relations—state, civil society, and family—lose their cohesion as boundaries often converge and overlap in tangible places across the city politics of AIDS. Moreover, that new found imprecision, or murkiness in analysis, enables citizenship to emerge in locations across the city where it makes contextual sense to be: at sites where those relations are hybrid combinations.

When relations of state, civil society, and family are spatialized, we can appreciate the significance of their recent restructurings in both enabling and constraining citizenship. Geographically, these relations do not exist solely in one space, but are brought together, rub against, and overlap one another. As the state has become more diffuse, variegated, and rarefied throughout modern society, its monopoly on politics has surely declined. Urban politics no longer take place (if in fact they ever did) only at city hall or in the voting booth. Similarly, grassroots politics in civil society have invigorated public spaces across the city with various forms of identity politics. Still further complicating the map of social life, any singular notion of the family has been rejected, as people experiment and struggle with alternative forms of home life and kinship patterns. I have charted the ebb and flow of these social relations through a series of locations where their dualities were most evident to me during my ethnographic research into Vancouver's AIDS politics. As the AIDS crisis first affected gay men in Vancouver, its structuration with state, civil society, and family produced complicated political geographies in the city. The retrenchment of the welfare state and neoconservative ideology made the state an unlikely venue for radical politics. Grassroots movements in the gay community, however, grew out of civil society and partially took the place of the welfare state. A shadow state of AIDS organizations emerged somewhere between state and civil society. One of the earliest and most important efforts that AIDS service organizations made was to provide support to people living with AIDS through buddy-volunteers. Turning out to be much more than social workers of the state apparatus, however, these volunteers came to provide families for people who in many cases had been painfully alienated from their own biological kin. Finally, at the NAMES Project Quilt display, we can see family and civil society woven together in place. The display was a venue where strangers could come together in public to raise funds and awareness for ASOs. It was a prominent space where family and friends could openly remember and memorialize their dead.

In a sense, such categorical fuzziness hearkens back to a long-standing point of social geography: that space and place often have multiple, contradictory meanings across different social worlds (Ley & Samuels, 1978). The critique of political theory's geographies, however, extends that basic point considerably. My argument is less that particular spaces in the city have different meanings across social groups, and more that it was the overlap of structures and meanings associated with separate spheres in material spaces that constrained and enabled radical citizenship across the city of Vancouver. So there is a danger in assuming, as Mouffe's spatial metaphors imply, a fixed definition to those spaces by not considering how their restructurings enable or inhibit political engagement. The poststructural quest for de-centered subjects fails to take into account the ways changing spatial contexts contribute to subjects' lack of fixity. What makes that failure both ironic and problematic is that these spaces enabled citizenship to be articulated in various forms of social relations. So much of radical citizenship's theoretical value stems from its insistence that social subjects not be reduced to essentials. Avoiding geographic metaphor and paying close attention to the spatiality of social relations would bolster the general argument considerably. To this end, I outline below the reasons why poststructural political theory must come to grips with the geography.

SPACES EMPOWERING CITIZENSHIP

The hybrid spaces amidst relations of state, civil society, and family do not just reflect citizens' empowerment across so many spheres of life. The spatial overlap of these relations helped to empower citizens. It brought together sets of social relations through which citizens could be agonistic. In these particular spatial contexts, citizens responded to needs as best they could with the tools (and amid the constraints) at hand. They could recognize their duties and obligations to fellow citizens. In turn, they could fight for rights and entitlements successfully.

So, for example, Chapters 3 and 4 focused on the state–civil society connection. I began my search for new spaces of citizenship in civil society because voluntary groups in public spaces of the city (self-recognized as standing beyond the state's traditional locus of politics) have already been noted for their novel political location across many theoretical traditions. Spaces of civil society are pulled in the opposite directions of state and family. As Chapter 3 detailed, a direct-action group like ACT UP succeeded in venting the anger that grew out of so much death and stigma. It also worked more broadly in disciplining state and medical power structures to recognize that people fighting AIDS should be taken seriously. Still, other gay organizations in civil society were more successful in meeting the needs of people living with HIV and AIDS. Thus, we saw in Chapter 4 that gay volunteer organizations that began in civil society, as outlets for people's charity have grown away from the grassroots and toward being arms of the shadow-state apparatus. The actual spaces they occupy (e.g., AIDS Vancouver, PWA, PARC) have changed in the tugs between discourses. And citizens who joined together in self-help groups to resist state and medical authority now find that some results of that authority (in the form of clientization) are working through their own associations. These changes reflect and reinforce the welfare state's ongoing shift, as well as its reluctance to take on board AIDS and/or gay and lesbian issues through the 1980s. Also at work is the growth in needs; that is, as the AIDS crisis expands in the city, it makes more sense to bureaucratize and develop closer links to the state in order to meet those needs.

Chapter 5 explored the nexus of state and family, while Chapter 6 treated the overlap of social relations associated with family and civil society. The restructuring of the family is another broad undercurrent enabling citizenship in "private" spaces where discourses of the family loom large. The de-centered character of buddy relationships (Chapter 5) demonstrates that it is not merely the rise of the shadow state that affects where new spaces of citizenship in the city are found. While buddies did often act as "eyes and ears" of state surveillance in the clients' homes, they were also creating family spaces by forging intimate relations in a context where new forms of gay and lesbian kinship were already being reworked. The lack of biological family ties (or the enormous strains placed upon them by AIDS) was (at least partially) compensated for by buddies' support. In turn, these shadow-state volunteers were woven into the kinship networks of people living with AIDS, and vice versa. Situations like the home, the park, and even the hospital room were all locations where familial relations were forged in place between buddies. Finally, events like the Quilt display (Chapter 6) reveal not just a political civil society but also a space of mourning and grief for the family and friends of the dead. Family space also was remapped with civil society at the Quilt display. Here, kin's need for open, public grief and mourning (prompted in part by the stigma some attach to AIDS) melded with the need for fund-raising and public education. Consequently, a space of kin and strangers was forged on the floor of the display. Debates over the relative salience of politics and grief that surround the Quilt, I argue, miss the point of the Quilt's success: that it is (in Crimp's words) both mourning and militancy.

Spaces Disempowering Citizens

But if empowerment can be witnessed at these spatial junctures, so too can disempowerment. New spaces for politics do not always guarantee the success of the politics, any more than new *forms* of politics do. A failure to understand the overlap between state and civil society, for example, made the radical democratic practices of

ACT UP rather ineffectual and out of place (Chapter 3). The allure of radical, direct-action protest embodied in ACT UP was lost on most activists in the city. It set up a false dichotomy between the state and civil society, which were overlapping in shadow-state organizations. By inadvertently placing strains on clandestine efforts to channel money and resources toward AIDS, it had the ironic effect of *antagonizing* participants in the emerging coalition of gays and government. While questions of political incorporation are surely important here, one cannot deny that most activists in the city felt ACT UP did more harm than good, or that its time had passed.

Also along the state–civil society overlap, the increasing shift toward the state that AIDS organizations were experiencing threatened to replay the problems of clientization that modern state theory has highlighted. AIDS Vancouver and the PWA Society became more financially and programmatically incorporated into the state apparatus as they bureaucratized and demands on them increased. Concomitantly, they lost a great deal of their grassroots ethos and became more "statelike." Consequently, citizen-volunteers who provided services became more and more like state bureaucratic experts, and service recipients became more like clients. Processes of statization were also apparent through these organizations, as the reach of the state into people's private lives increased. So, what began as relations of equality (where citizens helped citizens) was tending toward relations of inequality and dependency. This process was even taking place at the Vancouver Persons With AIDS Society, which was explicitly a self-help group. Yet, had these financial tie-ins with the state not been created, the organizations would have been unable to cope with the level of demands they were confronting. Their agonism demanded that they incorporate into the state apparatus. The buddy program was a clear example of this more general process, albeit entailing some incursions into the client's private sphere.

One might also read a degree of disempowerment into events like the Quilt display, even though this research did not specifically find that consequence in Vancouver. By downplaying the antagonistic nature of politics, some critics feel it saps participants' energies that would be better put toward meeting others' needs. One might reasonably question just how efficacious it was for familial relations to be put on display in public space. Who else bears witness to their pain? Who gains an understanding of the crisis?

My point in raising these counterclaims on citizens' empowerment is not to dismiss its potential in new, hybrid spaces. It is merely to admit that such spaces are not necessarily a royal road to radical democracy. As social relations mix in particular locations at particular times, there can be both the potential success and failure of radical democratic citizenship. Here, again, the need for a more robust geographical imagination in political philosophy is underscored. Since all social relations are spatial (and temporal), their lived contexts must not be ignored.

GEOGRAPHY LESSONS

There are, I think, three conceptual points to be brought back to a theory of radical democratic citizenship from this ethnography of AIDS politics in Vancouver. First, it has shown that it makes little sense to emphasize de-centered subjectivity in agents, while keeping the political spaces they occupy fixed or static. By spatializing those sets of social relations in a particular context, I have tried to show that Mouffe's larger project cannot meet its stated ends unless her treatment of "new spaces" incorporates the actual shifts in material space that are integral to new forms of politics. This point hinges on the acknowledgment that all social relations are spatial, a point geographers have been emphasizing for at least a decade (Gregory & Urry, 1985; Massey, 1984). Even with reference to the current attraction of spatial metaphors in poststructuralism, geographers have warned against only deploying spatial vocabulary to emphasize fixity and stasis (Massey, 1993). Place and situation are sets of social relations that are perpetually "becoming" and contingent (Pred, 1984; Keith & Pile, 1993); that contingency is not only historical but also geographical, occupying and referring to many spatial scales at once (Brown, 1995b). In other words, particular locations in the city can be structured by a wide set of social relations simultaneously, or through a period in time. Without taking these fuzzy geographies on board, poststructural political theory runs the risk of allowing its abstractions to fix its de-centered subjects in ways that at best misrepresent politics (e.g., the friend-versus-enemy dynamic forced onto the Quilt display) in the city and at worst conceal them (by theoretically favoring ACT UP's demonstrations over the work undertaken by organizations like AIDS Vancouver and PWA). The consequences could be an inability to link different struggles together, and to privilege certain struggles more easily seen with a fixed spatial context; more occluded politics would be ignored or misrepresented. These consequences are exactly the pitfalls that the radical democratic project is trying to avoid!

Contrasting Chapters 3 and 6 demonstrates this point. In Chapter 3, I argued that ACT UP Vancouver should have been the prime example of radical democratic citizenship according to theory. Conversely, the Quilt display (lacking a friend-versus-enemy dynamic) should not have allowed citizenship to emerge at the B.C. Enterprise Hall. ACT UP Vancouver, however, did not enable successful citizenship in spaces of civil society, because it misunderstood and misrepresented changes in local political culture and structures. Nevertheless, the Quilt enabled citizenship because at its display politics grew from the convergence of family and civil society, as elements of citizenship (rights, duties, community) were made salient in a context of grief and mourning.

Second, radical democracy must acknowledge the ways that spaces restructure, and that those changes are not necessarily linear nor absolute transformations, because it is these changes that helped to enable radical citizenship in Vancouver's AIDS politics. Struggles over rights, duties, and responsibilities did not only take place in conventional areas of the state because the state was unwilling and/or unable to accommodate those struggles. Nor did they only take place in the family or civil society, because the scale of the AIDS crisis in Vancouver demanded state intervention. These reasons do contribute to an explanation of citizenship's geographies in Vancouver. Still, the statization that has resulted is, in turn, resisted by elements of family and civil society. In other words, the changes in those spaces and the hybrid combinations they produce are constantly being remade *and* challenged. Changes in the structures and meanings associated with the PWA Society, for instance, are not only a simplistic linear progression from grassroots, self-help coalition to a social service bureaucratic arm of the state. The PWA Society, like other AIDS organizations in the city, manifested a combination of those two extremes as it grew. Here is where radical democracy's refusal to fix citizen's identities can signal the shifting spaces of politics. In the same way that poststructuralism refuses to fix identities of social subjects, so too must it reject fixing assumptions about the content of the spaces they inhabit. By extending this flexibility, radical democracy can more accurately reflect the shifts and fluidity not only of identity but social institutions as well. Terms like *state, family,* and *civil society* refer to very different kinds of places at the end of the twentieth century than they did at its midpoint. These changes structure—and are structured by—the capacity for politics to exist through them.

It is not enough, in other words, to look for "new" spaces of citizenship, leaving the old ones behind. We must look at how new spaces and old spaces are being redefined. It is interesting to note, for instance, that one implication of this study is that there has been a sort of "return" to the state—as ASOs become more incorporated into its apparatus. Does this mean there should be a concurrent theoretical return to the state or to questions of relative autonomy? If so, as Kirby (1993) argues, it needs to be much more sophisticated. Searching for new forms of politics in actual locations, I found political theory's spatial vocabulary awkward and inhibiting. It was more accurate to map the simultaneous spaces: where state and civil society overlapped, where civil society and family overlapped, and where family and state overlapped. Employing these hybrids did not mean completely rejecting "old" spaces like the state for "new" spaces like the family. Simultaneous spaces provided evolving contexts that allowed citizenship not merely to emerge but to do so in ways that were efficacious and made sense in Vancouver's political culture.

The third implication for radical democracy is to implore its theorists to eschew the high levels of abstraction traditional to political theory and to move toward greater engagement between theory and empirics. This is not the same as arguing that radical democracy needs to be more geographical! Operating at a lower level of abstraction, political philosophy might lead to more agile theory, and perhaps enable subjects to see their own citizenship emerge in unorthodox places, beyond the voting booth or city hall. A conversation needs to emerge between scholarship in political science and political theory as it relates to urban politics. Certainly these intradisciplinary traditions have never been held completely apart (e.g., Syed, 1966; Wickwar, 1970; Frug, 1980; Saunders, 1979). They have, however, rarely engaged each other (Ricci, 1984; Gunnell, 1993). Urban political inquiry has lacked any extensive philosophical engagement, leaving it largely descriptive and limited in its insightfulness (Elkin, 1987; cf. Arkes, 1981, and Schabert, 1989). Radical democracy can, I think, play a pivotal role here because the study of local politics has long been understood as the best embodiment of democratic practice, even during modernity (Mill, 1958; Dahl, 1967; Hill, 1974; Young, 1989). Even critics of modern urban politics acknowledge its participatory potential (Cox & Johnston, 1981; Harvey, 1986). Radical democratic theory could open up the content and meaning of what passes for city politics beyond narrow issues of service delivery and urban redevelopment, which have been its mainstays (Brown, 1995b). In short, the metaphors of space must be supplemented with the spatiality of social relations in order to understand political practice.

LIMITATIONS

Despite these implications, there are several limitations of this research that I would like to discuss. The first is the difficulty in talking about *all* the potential spaces in any given politics. For instance, in this study, the "older" spaces of the state were largely ignored. Yet, surely the state is still important in AIDS issues. This point was hinted at, for instance, in the funding arrangements and contracts of the shadow state. AIDS organizations and activists do continue to lobby government. Legislatures do continue to decide on increasing or decreasing public funds for people living with AIDS. In our haste to remap citizenship, we should not leave the assumption behind that older forms of citizenship have been whisked away. The voting booth, the Parliament, the nation—these are still locations of citizenship. Likewise, as Canada's ongoing constitutional debacle and a recent series of essays demonstrate, debates over what Canadian citizenship means still occur even within the traditional *national* definition of "the citizen" (Kaplan, 1993).

Likewise, a serious limitation of this study is that is has only looked at AIDS politics in a single place at a single time. Vancouver's experience with AIDS and, hence, its politics look very different from places in, say, Africa or Asia. The experience gay men have had responding to this crisis is not necessarily the same as other identities. So there are certainly alternate political geographies of AIDS to be written—even on Vancouver. The point of the research, then, is not to provide a definitive urban political geography of AIDS but rather to provide an account of a particular place from which insights might be transferred. The same postmodern qualifier can be made with respect to time within space. On several occasions since I finished the study I have explained my conclusions to people presently involved in Vancouver's response to AIDS. Some worry that I have misrepresented the local context, offering several current examples. I must remind them that the study is based on research conducted in 1992–1993. Since I left the field, citizens and their spaces have changed. The geography I have written has already become an *historical* geography.

A second problem falls under the issue of representation. I have described citizenship throughout this book as emerging in hybrid, simultaneous spaces. Nonetheless, the axes of those combinations were faulted for their inflexibility. While these hybrids better capture the geographies of citizenship across the restructuring of social institutions, the argument could certainly be pushed that they, too, ultimately fix political spaces. How, then, are we ever to describe spaces of citizenship without introducing elements of fixity and closure? Smith (1991) lodged a similar criticism against Laclau and Mouffe more generally when he argued that their subjects are too radically indeterminate. This criticism, of course, is voiced against deconstruction more generally. Writing fixes spaces and citizens in a way that makes its representations static. Critiques of these representations, then, must be perpetual.

An associated criticism deals with the specific categories I have used (state, civil society, and family). If these categories are so limiting, how can I justify using them at all? The simple answer is that they were not *completely* useless to understanding the organization of social life and how politics weaves through it. While I have tried to stress the spatial overlap of these categories, I have not shown that these locations can often be discrete locations in Vancouver. For example, I have not discussed the ways that biological families support people living with AIDS, outside of the state; or how they mourn and grieve outside of civil society. I have not discussed voluntary organizations that do not have ties with the state, or state programs that do not rely on the shadow state to execute policies.

I have not discussed activists like Dr. Peter, who used the television news as a cyberspace of civil society to promote AIDS awareness (see Gawthrop, 1994). In other words, while this research has demonstrated the ways that spatial categories may well blur so as to enable citizenship, I am not arguing that the continuing relevance of traditional categories has (or should be) totally wiped out. On a more philosophical plane, I suppose, the point I would stress is that, even though many scholars are actively engaged in rejected and transgressing dualisms, these are inevitable. They are part of the way meaning is produced in language. To reject dualisms is not the same thing as to interrogate their effects perpetually, as is appropriate.

THE CITIZEN IS *HERE*

Just after this study was completed, Jeffrey Schmalz wrote a *New York Times Magazine* article that began

> Once AIDS was a hot topic in America—promising treatments on the horizon, intense media interest, a political battlefield. Now, 12 years after it was first recognized as a new disease, AIDS has become normalized, *part of the landscape. It is at once everywhere and nowhere,* the leading cause of death among young men nation wide, but little threat to the core of American political power, the white heterosexual suburbanite. No cure or vaccine is in sight. And what small treatment advances had been won are now crumbling. The world is moving on, uncaring, frustrated, and bored, leaving by the roadside those of us who are infected and who can't help but wonder. (quoted in Miller, 1995, p. 546; emphasis added)[1]

The passage reiterates the spatial confusion that radical democracy has exemplified. If politics are indeed everywhere, it is not the same thing to say that they are nowhere. They happen at particular times and particular locations. These contexts affect, and are affected by, those politics.

There is another reason to reject the notion that AIDS politics

---

[1]The original source is Jeffrey Schmalz, "Whatever happened to AIDS?" *The New York Times Magazine,* November 28, 1993.

are nowhere. I have given a number of talks and classroom lectures on radical citizenship in Vancouver's AIDS politics. I find a recurring skepticism about the idea of citizenship to convey the processes I describe. The common theme to these criticisms is: what are the stakes in calling the people I describe "citizens?" Most broadly, using the term "citizenship" joins the disparate, often disjointed and contradictory, responses to AIDS in an explicitly *political* way. By doing this, I have tried to show that issues about individuals' rights, duties to others, and membership in a community of equals *do* take place through the AIDS crisis. This point is necessary within geography given the apolitical representation of the pandemic as a story of viral diffusion. But it also needs to be made because in the second decade of the crisis people (citizens) are already asking (for different reasons), "Whatever happened to AIDS?"

Reading radical citizenship through AIDS issues conveys a sense of how significant people's efforts are—and the often overwhelming extent of sickness and death—in a context of erasure, concealment, and stigma. In such an extreme context "just being there" as a buddy and attending a Quilt display *are* extraordinary city politics. I know of no better way to convey a sense of these stakes than quoting from Vito Russo's (1992) eloquent ACT UP speech, given in Albany, New York, in 1988: "AIDS is not what it appears to be at this moment in history. It is more than just a disease that ignorant people have turned into an excuse to exercise bigotry they already feel. It is more than a horror story to be exploited by the tabloids. *AIDS is a test of who we are as a people*" (pp. 301–302, emphasis added). This, it seems to me, is the promise of radical democratic theory: to see AIDS as political, and the people responding to it in so many different ways as radical citizens. The promise of geography is to insist that *where* those struggles are being waged matters to both their forms and their outcomes.

BIBLIOGRAPHY

Acting stupid: AIDS group only hurts its own cause, editorial, *The Province* (Vancouver), 28 April 1990, p. 24

Adam BD, 1992, Sex and caring among men: Impacts of AIDS on gay people, in K Plummer, Ed, *Modern Homosexualities: Fragments of Lesbian and Gay Experience* (Routledge, New York), pp. 175–186

Adams R, 1990, *Self-Help, Social Work, and Empowerment* (Macmillan, London)

Adler S, Brenner J, 1992, Gender and space: Lesbians and gay men in the city, *International Journal of Urban and Regional Research, 16,* 24–33

AIDS protesters jostle, spit at Vander Zalm, knock wife to the ground, *Winnipeg Free Press,* 26 August 1990, p. 8

Altman D, 1988, Legitimation through disaster: AIDS and the gay movement, in E Fee, DM Fox, Eds, *AIDS: The Burdens of History* (University of California Press, Berkeley), pp. 301–315

Altman D, 1994, *Power and community: Organisational and cultural responses to AIDS* (Taylor & Francis, London)

Andrews N, 1994, *Family: A Portrait of Gay and Lesbian America* (Harper Collins, New York)

Annetts J, Thompson B, 1992, Dangerous activism? in K Plummer, Ed, *Modern Homosexualities: Fragments of Lesbian and Gay Experience* (Routledge, New York), pp. 227–236

Arkes H, 1981, *The Philosopher in the City: The Moral Dimensions of Urban Politics* (Princeton University Press, Princeton)

Arno P, 1986, The non-profit sector's response to the AIDS epidemic: Community-based services in San Francisco, *American Journal of Public Health, 76,* 1325–1330

Arno P, 1991, An expanded role for community-based organizations, in N MacKenzie *The AIDS Reader: Social, Political, Ethical Issues* (Meridian, New York), pp. 497–504

Arrests, disruptions mark first day of AIDS Convention, *Vancouver Sun,* 21 June 1990, p. A-4

Ball E, 1987, The great sideshow of the Situationist International, in A Kaplan, K Ross, Eds, *Yale French Studies* (Yale University Press, New Haven), pp. 21–27

Banzhat M, 1990, *Women, AIDS, and Activism* (Between the Lines, Toronto)

Barnes T, Duncan J, 1992, *Writing Worlds: Discourses, Texts, and Metaphors in the Representation of Landscape* (Routledge, London)

Barrett T, 1987, AIDS comment no slur, Dueck says, *Vancouver Sun*, 11 June, p. B-3

Beauchamp DE, 1991, Morality and the health of the body politic, in N MacKenzie, Ed, *The AIDS Reader: Social, Political and Cultural Issues* (Meridian, New York), pp. 408–421

Bell D, 1995, Pleasure and danger: The paradoxical spaces of sexual citizenship, *Political Geography, 14,* 139–153

Benhabib S, 1992, Models of public space: Hannah Arendt, the liberal tradition, and Jurgen Habermas, in C Calhoun, Ed, *Habermas and the Public Sphere* (MIT Press, Cambridge), pp. 73–98

Benkov LA, 1994, *Reinventing the Family: The Emerging Story of Gay and Lesbian Parents* (Crown, New York)

Benn SI, Gauss GF, 1983, *Public and Private in Social Life* (St. Martin's, New York)

Berkowitz B, 1987, *Local Heroes: The Rebirth of Heroism in America* (Lexington Books, Lexington, MA)

Berlant L, Freeman E, 1993, Queer nationality, in M Warner, Ed, *Fear of a Queer Planet* (University of Minnesota Press, Minneapolis), pp. 193–229

Berlin I, 1984, Two concepts of liberty, in M Sandel, Ed, *Liberalism and Its Critics* (New York University Press, New York), pp. 15–36

Berry J, Portney K, Thompson K, 1993, *The Rebirth of Urban Democracy* (Brookings Institution, Washington)

Blair C, Jeppeson MS, Pucci E, 1991, Public memorializing in postmodernity: The Vietnam Veterans Memorial as prototype, *Quarterly Journal of Speech, 77,* 263–288

Bock G, James S, 1992, *Beyond Equality and Difference: Citizenship, Feminist Politics, and Female Subjectivity* (Routledge, New York)

Bodnar J, 1992, *Remaking America: Public Memory, Commemoration, and Patriotism in the Twentieth Century* (Princeton University Press, New Jersey)

Brown J, Ed, 1992, *A Promise to Remember: The NAMES Project Book of Letters* (Avon, New York)

Brown MK, 1986, *Remaking the Welfare State: Retrenchment and Social Policy in America and Europe* (Temple University Press, Philadelphia)

Brown MP, 1992, The possibility of local autonomy, *Urban Geography, 13*(3), 257–279

Brown MP, 1994, The work of city politics: Citizenship through employment in the local response to AIDS, *Environment and Planning A, 26,* 873–894

Brown MP, 1995a, Ironies of distance: An ongoing critique of the geographies of AIDS, *Environment and Planning D: Society and Space, 13,* 159–183

Brown MP, 1995b, Sex, scale, and the "new urban politics": HIV-prevention strategies from Yaletown, Vancouver, in D Bell, G Valentine, Eds, *Mapping Desire* (Routledge, London), pp. 245–263

Brown MP, 1995c, Time-space and the recent historical geography of AIDS, paper presented to the New Zealand Geographical Society Conference, Christchurch, New Zealand, August 1995

Brownhill S, Halford S, 1990, Understanding women's involvement in local politics: How useful is the formal/informal dichotomy? *Political Geography Quarterly, 9,* 396–414

Browning F, 1993, *The Culture of Desire: Paradox and Perversity in Gay Lives Today* (Crown, New York)

Bull C, 1993, Us vs. them, *The Advocate, 641,* 2 November, 41–45

Butcher JR, 1986, Public sector restraint and the social services: The case of the voluntary sector provision of personal social services in British Columbia, MA Thesis, Department of Geography, University of British Columbia

Buttle J, 1990, AIDS activists won't stop confrontations, protests, *Vancouver Sun,* 13 September, p. A-17

Buttle J, 1991, Activists invade Campbell camp, *Vancouver Sun,* 30 November, p. B-10

Calfia P, Fuller J, 1995, *Forbidden Passages: Writings Banned in Canada* (Cleis Press, San Francisco)

Callen M, Ed, 1992, *Surviving and Thriving With AIDS* (Persons With AIDS Coalition, New York)

Callen M, Grover JZ, Maggenti M, 1991, Roundtable, in B Wallis, Ed, *Democracy: A Project by Group Material* (Bay Press, Seattle), pp. 241–258

Canel E, 1992, New social movement theory and resource mobilization: The need for integration, in W Carroll, Ed, *Organizing Dissent: Contemporary Social Movements in Theory and Practice* (Garamond, Toronto), pp. 22–51

Carter V, 1992, Absence makes the heart grow fonder: Lesbian and gay campaigning tactics and Section 28, in K Plummer, Ed, *Modern Homosexualities: Fragments of Lesbian and Gay Experiences* (Routledge, New York), pp. 217–226

Castells M, 1983, *The City and the Grassroots: A Cross Cultural Theory of Urban Social Movements* (University of California Press, Berkeley)

Chambre SM, 1991, Volunteers as witnesses: The mobilization of AIDS volunteers in New York City, 1981–1988, *Social Service Review, 65,* 531–547

Chauncey G, 1994, *Gay New York: Gender, Urban Culture, and the Making of the Gay Male World, 1890–1940* (Basic Books, New York)

Chesler M, 1990, The dangers of self-help groups: Understanding and challenging professionals' views, in T Powell, Ed, *Working With Self-Help* (National Association of Social Workers Press, Silver Spring, MD), pp. 301–324

Chew S, 1993, What's going down with ACT UP? *Out,* November, pp. 72–137

Clark G, Dear M, 1984, *State Apparatus* (Unwin Hyman, Boston)

Cliff AD, Haggett P, 1989, Spatial aspects of epidemic control, *Progress in Human Geography, 13,* 315–347

Cohen E, 1991, Who are "we"? Gay "identity" as political (e)motion (a theoretical rumination), in D Fuss, Ed, *Inside/Out: Lesbian Theories, Gay Theories* (Routledge, New York), pp. 71–92

Cohen JL, Arato A, 1993, *Civil Society and Political Theory* (MIT Press, Cambridge)

Cooper D, 1994, *Sexing the City: Lesbian and Gay Politics in the Activist State* (Rivers Oram Press, London)

Cox K, Johnston RJ, Eds, 1981, *Conflict, Politics and the Urban Scene* (Longman, London)

Creswell T, 1996, *In Place/Out of Place: Geography, Ideology, Transgression* (University of Minnesota Press, Minneapolis)

Crimp D, Ed, 1988a, *AIDS: Cultural Analysis/Cultural Activism* (MIT Press, Cambridge)

Crimp D, 1988b, How to have promiscuity in an epidemic, in D Crimp, Ed, *AIDS: Cultural Analysis/Cultural Criticism* (MIT Press, Cambridge), pp. 237–271

Crimp D, 1989, Mourning and militancy, *October, 51,* 3–18

Crimp D, 1992a, Portraits of people with AIDS, in L Grossberg, C Nelson, P Treichler, Eds, *Cultural Studies* (Routledge, New York), pp. 117–133

Crimp D, 1992b, AIDS demo graphics, in A Klusacek, K Morrison, Eds, *A Leap in the Dark: AIDS, Art and Contemporary Culture* (Vehicule, Montreal), pp. 47–57

Crimp D, 1993, Right on, Girlfriend! in M Warner, Ed, *Fear of a Queer Planet: Queer Politics and Social Theory* (University of Minnesota Press, Minneapolis), pp. 300–320

Crimp D, Rolston A, 1990, *AIDS Demo Graphics* (Bay Press, Seattle)

Dahl R, 1967, The city and the future of democracy, *American Political Science Review, 61*(4), 953–970

Dear M, 1986, Theory and object in political geography: editorial comment, *Political Geography Quarterly, 5,* 295–297

D'Emilio J, 1983, *Sexual Politics, Sexual Communities: The Making of a Homosexual Minority in the United States 1940–1970* (University of Chicago Press, Chicago)

Donaldson D, 1985, On the provision of public services by the voluntary sector, Paper #P-85-6, Economic Policy Institute, University of British Columbia

Dorn M, Laws G, 1994, Social theory, body politics, and medical geography, *The Professional Geographer, 46,* 106–110

Douglas, M, 1993, The idea of home: A kind of space, in A Mack, Ed, *Home: A Place in the World* (New York University Press, New York), pp. 261–281

Dowling R, 1997, Neotraditionalism in the suburban landscape, *Urban Geography* (forthcoming)

Duberman M, 1993, *Stonewall* (Plume, New York)

Duchense D, 1989, *Giving Freely: Volunteers in Canada* (Supply and Services Canada, Ottawa)

Dunn J, 1996, *The History of Political Theory and Other Essays* (Cambridge University Press, New York)

Dutt AK, Miller D, Dutta HM, 1990, Reflections on the AIDS distribution pattern in the United States of America, in RW Thomas, Ed, *Spatial Epidemiology*, London Papers in Regional Science #21 (Pion, London), pp. 183–196

Dutt AK, Monroe C, Dutta HM, Prince B, 1987, Geographical patterns of AIDS in the United States, *Geographical Review, 77*, 456–471

Easton S, 1992, Longest B.C. survivor declined hero status, *The Province* (Vancouver), 16 November, p. A-5

Elkin S, 1987, *City and Regime in the American Republic* (University of Chicago, Chicago)

Elshtain J, Ed, 1983, *The Family in Political Thought* (University of Massachusetts Press, Amherst)

Evans DT, 1993, *Sexual Citizenship: The Material Construction of Sexualities* (Routledge, London)

Fairclough T, 1985, The gay community of Vancouver's West End: The geography of a modern urban phenomenon, MA Thesis, Department of Geography, University of British Columbia

Fauci A, 1991, The human immunodeficiency virus: Infectivity and mechanisms of pathogenesis, in N MacKenzie, Ed, *The AIDS Reader: Social, Political, Ethical Issues* (Meridian, New York), pp. 25–41

Ferguson K, 1984, *The Feminist Case Against Bureaucracy* (Temple University Press, Philadelphia)

Fernandez E, 1991, A city responds, in N Mackenzie, Ed, *The AIDS Reader: Social, Political, Ethical Issues* (Meridian, New York), pp. 577–585

FitzGerald F, 1986, *Cities on a Hill: A Journey Through Contemporary American Cultures* (Simon & Schuster, New York)

Flather P, 1987, AIDS law protesters jeer Socred fundraiser, *Vancouver Sun*, 3 December, p. A-14

Fraser K, 1992, Dr. Peter dies in his sleep: AIDS activist put human face to deadly disease, *The Province* (Vancouver), 16 November, p. A-1

Fraser N, 1989, *Unruly Practices: Power, Discourse and Gender in Contemporary Society* (University of Minnesota Press, Minneapolis)

Fraser N, 1990, Rethinking the public sphere: A contribution to the critique of actually existing democracy, *Social Text, 25/26*, 56–80

Freud S, 1937, Mourning and melancholia, in J Rickman (1953), *A General Selection from the Works of Sigmund Freud* (Clarke Irwin, Toronto), pp. 142–162

Frish M, 1990, *A Shared Authority* (Temple University Press, Philadelphia)

Froman JK, 1992, *After You Say Goodbye: When Someone You Love Dies of AIDS* (Chronicle, San Francisco)

Frug G, 1980, The city as a legal concept, *Harvard Law Review, 93,* 1059–1154

Fuller J, Blackley S, 1995, *Restricted Entry: Censorship on Trial* (Press Gang Books, Vancouver)

Fyfe NR, 1995, Law and order policy and the spaces of citizenship in Contemporary Britain, *Political Geography, 14,* 177–189

Gairdner WD, 1992, *The War Against the Family: A Parent Speaks Out on the Political, Economic, and Social Policies That Threaten Us All* (Stoddart, Toronto)

Gamson J, 1991, Silence, death and the invisible enemy: AIDS activism and social movement "newness," in M Burawoy, Ed, *Ethnography Unbound: Power and Resistance in the Modern Metropolis* (University of California Press, Berkeley), pp. 35–57

Gardner LI, Brundage JF, Burke DS, McNeil JG, Visintine R, Miller RN, 1989, Spatial diffusion of the human immunodeficiency virus infection epidemic in the United States, 1985–1987, *Annals of the Association of American Geographers, 79,* 25–43

Gates J, 1992, Global responsibility, *Vancouver PWA Newsletter* (Vancouver Persons With AIDS Society, Vancouver), 1–4

Gawthrop D, 1994, *Affirmation: The AIDS Odyssey of Dr. Peter* (New Star, Vancouver)

Gay Men's Oral History Group, 1989, *Walking After Midnight: Gay Men's Life Stories* (Routledge, New York)

Gays seeking city money: Alderman seek more data, *Vancouver Sun,* 27 September 1974, p. 11

Geltmaker T, 1992, The queer nation acts up: Health care, politics, and sexual diversity in Los Angeles, *Environment and Planning D: Society and Space, 10,* 609–650

Giddens A, 1987, *The Nation State and Violence: Volume Two of a Contemporary Critique of Historical Materialism* (University of California Press, Berkeley)

Goldberg S, Collins J, 1991, *An External Evaluation of the Vancouver Persons With AIDS Society,* unpublished manuscript, PARC, 1107 Seymour St., Vancouver, B.C.

Goldberg M, Mercer J, 1986, *The Myth of the North American City* (University of British Columbia Press, Vancouver)

Gould P, 1991a, Thinking like a geographer, *Canadian Geographer, 35,* 324–331

Gould P, 1991b, Modelling the geographic spread of AIDS for educational intervention, in R Ulack, WF Skinner, Eds, *AIDS and the Social Sciences* (University of Kentucky Press, Lexington), pp. 30–44

Gould P, 1993, *The Slow Plague* (Blackwell, Cambridge, England)

Gould SJ, 1991, The terrifying normalcy of AIDS, in N MacKenzie, Ed, *The AIDS Reader: Social, Political, Ethical Issues* (Meridian, New York), pp. 100–103

Gray J, 1986, *Liberalism* (University of Minnesota Press, Minneapolis)

Gregory D, 1994, *Geographical Imaginations* (Blackwell, Cambridge)

Gregory D, Urry J, 1985, *Social Relations and Spatial Structures* (St. Martins, New York)

Grover JZ, 1988, AIDS: Keywords, in D Crimp, Ed, *AIDS: Cultural Analysis/Cultural Activism* (MIT Press, Cambridge), pp. 17–30

Grover JZ, 1992, AIDS, keywords and cultural work, in L Grossberg, C Nelson, P Treitchler, Eds, *Cultural Studies* (Routledge, New York), pp. 227–239

Gunnell JG, 1993, *The Descent of Political Theory: The Genealogy of an American Vocation* (University of Chicago Press, Chicago)

Guttman E, Ed, 1988, *Democracy and the Welfare State* (Princeton University Press, Princeton)

Habermas J, 1984, *A Theory of Communicative Action* (Beacon Press, Boston)

Habermas J, 1991, *The Structural Transformation of the Public Sphere* (MIT Press, Cambridge)

Halley JE, 1993, The construction of heterosexuality in M Wanner, Ed, *Fear of a Queer Planet: Queer Politics and Social Theory* (University of Minnesota Press, Minneapolis), pp. 82–102

Haraway DJ, 1991, *Simians, Cyborgs, and Women: The Reinvention of Nature* (Routledge, New York)

Harvey D, 1986, *Consciousness and the Urban Experience* (Johns Hopkins University Press, Baltimore)

Hasson S, Ley D, 1994, *Neighborhood Organizations and the Welfare State* (Toronto University Press, Toronto)

Hawkins PS, 1993, Naming names: The art of memory and the NAMES Project AIDS Quilt, *Critical Inquiry, 19*, 752–779

Health and Welfare Canada, 1990, *AIDS Surveillance Report* (Supply and Services Canada, Ottawa)

Health and Welfare Canada, 1994, *Quarterly Surveillance Update: AIDS in Canada,* July 1994 (Supply and Services Canada, Ottawa)

Heater D, 1990, *Citizenship: The Civic Ideal in World History, Politics and Education* (Longman, New York)

Hegel G, 1991, *Elements of the Philosophy of Right,* Trans. HB Nisbet, Ed, AW Wood (Cambridge, New York)

Held D, 1987, *Models of Democracy* (Stanford University Press, Stanford)

Held D, 1990, *Political Theory and the Modern State* (Stanford University Press, Stanford)

Helig P, Mundt RJ, 1984, *Your Voice at City Hall* (State University of New York Press, Albany)

Hill DM, 1974, *Participation in Local Affairs* (Penguin, Harmondsworth, England)

Hoffman J, 1995, *Beyond the State: An Introductory Critique* (Polity, London)

Horton M, 1989, Bugs, drugs, and placebos: The opulence of truth, or how to make a treatment decision in an epidemic, in E Carter, S Watney, Eds, *Taking Liberties: AIDS and Cultural Politics* (Serpents Tail, London), pp. 161–182

Horwood H, 1989, AIDS rally irks some, *The Province* (Vancouver), 5 September, p. 8

Hunter N, 1995, Marriage, law, and gender: A feminist inquiry, in L Duggan, N Hunter, Eds, *Sex Wars: Sexual Dissent and Political Culture* (Routledge, New York), pp. 107–122

Ignatieff M, 1989, Citizenship and moral narcissism, *The Political Quarterly, 60,* 63–74

Ismael JS, Vaillancourt Y, 1988, *Privatization and Provincial Social Services in Canada: Policy Administration and Service Delivery* (University of Alberta, Edmonton)

Jencks C, 1986, *What Is Postmodernism?* (St. James Press, New York)

Johnston RJ, 1994, Civil society, in RJ Johnston, D Gregory, DM Smith, Eds, *The Dictionary of Human Geography,* third ed, pp. 68–69

Jones KB, 1990, Citizenship in a women-friendly polity, *Signs, 15,* 781–812

Judd DR, Swanstrom T, 1995, *City Politics: Private Power and Public Policy* (Harper Collins, New York)

Kaplan A, Ross K, 1987, Introduction, in *Yale French Studies* (Yale University Press, New Haven), pp. 1–20

Kaplan W, Ed, 1993, *Belonging: The Meaning and Future of Canadian Citizenship* (McGill/Queens University Press, Montreal)

Katz A, 1993, *Self-Help in America: A Social Movement Perspective* (Twayne, New York)

Katz A, Bender E, 1990, *Helping One Another: Self-Help Groups in a Changing World* (Third Party, Oakland, CA)

Katznelson I, 1981, *City Trenches: Urban Politics and the Patterning of Class in the United States* (Pantheon Books, New York)

Kayal PM, 1993, *Bearing Witness: Gay Men's Health Crisis and the Politics of AIDS* (Westview Press, Boulder, CO)

Keane J, 1988, *Democracy and Civil Society* (Verso, London)

Kearns AJ, 1992, Active citizenship and urban governance, *Transactions of the Institute of British Geographers, 17,* 20–34

Kearns AJ, 1995, Active citizenship and local governance: Political and geographical dimensions, *Political Geography, 14,* 155–175

Kearns R, 1994, Putting health and health care into place: An invitation accepted and declined, *The Professional Geographer, 46,* 11–115

Keith M, Pile S, 1993, *Place and the Politics of Identity* (Routledge, London)

Kines L, 1990, AIDS activist to take his life this week, *Vancouver Sun,* 20 August, p. B-6

King D, 1987, *The New Right: Politics, Markets and Citizenship* (Macmillan, Basingstoke, England)

King E, 1993, *Safety in Numbers: Safer Sex and Gay Men* (Routledge, London)

Kinsman G, 1987, *The Regulation of Desire: Sexuality in Canada* (Black Rose Books, Montreal)

Kirby A, 1993, *Power/Resistance, Local Politics and the Chaotic State* (University of Indiana Press, Bloomington)

Kofman E, 1995, Citizenship for some but not for others: Spaces of citizenship in contemporary Europe, *Political Geography, 14,* 121–137

Koontz S, 1992, *The Way We Never Were: American Families and the Nostalgia Trap* (Basic Books: New York)

Kramer L, 1989, *Reports from the Holocaust: The Makings of an AIDS Activist* (St. Martin's, New York)

Krefetz S, 1977, *Welfare Policy-Making and City Politics,* (Praeger, New York)

Kubler-Ross E, 1970, *On Death and Dying* (Macmillan, New York)

Kuklin S, 1989, *Fighting Back: What Some People Are Doing About AIDS* (GP Putnam's Sons, New York)

Kymlicka W, 1990, *Contemporary Political Philosophy: An Introduction* (Oxford, Toronto)

La Novara P, 1993, *A Portrait of Families in Canada* (Statistics Canada, Ottawa) K1A 0T6

Laclau E, Mouffe C, 1985, *Hegemony and Socialist Strategy* (Verso, London)

Lapovsky-Kennedy E, Davis MD, 1993, *Boots of Leather, Slippers of Gold: The History of a Lesbian Community* (Penguin, New York)

Lasswell H, 1950, *Politics: Who Gets What, When, How* (Smith, New York)

Latour B, 1987, *Science in Action: How to Follow Scientists and Engineers Through Society* (Harvard University Press, Cambridge)

Lefort C, 1986, *Democracy and Political Theory* (Polity, Cambridge)

Leslie G, 1991, *Breach of Promise: Socred Ethics Under Vander Zalm* (Harbour Publishing: Madeira Park, B.C.)

Letts C, 1992, Buddy Volunteers at AIDS Vancouver: An Exploration of Their Experiences, unpublished BA Honors Thesis, Simon Fraser University, Burnaby, B.C.

Ley D, Duncan J, 1993, *Place/Culture/Representation* (Routledge, New York)

Ley D, Olds C, 1988, Landscape as spectacle: Worlds fairs and the culture of heroic consumption, *Society and Space 6,* 191–212

Ley D, Samuels M, 1978, *Humanistic Geography* (Maaroufa, Chicago)

Lineberry RL, Sharkansky I, 1978, *Urban Politics and Public Policy,* third ed (Harper & Row, New York)

Lipsky M, 1980, *Street Level Bureaucracy: Dilemmas of the Individual in Public Services* (Russell Sage, New York)

Lowe S, 1986, *Urban Social Movements: The City After Castells* (St. Martins, New York)

Loyotonnen M, 1991, The spatial diffusion of the human immunodeficiency virus type I in Finland, 1982–1987, *Annals of the Association of American Geographers, 81,* 127–151

MacIntyre A, 1984, *After Virtue* (University of Notre Dame Press, South Bend)

MacKenzie N, Ed, (1991) *The AIDS Reader: Social, Political, Ethical Issues* (Meridian, New York)

Mack A, 1993, *Home: A Place in the World* (NYU Press, New York)

MacKian S, 1995, "That great dust-heap called history": Recovering the multiple spaces of citizenship, *Political Geography, 14,* 209–216

Magnusson W, 1985, Bourgeois theories of local government, *Political Studies, 34,* 1–18

Magnusson W, 1986, Local Autonomy and Community Politics, in W Magnusson, Ed, *After Bennett: A New Politics for British Columbia* (New Star Books, Vancouver), pp. 227–242

Magnusson W, 1992, Decentering the state or looking for politics, in W Carroll, Ed, *Organizing Dissent: Contemporary Social Movements in Theory and Practice* (Garamond, Toronto), pp. 69–80

Magnusson W, Carroll WK, Doyle C, Langer M, Walker RBJ, Eds, 1984, *The New Reality: The Politics of Restraint in British Columbia* (New Star Books, Vancouver)

Mann M, 1987, Ruling class strategies and citizenship, *Sociology, 21,* 339–354

Marston SA, 1990, Who are "the people"? Gender, citizenship, and the making of the American nation, *Environment and Planning D: Society and Space, 8,* 449–458

Marston SA, 1995, Commentary: The private goes public: Citizenship and the new spaces of civil society, *Political Geography, 14,* 194–198

Marston SA, St. Germain M, 1991, Urban restructuring and the emergence of new political groupings: Women and neighborhood activism in Tuscon, Arizona, *Geoforum, 22,* 223–236

Marston SA, Staeheli L, 1994, Citizenship, struggle, and political and economic restructuring, Guest editorial, *Environment and Planning A, 26,* 840–848

Mason G, Baldrey K, 1989, *Fantasyland: Inside the Reign of Bill Vander Zalm* (McGraw-Hill Ryerson, Toronto)

Massey D, 1984, *Spatial Divisions of Labour* (St. Martin's Press, New York)

Massey D, 1993, Politics and space/time, in M Keith, S Pile, Eds, *Place and the Politics of Identity* (Routledge, London), pp. 141–161

Massey D, 1994, *Space, Place, and Gender,* (Minnesota, University of Minnesota Press)

Massey D, 1995, Thinking radical democracy spatially, *Society and Space, 13,* 283–288

McDowell L, 1995, Body Work: Heterosexual gender performances in City workplaces, in D Bell, G Valentine, Eds, *Mapping Desire* (Routledge, London), pp. 75–95

McInnes C, 1989, Homophobia guides BC AIDS policy, activist says, *Toronto Globe and Mail,* 18 August, p. A-9

McLeod DW, 1996, *Lesbian and Gay Liberation in Canada: A Selected Annotated Chronology 1964–1975* (ECW Press/Homewood Books, Toronto)

Metropolitan Vancouver Athletics and Arts Association, 1990, *Celebration '90: Gay Games III and Cultural Festival Official Program* (MVAAA, 1170 Bute St., Vancouver V6E 1Z6)

Mill JS, 1958 [1859], *On Liberty,* G Himmelfarb, Ed (Penguin, London)

Miller J, curator, 1992, Visual aids: Uncensoring the aids crisis, an exhibition of International AIDS Awareness Posters, November 30–December 4, 840 Howe Street, Vancouver, B.C.

Miller N, 1995, *Out of the Past: Gay and Lesbian History from 1869 to the Present* (Random House, New York)

Mishra R, 1990, *The Welfare State in Capitalist Society: Policies of Retrenchment and Maintenance in Europe, North America, and Australia* (University of Toronto Press, Toronto)

Mitchell D, 1996, Public space and the city, *Urban Geography, 17,* 127–131

Mohr R, 1993, On some words from ACT UP: Doing and being done, *Gay Ideas: Outing and Other Controversies* (Beacon Press, Boston), pp. 49–53

Monette P, 1992, *Becoming a Man* (Harper Collins, New York)

Mouffe C, 1991, Citizenship and political community, in Miami Theory Collective, Ed, *Community at Loose Ends* (University of Minnesota, Minneapolis), pp. 70–82

Mouffe C, 1992, *Dimensions of Radical Democracy: Pluralism, Citizenship, Community* (Verso, London)

Mouffe C, 1993, *The Return of the Political* (Verso, London)

Mouffe C, 1994, For a politics of nomadic identity, in G. Robertson et al., Eds, *Travellers' Tales: Narratives of Home and Displacement* (Routledge, London), pp. 105–113

Mouffe C, 1995, Post-Marxism: Democracy and identity, *Society and Space, 13,* 259–265

Nardi P, Sanders D, Marmour J, 1994, *Growing Up Before Stonewall: Life Stories of Some Gay Men* (Routledge, New York)

Navarre M, 1988, Fighting the victim label: PWA Coalition portfolio, in D Crimp, Ed, *AIDS: Cultural Analysis/Cultural Activism* (MIT Press, Cambridge), pp. 147–166

Newman JL, 1990, On the transmission of AIDS in Africa, *Association of American Geographers, 80,* 300–301

Newton E, 1993, *Cherry Grove, Fire Island: Sixty Years in America's First Gay and Lesbian Town* (Beacon Press, Boston)

Northrop A, 1992, The radical debutante, in E Marcus, Ed, *Making History: The Struggle for Gay and Lesbian Equal Rights, 1945–1990, An Oral History* (Harper Collins, New York), pp. 474–490

Oakeshott M, 1975, *On Human Conduct* (Oxford University Press, New York)

Offe C, 1985, New social movements: Challenging the boundaries of institutional politics, *Social Research, 52,* 817–868

Okin S, 1991, Gender, the public, and the private, in D Held, Ed, *Political Theory Today* (Stanford University Press, Stanford), pp. 67–90

Olander W, 1991, The window on Broadway by ACT UP, in B Wallis, Ed, *Democracy: A Project By Group Material* (Bay Press, Seattle), pp. 277–279

Osborn J, 1991, Prevention: Can we mobilize what has been learned? in N MacKenzie, Ed, *The AIDS Reader: Social, Political and Ethical Issues* (Meridian, New York), pp. 366–375

Ouster of B.C. minister demanded after AIDS remark, *Toronto Globe and Mail,* 16 August 1990, p. A-13

Painter J, Philo C, 1995, Spaces of citizenship: An introduction, *Political Geography, 14,* 107–120

Parton N, 1993, Master's death means dog must go, *Vancouver Sun,* 3 March, p. A-1

Pateman C, 1989, *The Disorder of Women: Democracy, Feminism and Political Theory* (Stanford University Press, Stanford)

Pattie CJ, 1994, Forgetting Fukuyama: New spaces of politics, Editorial in *Environment and Planning A, 26,* 1007–1010

Patton C, 1985, *Sex and Germs: The Politics of AIDS* (South End, Boston)

Patton C, 1989, The AIDS industry: Construction of "victims," "volunteers" and "experts," in E Carter, S Watney, Eds, *Taking Liberties: AIDS and Cultural Politics* (Serpent's Tail, London), pp. 113–126

Patton C, 1990, *Inventing AIDS* (Routledge, New York)

Perrow C, Guillen MF, 1990, *The AIDS Disaster: The Failure of Organizations in New York and the Nation* (Yale University Press, New Haven)

Persky S, 1989, *Fantasy Government: Bill Vander Zalm and the Future of Social Credit* (New Star Books, Vancouver)

Phelan S, 1989, *Identity Politics: Lesbian Feminism and the Limits of Community* (Temple University Press, Philadelphia)

Pincel S, 1994, Challenges to citizenship: Latino immigrants and political organizing in the Los Angeles area, *Environment and Planning A, 26,* 895–914

Pinch S, 1985, *Cities and Services: The Geography of Collective Consumption* (Routledge & Keegan Paul, Boston)

Police hassling clubs—gays, *The Province* (Vancouver), 25 November 1974, p. 9

Postone M, 1992, Political theory and historical analysis, in C Calhoun, Ed, *Habermas and the Public Sphere* (MIT Press, Cambridge), pp. 164–180

Powell T, 1990, Differences between national self-help organizations and local self-help groups: Implications for members and professionals, in T Powell, Ed, *Working With Self-Help* (National Association of Social Workers Press, Silver Spring, MD), pp. 50–70

Pratt G, 1991, Feminist politics: The dangers of difference, the place of geography, paper presented at the Annual Meeting of the Association of American Geographers, Miami, FL, April 1–3

Pratt G, 1992, Spatial metaphors and speaking positions, commentary, *Society and Space, 10,* 241–244

Pratt G, 1994, Poststructuralism, in RJ Johnston, D Gregory, D Smith, Eds, *The Dictionary of Human Geography* (Blackwell, Oxford, England), p. 468

Pred A, 1984, Place as a historically contingent process, *Annals of the Association of American Geographers, 74,* 279–297

Preston J, 1991, *Hometowns: Gay Men Write About Where They Belong* (Dutton, New York)

Preston J, 1992, *A Member of the Family: Gay Men Write About Their Families* (Dutton, New York)

Price-Chalita P, 1994, Spatial metaphor and the politics of empowerment, *Antipode, 26,* 236–254

Priegert P, 1994, Family ties still bind despite slings, arrows of changing times, *Vancouver Sun,* 19 July, p. A-5

Rappoport J, 1988, *AIDS Inc: Scandal of the Century* (Human Energy Press, San Bruno, CA)

Rayside DM, Lindquist EA, 1992, AIDS activism and the state in Canada, *Studies in Political Economy, 39*, 37–76

Rebalski M, 1989, AIDS activists stage protest at Fantasy Gardens, *Vancouver Sun*, 5 September, p. A-1

Reimer S, 1992, Gender, flexibility and the public sector in British Columbia, MA Thesis, Department of Geography, University of British Columbia

Rekart J, 1993, *Public Funds, Private Provision: The Role of the Voluntary Sector* (University of British Columbia, Vancouver)

Rekart ML, Roy JL, 1993, *AIDS Update, Quarterly Report: Third Quarter 1993* (British Columbia Centre for Disease Control, Vancouver)

Rekart ML, Wong E, 1994, *AIDS Update, Quarterly Report: First Quarter 1994* (British Columbia Centre for Disease Control, Vancouver)

Resnick P, 1992, *Isonomia, isegoria, isomoiria* and democracy at the global level *Praxis International, 12*, 35–49

Ricci D, 1984, *The Tragedy of Political Science* (Yale University Press, New Haven)

Richstone J, Russell J, 1981, Comment: Shutting the gate: Gay civil rights in the Supreme Court of Canada, *McGill Law Journal, 27*, 92–117

Roche M, 1992, *Rethinking Citizenship: Welfare, Ideology and Change in Modern Society* (Polity, London)

Rose G, 1988, Locality, politics, culture: Poplar in the 1920s, *Environment and Planning D: Society and Space, 6*, 151–168

Rose G, 1990, The struggle for political democracy: Emancipation, gender and geography, *Environment and Planning D: Society and Space, 8*, 395–408

Rose G, 1991, Citizenship, community and locality: A feminist critique of the public sphere, paper delivered at the Association of American Geographers Annual Meeting, Miami, FL, April 1–3

Rose G, 1993, *Feminism and Geography: The Limits of Geographical Knowledge* (University of Minnesota Press, Minneapolis)

Ruskin C, 1988, *The Quilt: The stories from the NAMES Project* (Pocket Books, New York)

Russo V, 1991, A test of who we are as a people, in B Wallis, Ed, *Democracy: A Project By Group Material* (Bay Press, Seattle), pp. 299–302

Russo V, 1992, The film historian, in E Marcus, Ed, *Making History: The Struggle for Gay and Lesbian Equal Rights 1945–1990, An Oral History* (Harper Collins, New York), pp. 407–419

Saalfield C, Navarro R, 1991, Shocking pink praxis: Race and gender on the ACT UP frontlines, in D Fuss, Ed, *Inside/Out: Lesbian Theories, Gay Theories* (Routledge, New York), pp. 291–311

Sandel M, 1984, *Liberalism and Its Critics* (New York University Press, New York)

Sandel M, 1982, *Liberalism and the Limits of Justice* (Cambridge University Press, New York)

Sarup M, 1993, *An Introductory Guide to Post-Structuralism and Post-Modernism* second ed (Harvester Wheatsheaf, Sydney)

Sarup M, 1994, Home and identity, in G Robertson, M Mash, L Tickner, J Bird, B Curtis, T Putnam, Eds, *Travellers' Tales: Narratives of Home and Displacement* (Routledge, London), pp. 93–104

Sasson A, 1987, *Women and the State: The Shifting Boundaries of Public and Private* (Hutchinson, London)

Saunders P, 1979, *Urban Politics: A Sociological Interpretation* (Penguin, Harmondsworth, Middlesex)

Schabert T, 1989, *Boston Politics: The Creativity of Power* (Walter de Gruyter, Berlin)

Schmitt C, 1976, *The Concept of the Political,* George Schwab, Trans (Princeton University Press, Princeton)

Scruggs JC, Swerdlow JL, 1985, *To Heal a Nation: The Vietnam Veterans Memorial* (Harper & Row, New York)

Seven AIDS protesters arrested: Occupied John Jansen's office, *Vancouver Sun,* 1 December 1990, p. A-2

Shannon GW, 1991, AIDS: A search for origins, in R Ulack, WF Skinner, Eds, *AIDS and the Social Sciences* (University of Kentucky Press, Lexington), pp. 8–29

Shannon, GW, Pyle GF, 1989, The origin and diffusion of AIDS: A view from medical geography, *Annals of the Association of American Geographers, 79,* 1–24

Shannon, GW, Pyle GF, Bashshur RL, 1991, *The Geography of AIDS: Origins and Course of an Epidemic* (Guilford Press, New York)

Shapiro M, 1992, *Reading the Postmodern: Political Theory as Textual Practice* (University of Minnesota Press, Minneapolis)

Shariff S, 1990, Anger alone isn't enough, *Vancouver Sun,* 11 July, p. A-1

Shaw N, 1991, Preventing AIDS among women: The role of community organizing, in N MacKenzie, Ed, *The AIDS Reader: Social, Political, Ethical Issues* (Meridian, New York), pp. 505–521

Shilts R, 1982, *The Mayor of Castro Street: The Life and Times of Harvey Milk* (St. Martin's, New York)

Shilts R, 1987, *And the Band Played On: Politics, People, and the AIDS Epidemic* (Penguin, New York)

Shklar J, 1991, *American Citizenship: The Quest for Inclusion* (Harvard University Press, Cambridge)

Siltanen J, Stanworth M, 1984, *The Politics of Public Man and Private Woman: A Critique of Sociology and Politics* (Hutchinson, London)

Simpson S, 1989, Few tears shed for Dueck as outgoing Health Minister, *Vancouver Sun,* 2 November, p. B-1

Smallman-Raynor MR, Cliff AD, 1990, Acquired Immunodeficiency Syndrome (AIDS): The global spread of Human Immunodeficiency Virus Type 2 (HIV-2), in RW Thomas, Ed, *Spatial Epidemiology,* London Papers in Regional Science #21 (Pion, London), pp. 139–182

Smith A, 1986, Medical geography, in RJ Johnston, D Gregory, DM Smith, Eds, *Dictionary of Human Geography* second ed (Blackwell, Oxford, England), p. 293

Smith J, 1993a, Quilt-makers create patchwork of memories, *The Kitsilano News* (Vancouver), 17 February, pp. 1, 4

Smith J, 1993b, Above average: Bright young artist devotes his work to charity—despite HIV, *The West Ender* (Vancouver), 4 February, p. 6

Smith N, Katz C, 1993, Grounding metaphor: Towards a spatialized politics, in M Keith, S Pile, Eds. *Place and the Politics of Identity* (Routledge, London), pp. 67–83

Smith P, 1988, *Discerning the Subject* (University of Minnesota Press, Minneapolis)

Smith P, 1991, Laclau and Mouffe's secret agent in Miami Theory Collective, Ed, *Community at Loose Ends* (University of Minnesota Press, Minneapolis), pp. 99–110

Smith S, 1989, Society, space and citizenship: A human geography for the "new times"? *Transactions of the Institute of British Geographers, 14,* 144–156

Sorkin M, 1992, *Variations on a Theme Park* (Hill & Wang, New York)

Stacey J, 1988, Can there be a feminist ethnography? *Women's Studies International Forum, 11,* 21–27

Stacey J, 1991, *Brave New Families: Tales of Domestic Upheaval in Late Twentieth-Century America* (Basic Books, New York)

Staeheli L, 1994a, Restructuring citizenship in Pueblo, Colorado, *Environment and Planning A, 26,* 849–871

Staeheli L, 1994b, Empowering political struggle: Spaces and scales of resistance, *Political Geography, 13,* 387–391

Stone CN, Whelan RK, Murin WJ, 1986, *Urban Policy and Politics in a Bureaucratic Age,* second ed (Prentice-Hall, New York)

Sturken M, 1992, Conversations with the dead: Bearing witness in the AIDS Memorial Quilt, *Socialist Review, 92,* 77

Sun's ad policy opposes homosexuality: Inquiry told, *Vancouver Sun,* 1 March 1975, p. 16

Svara JH, 1990, *Official Leadership in the City: Patterns of Conflict and Cooperation* (Oxford University Press, New York)

Sword P, 1991, ACT UP pushes for anonymous AIDS tests, *Halifax Chronicle Herald,* 25 January, p. A-5

Syed A, 1966, *The Political Theory of American Local Government* (University of Massachusetts Press, Amherst)

Tatchell P, 1991, Equal rights for all: Strategies for lesbian and gay equality in Britain in K Plummer, Ed, *Modern Homosexualities: Fragments of Lesbian and Gay Experiences* (Routledge, New York), pp. 237–245

Tester K, 1992, *Civil Society* (Routledge, London)

Treichler P, 1988, Biomedical discourse: An epidemic of signification, in D Crimp, Ed, *AIDS: Cultural Analysis/Cultural Activism* (MIT Press, Cambridge), pp. 31–70

Trend D, 1995, *Radical Democracy: Identity, Citizenship and the State* (Routledge, London)

Turner O, 1964, Around town, *The Province* (Vancouver), 14 August, p. 21

Ulack R, Skinner WF, 1991, *AIDS and the Social Sciences* (University of Kentucky, Lexington)

Urry J, 1981, *The Anatomy of Capitalist Societies: The Economy, Civil Society, and the State* (Macmillan, London)

Ursel J, 1992, *Private Lives, Public Policy: One Hundred Years of State Intervention in the Family* (Women's Press, Toronto)

Valentine G, 1993, (Hetero)sexing Space, *Environment and Planning D: Society and Space, 11,* 395–413

van Hertum A, 1993, Members vote to shut down ACT UP, *The Washington Blade* (Washington, DC), 21 May, *24*(22), 1, 23

Vancouver Affiliate of The NAMES Project, 1993, *Volunteer Handbook to the 1993 Vancouver Display of the Canadian AIDS Memorial Quilt* (The Names Project, 1107 Homer St., Suite 304, Vancouver V6B 2Y1)

Varnell P, 1996, Family values: Ours and theirs, in B Bawer, Ed, *Beyond Queer: Challenging Gay Left Orthodoxy* (Free Press, New York), pp. 259–262

Veness A, 1993, Neither homed nor homeless: Contested definitions and personal lifeworlds of the poor, *Political Geography, 12,* 319–340

Vogel U, Moran M, 1991, *Frontiers of Citizenship* (Macmillan, London)

Wacher R, 1990, *The Fragile Coalition: Scientists, Activists, and AIDS* (St Martin's, New York)

Wallace R, Fullilove MT, 1991, AIDS deaths in the Bronx 1983–1988: Spatiotemporal analysis from a sociogeographic perspective, *Environment and Planning A, 23,* 1701–1724

Walzer M, 1989, Citizenship, in T Ball, J Farr, R Hanson, Eds, *Political Innovation and Conceptual Change* (Cambridge University Press, New York), pp. 211–219

Watney S, 1987, *Policing Desire: Pornography, AIDS, and the Media* (University of Minnesota Press, Minneapolis)

Watney S, 1988, The spectacle of AIDS, in D Crimp, Ed, *AIDS: Cultural Analysis/Cultural Activism* (MIT Press, Cambridge), pp. 71–86

Watney S, 1989, The subject of AIDS, in P Aggleton, G Hart, P Davies, Eds, *AIDS: Social Representations, Social Practices* (Falmer, New York), pp. 64–73

Watney S, 1990, Practices of freedom: "Citizenship" and the politics of identity in the age of AIDS, in J Rutherford, Ed, *Identity: Community, Culture, Difference* (Lawrence & Wishart, London), pp. 157–187

Watney S, 1991, Citizenship in the age of AIDS, in G Andrews, Ed, *Citizenship* (Lawrence & Wishart, London), pp. 164–182

Watts SJ, Okello R, 1990, Medical geography and AIDS, *Annals of the Association of American Geographers, 80,* 301–303

Weber M, 1968, G Roth, C Wittich, Eds, *Economy and Society* (University of California Press, Berkeley)

Weedon C, 1987, *Feminist Practice and Poststructuralist Theory* (Blackwell, Oxford, England)

Weeks J, 1989, AIDS, altruism and the new right, in E Carter, S Watney,

Eds, *Taking Liberties: AIDS and Cultural Politics* (Serpent's Tail, London), pp. 127–132

Weinberg J, 1992, The Quilt: Activism and remembrance, *Art in America*, 80, 1–3

Weston K, 1991, *Families We Choose: Lesbian and Gay Kinship* (Columbia, New York)

White S, 1988, Poststructuralism and political reflection, *Political Theory*, 16, 186–208

Whitehead T, 1989, The voluntary sector: Five years on, in E Carter, S Watney, Eds, *Taking Liberties: AIDS and Cultural Politics* (Serpents Tail, London), pp. 107–112

Whitmore G, 1991, Bearing Witness, in N MacKenzie, Ed, *The AIDS Reader: Social, Political, Ethical Issues* (Meridian, New York), pp. 586–594

Wicwar H, 1970, *The Theory of Local Government* (University of South Carolina Press, Columbia)

Wigwood R, 1992, Coping with AIDS' step-by-step death, *Vancouver Sun*, 27 April, p. B-3

Wigwood R, 1993, AIDS takes highest toll of all diseases, *Vancouver Sun*, 11 September, p. A-1

Williamson J, 1989, Every virus tells a story: The meanings of HIV and AIDS, in E Carter, S Watney, Eds, *Taking Liberties: AIDS and Cultural Politics* (Serpents Tail, London), pp. 69–80

Willms SM, Hayes MV, Hulchanski JD, 1991, *Choice, Voice, and Dignity: Housing Issues and Options for Persons With HIV Infections in Canada: A National Study* (UBC Centre for Human Settlements, Vancouver)

Wilson D, 1990, Militant tactics by AIDS groups dramatize frustration with crisis: Massive die-in staged to mark loss of life to the disease, *Toronto Globe and Mail*, 24 August, pp. A-1, A-8

Wilson E, 1977, *Women and the Welfare State* (Tavistock, London)

Wilton RD, 1996, Diminished worlds?: The geography of everyday life with HIV/AIDS, *Health and Place*, 2, 69–83

Wolch JR, 1989, The shadow state: Transformations in the voluntary sector, in J Wolch, M Dear, Eds, *The Power of Geography: How Territory Affects Social Life* (Unwin Hyman, Boston), pp. 197–221

Wolch JR, 1990, *The Shadow State: Government and the Voluntary Sector in Transition* (The Foundation Center, New York)

Wolfe A, 1989, *Whose Keeper? Social Science and Moral Obligation* (University of California Press, Berkeley)

Wood R, 1958, *Suburbia: Its People and Their Politics* (Houghton Mifflin, Boston)

Wood WB, 1988, AIDS north and south: Diffusion patterns of a global epidemic and a research agenda for geographers, *Professional Geographer*, 40, 266–279

Young IM, 1990, *Justice and the Politics of Difference* (Princeton University Press, Princeton)

INDEX

"f" following page number indicates figure; "t" indicates table; "n" indicates footnote.